THE Anguish

and Adventure

OF Adversity

FINDING JOY IN THE JOURNEY

CHERYL CARSON

Dedicated to Leah Jane Brower
whose persistent requests,
loving encouragement, and
unwavering support
provided the impetus for the
writing of this book.

COVER DESIGN: Sherrie Everett
COVER PHOTOS: Micheal D. Carson

First Printing, 2000
Revised and Expanded Edition

Copyright © 2000 by TrueHeart Publishing
256 North 2370 West, Provo, UT 84601
801-374-5686
All rights reserved
ISBN: 0-9655150-2-8

Printed by Press America

OTHER BOOKS BY CHERYL CARSON:

Forgiveness—The Healing Gift We Give Ourselves

*His Law Is Love: Offering Unconditional Love—Even to Those
    Who Don't Deserve It*

Contents

Introduction

SOMEHOW WE GROW up believing that most adversity can be avoided by living a good life. We think that there are guarantees. That living a life of obedience will bring its rewards. That proper choices and actions are always followed by positive consequences. That doing one's best to live well always brings peace and happiness. But having one's hopes shattered on the rocks of reality requires an adjustment in one's thinking.

The seeming injustices and unwarranted injuries in life may cause a faltering, a stumbling, a losing of the way. Sadly, some have suffered the only *real* loss: the loss of faith and hope.

But, being tested through tribulation, we become stronger through struggle as our personal priorities are proven through pain. Even through our tears we see more clearly the purposes of life and the promises of eternity.

When asked to speak at a single adult conference some years ago, I compiled everything I'd ever wanted to say about a subject which had always held an attraction for me: adversity. The unexpected result was the first edition of this book. Six years later the book was enlarged and expanded. To know that others have been touched with your writing—that's about as fulfilling an experience as a writer can have. During a particularly difficult time in my own life, I recall turning to a friend for comfort. "I have a book you ought to read," she said, smiling. "In fact, *you* wrote it."

I am aware that one must earn the right to speak or write on any subject. You may wonder if I qualify. Without being specific at this point, may I simply say: I don't want to be any more qualified than I am! In the eighteen years since the first edition, and especially in the twelve years since the second, I have learned more about adversity than I ever wanted to know.

When my little girl Merrie Anne was four and a half, she fell and broke her arm. After returning home from her visit to the doctor, in her childlike innocence she said sweetly, "Mama, I never wanted to have a broken arm; I never wished for one." Isn't that how we all feel about adversity? We never want it; we never wish for it.

I love life—on the printed page. A woman wrote me: "I finished your book on adversity and could relate personally to almost everything in it. I really would rather just read about adversity than experience it first hand, but that isn't an option for me right now."

I once recorded a similar feeling in my journal: *I wish that I only had to experience adversity vicariously—that I could merely be assigned to interview someone else who had gone through it.*

Mark Twain quipped, "By trying, we can easily learn to endure adversity. Another man's, I mean."

It has been said that everyone has about as much adversity as he can sustain at any given time. Someone observed: "Suffering is universal; how we deal with it is individual." Now I might offer an added dimension: *pain* is universal, but *suffering* is optional.

Some adversity is to pass through, some is to live with. Some we can control and some we cannot. Whatever its genre, we have the opportunity to know not only of the anguish, but also the adventure of adversity.

As we compare our circumstances to some of those recounted within these pages, the courage and faith demonstrated strengthens us in facing our own challenges. Here we are also offered practical, real-life suggestions for dealing with adversity. Most importantly, we gain an eternal perspective as we review God's promises that are ours if we endure well. The more we understand the big picture, the more we are able to handle the details.

So where do all these stories and ideas come from? Besides my own experiences and interviews with others, I've been collecting them on scraps of paper and in my "Thought Books" for a very long time. Unfortunately, many will not have names attached to them; their sources are Unknown.

For years I've been saying that I've never had an original thought in my life—but, upon hearing two others say the same thing on different occasions, I realize now that even *that* expression was not original with me. So, as you read, you may assume that there's a good chance someone said it before I did. A line, a phrase, a catchy string of words all wove themselves into this work. (But when you find something *really* outstanding, you may assume that *I* was the one to write it.)

As for the scripture references, I don't always note the book, chapter and verse. In the past, some of my best times have been spent searching out the location of a verse whose source was unknown. I want others to enjoy this same pleasure.

I have no pretense of superiority, only a passionate desire to share what I have learned through personal experience. "If I can stop one heart from aching, I shall not live in vain."

As Luciano De Crescenzo mused, "We are all angels with but one wing, and only by embracing each other can we fly."

Dear Reader, may your heart be as touched in the pondering as mine has been in the preparation of this book.

> May you experience peace
> and joy in the journey,
> feeling the love of
> Father in heaven
> as He reaches out
> to comfort and to strengthen.
> I, too, have
> felt His kindness and
> know that His love is constant
> and eternal.

WHY MUST I be hurt?
Suffering and despair,
Cowardice and cruelty,
Envy and injustice,
All of these hurt.

Grief and terror,
Loneliness and betrayal
And the agony of loss or death—
All these things hurt.

Why? Why must life hurt?
Why must those who love generously,
Live honorably, feel deeply
All that is good—and beautiful
Be so hurt,
While selfish creatures
Go unscathed?

That is why—Because they can feel.
Hurt is the price to pay for feeling.
Pain is not accident,
Nor punishment, nor mockery
By some savage god.

Pain is part of growth.
The more we grow
The more we feel—
The more we feel—the more we suffer,
For if we are able to feel beauty,
We must also feel the lack of it—
Those who glimpse heaven
Are bound to sight hell.

To have felt deeply is worth
Anything it cost.
To have felt Love and Honor,
Courage and Ecstasy
Is worth—any price.

And so—since hurt is the price
Of larger living, I will not
Hate pain, nor try to escape it.
Instead I will try to meet it bravely,
Bear it proudly:
Not as a cross, or a misfortune, but an
Opportunity, a privilege, a challenge—
To the god that gropes within me.

    —Elsie Robinson

CHAPTER ONE
Life Is Suffering

SEVERAL WOMEN WERE discussing the possible causes or purposes of adversity. One said that it is simply the nature of life, that "stuff happens." Another observed that some adversity we bring on ourselves through poor choices, and some we suffer because of the poor choices of others whose lives touch ours. A third stated that the purpose of adversity is to test us, to prove our mettle. A fourth expressed her belief that, since God loves us, adversity must be for our own good, to teach us and make us stronger. That sometimes our suffering is for the benefit of others, and sometimes others' suffering is for *our* benefit. Still another said she believed that, since God loves us and would not hurt us, the source of all adversity is the devil who presents obstacles to trip us up.

Whether adversity's purpose is to test us or teach us, to prove us or prepare us, whether it is sent from heaven or comes straight from hell—there is always a lesson in it for us, something we can learn.

Everything that happens to us is a gift. And if we are not yet able to feel gratitude for the experience, it is because we haven't completely unwrapped the gift. It is not easy to accept difficult times as gifts rather than unjust punishments. "I don't care if there *is* some lesson in this," your spirit screams from within, "I just want the pain to stop!" We wouldn't be human if we didn't recoil from pain.

Some assume that suffering is a sign that one is being punished for his weaknesses or mistakes. But if we attach tragedy or suffering to sin only, how do we explain the suffering of Christ? He who was least deserving of tribulation and torment endured the most. St. Augustine said, "God had one son on earth without sin, but never one without suffering."

Job's "comforters" assumed that because he was suffering, he must have sinned. Yet, in the words of the scriptures, he was "perfect and upright." So it is not surprising that Job, himself, wondered: "I am full of confusion; therefore, see thou mine affliction; If I be wicked, woe unto me; and if I be righteous, yet will I not lift up my head."

We needn't be confused. Trouble is the common denominator of living. Adversity is an integral part of this life—for everyone. "He destroyeth the perfect *and* the wicked." No matter how good or how bad you are, you will still have trouble. The rains descend on the house built on the rock as well as the house built on sand (see Matthew 7:25). The scriptures also tell us, "Yet man is born into trouble, as the sparks fly upward" (Job 5:7).

It is true that suffering is universal. The first of Buddha's four noble truths is that "life is suffering." (If you haven't been through adversity, then where *have* you been?) Circumstances may vary, but no one is exempt, though it may seem so from outward appearances. We may not know the weight of another's burden.

Longfellow said, "Believe me, every man has his secret sorrows, which the world knows not; and oftentimes we call a man cold when he is only sad."

Someone else admonished, "Let us be kind to one another, for most of us are fighting a hard battle."

> For some, the path seems easy
> As we outwardly compare.
> No one knows the inner struggles
> That gives each his cross to bear.

Beverly Sills, famous opera singer, has a millionaire husband and a family. *The Woman Who Has Everything—Almost*, the magazine article title stated. Their first child was born deaf, profoundly deaf. Her mother's world of soaring music will always be, for her, a world of stifling silence. Their second child was autistic, epileptic, and so severely retarded that he couldn't continue to live at home. Beverly Sills has had surgery for cancer and has suffered a number of other things. "Perhaps more than anything else they have done together, Beverly Sills and her husband Peter have ached together."

Just because your trials are many,
Don't think others haven't any.
And though to us it seems one-sided,
Trouble is pretty well divided.

If we could look in every heart,
We'd find that each one has its part.
And those who travel fortune's road
Sometimes carry the biggest load.

* * * *

A legend from the Far East relates how a woman in deep sorrow over the death of her only son went to a holy man to plead with him to restore life to her son. He replied that she must first go throughout the land and gather flowers from the dooryards of those whose homes had known no sorrow. Of these flowers she was to make a garland and bring it to him.

Time passed and finally the woman returned, but without the garland. "In all the land," she said, "I could find no homes whose families have known no sorrow. Now I can be content with my lot."

None of us are free from tribulation or weighty loads on life's journey, our personal earth adventure. Nor is the path always lined with love. Habitual grumblers may say, "Life is a disease with a very bad prognosis: it lingers on for years and ends with death."

The world teaches us that we should try to avoid pain, to escape hardship and difficulty, that we must somehow extricate ourselves from situations which cause us discomfort. But where was it ever promised that life in this world would be easy, free from conflict and uncertainty, devoid of anguish and wonder? When was it ever promised that life would be fair? If it's fair, then it's not a true test! Expecting the world to treat you fairly because you are a good person is like expecting the bull not to charge because you are a vegetarian.

Much of what we must endure in life is caused by circumstances beyond our control leading to undeserved pain. I was saddened to hear on the news about five teenagers in a stolen pick-up. The high speed chase by police on the freeway led into the city streets, where they ran a red light and broadsided a car where a four-year-old boy was seated. Both the little boy and the driver were critically injured and flown by helicopter to the hospital. Two of the teenagers in the pick-up were slightly injured. Life isn't fair. And none of us knows from one moment to the next what may hit us.

Life is not fair in the mortal sense, but life is always fair in the eternal sense. This world is not our ultimate home. No matter what happens to us, all the things that matter eternally *are* within our control. Like life, adversities are temporary. But what we become by them is permanent, lasting, eternal.

According to Jenkins Lloyd Jones: "Anyone who imagines that bliss is normal is going to waste a lot of time running around and shouting that he has been robbed. . . . Life is like an old-time rail journey—delays, sidetracks, smoke, dust, cinders, and jolts, interspersed only occasionally by beautiful vistas and thrilling bursts of speed. The trick is to thank the Lord for letting you have the ride."

Many of us look forward to a time when we will be able to "sit back and relax," feeling that we deserve a happy ending. But, as one man stated, "Perhaps one of the most mature moments in our lives will be when we stop looking for the day when we will have overcome all our problems. When we realize that that day will never come—that happiness is not in getting *past* the problems, but in learning to grow as we deal with them—perhaps that day will be a turning point in our lives."

"We must free ourselves of the hope that the sea will ever rest. We must learn to sail in high winds," said Hanmer Parsons.

Tennessee Williams advised, "Don't look forward to the day when you stop suffering. Because when it comes, you'll know you are dead."

* * * *

In updating the previous edition of this book, I attempted to contact people whose stories had been shared twelve years before. Several of them had died—some of them unexpectedly. As I telephoned those I could, for some reason I was hopeful that I would learn that their trials had let up, that their obstacles had been overcome, and that they were now enjoying a smooth ride. But, while I was happy that their spirits seemed strong and optimistic—even more than before—their challenges continue. I guess they always will.

Life is not a problem to be solved once; it is a continuing challenge to be met day by day. For who is there who has reached that point in life when he can afford to allow himself to stop growing or to stop improving? If happiness depended on the end of trials, we would often be disappointed, for the parade of problems continues; when one trial is ended, be assured that there will be another on its way.

We think life should flow smoothly with an unbroken chain of green lights and with empty parking spaces right next to our intended destinations. If not, we become frustrated and discouraged. As Michael McLean, songwriter and performer, said, "Most of us think life is supposed to be long, long periods of bliss, punctuated occasionally by challenges, which we overcome through righteousness, and move on to another long, long period of happiness and bliss. But in truth, it's the other way around."

Perhaps the first thing we can do with adversity—is to expect it. Then we won't be caught unprepared or be overcome by deepening despondency when it arrives. Yet, sometimes this is impossible, as we are thrown into new, adverse circumstances or receive painful knowledge in shocking ways, and we are not at all prepared. One minute the world seems to be on an even keel; the next, we may be reeling in horrifying pain.

Learning of the premature death of a mate is often unexpected, but it came as an even greater shock to one woman, the mother of seven young children. Her husband, a pilot, was killed when the private plane he was flying crashed. For some reason, the proper authorities failed to notify her. She was not unduly concerned when her husband failed to arrive home in time for supper; it was not uncommon for him to be late.

Some friends, having learned of the accident, called to offer her their condolences. But when they began talking to her on the phone, it was evident that she had not heard the news, and they ended the conversation without her suspecting anything to be amiss.

Her first indication that he was dead came when she received another telephone call: "This is the coroner. Could you give me your late husband's full name?"

* * * *

I met a young woman who had learned of her husband's infidelity when she went to her doctor with a painful physical condition. He informed her that she had a venereal disease. "That is impossible," she said. "I have been faithful all my life."

"Then we'd better check your husband," was his reply.

I could not have known that I would have a similar experience in my first marriage. In the course of our infertility studies, when the results of my test for chlamydia came back positive, it was easily cured with antibiotics, although the disease had already done some damage. That was in 1983, and doctors were just learning about chlamydia. A year or two later, when I learned how the disease was transmitted, I questioned the doctor and nurse: "Why didn't you *tell* me that chlamydia was a venereal disease?"

"Because we are not in the business of wrecking marriages," they replied.

Although the thirteen-year marriage had already just ended by that time, I remember my agony, of thinking that I wanted to die. Suddenly, my whole life seemed a farce, a big, cruel joke. That this woman who had saved all her kisses for her husband should have contracted a venereal disease within her marriage seemed the height of irony. Besides, the one thing that had kept me in that pain-filled marriage was my belief that the only acceptable grounds for divorce was marital infidelity. Even through all the pain, I had repeatedly thought to myself: "No matter how he treats me, at least he is faithful."

* * * *

Some years ago we were licensed foster and shelter care providers, temporarily caring for children removed from their parents for abuse or neglect or for other reasons. Late one night we were asked to take in two little children, ages two and one, who had been neglected and left alone by their mother. They were with us for a week.

On Sunday we took them to church with us. During a break between meetings, we were approached by a good couple in their fifties. "May we take those two children for awhile?" asked the woman.

At first, I thought she was merely trying to be helpful, since we also had our own one-year-old to care for, and both my husband and I had responsibilities to attend to. But the look of intensity on her face and her tone of voice led me to believe that there was something more. "Do you know these children?" I asked.

Then I saw her husband. With tears streaming down his face, he said, "Those are our grandchildren!"

* * * *

Perhaps it is impossible to be fully prepared for some types of adversity. Similar threads run through the descriptions of shock and pain that come from an unexpected blow. One mother, after learning that her two-year-old had cancer, wrote: "I remember looking out at other people from my dark, bleak soul and wondering how life could go on as if things were still normal. How could people still laugh and joke and discuss the weather when the life of my little girl was in such peril?"

Another mother remembered walking out of the hospital into the darkened evening just before Christmas after learning of a life-threatening illness of her child. She wondered how people could be so happy and cheerful and why the Christmas carols were still playing. Had she been able to see beyond her anguish, she would have realized that those Christmas carols heralded the very reason we can still rejoice, even in the face of heart-wrenching loss.

CHAPTER TWO

A Blessing or a Burden

THE VARIOUS KINDS and degrees of adversity are legion; pages could be filled by listing them. And, interestingly, a circumstance that may be an advantage to one may be a trial to another.

WEALTH, PRESTIGE

Wealth can be a blessing or a burden. One woman looked back on the days when she had little, saying how much more difficult and complicated her life had become since the acquisition of wealth. "I can hardly sleep at night now, for worrying over it." She had come to believe that all ownership is a form of bondage.

Another person's wealth caused him to become selfish and suspicious of others. When a younger man came to him for some advice, he immediately assumed the man was motivated by a desire to get his money. Wealth had become his test, as well.

What may seem to be advantages—such as prosperity, possessions, power, and prestige—may actually be severe trials. Adulation can be our ruination. Receiving the plaudits and praise of others may distort one's perspective and could be the beginning of his spiritual downfall.

MARRIAGE, DIVORCE

Many people think that getting married is going to solve all their problems. Later, they may think that getting divorced is going to solve all their problems. The truth is, about 25% of problems come from being single, about 25% come from being married, and about 50% come from being human. There's no way to avoid problems.

One marriage and family therapist stated that *every* marriage has grounds for divorce. And when one marries a second time, rather than experiencing an absence of marital problems as might have been hopefully anticipated, one may simply acquire a different set of problems.

Second marriages fail at the same rate as first marriages, though for different reasons, perhaps. (This statistic, depressing as it may seem at first, may be viewed in a more positive light: while nearly all the parties involved in second marriages failed the first time around, only half of them will fail on the second try.)

Up to 75% of second or subsequent marriages fail when children are involved, despite the unrealistic expectation that they will all, from the beginning, be one big, happy family. Stepmotherhood is one of the most complex family roles a woman can undertake—something akin to walking across a mine field. It wasn't until I read the book *Step-Mothering: How to Survive without Feeling Frustrated, Left Out, or Wicked*, that I realized I was not alone. "I didn't know it would be like this," they say.

HOME, CHILDREN

Many situations carry seeds of both heartache and joy. Home life can be either heaven or hell. Our homes are not all houses of prayer and havens of security. "Home should be a refuge from the storm, not the storm," said one person who had realized that he must either break away or break apart.

Marriage either becomes or gives birth to life's greatest challenges. One woman considers bearing and rearing children to be a great blessing, while another finds the rigors and challenges that come with raising a family to be filled with trials. And, while it is hoped that having children will be a source of happiness, one woman said to me, "No one can hurt you like your own children can."

REARING A HANDICAPPED CHILD

Some might consider parenting a handicapped child to be a problem—others, a privilege, as expressed by one mother: "My husband and I have the privilege of raising a child with mental and physical disabilities. In her eyes is a depth that speaks to the divinity of life and the beauty of the soul."

ADOPTION

For those not able to bear children, adoption seems a desirable alternative. Yet it, too, may be accompanied with negative emotions. The couple has probably gone through extensive efforts and many disappointments and frustrations in their attempts to conceive. Psychologically, it is painful to realize that there can be no "natural" children. When one man learned that that was the case, he walked the streets all night, struggling with acceptance. "It's like all the children you ever hoped to have, have all just died," said one woman.

Even when adoption is the option, one may expect more challenges. While adoption may be considered a blessing, there is also a disproportionately high percentage of adoptees in therapy; a more widespread rejection of parental values among children who are adopted; and a higher incidence of serious problems such as imprisonment or unwed pregnancies experienced by adoptees. "It just seems so difficult for these children to overcome the feelings of being rejected by the one person who should have wanted them the most," observed one parent.

I know a man who has chosen to adopt several troubled teenage children. "Everyone has to suffer, so you might as well suffer for a good cause," he said.

THE GOLDEN YEARS

And what of the "golden years"? One thing is certain: growing old isn't for sissies. "No one wants to grow old, but it's better than the alternative," quipped one. In most cases, the body wears out long before we're ready to vacate the premises. (Personally, I think that people should be born old and then achieve youth when they have earned the right to enjoy it.)

To some, these years are a burden, to others, a blessing, depending upon their outlook. Aging often brings limitations, yet in the ripeness of age, the spirit can bloom. "Rather than thinking that time is *on* my hands, I realized that time is *in* my hands," said one active senior citizen.

"There is a compensation for growing older," said another. "When you don't look so good, you can't see so well, either."

Aging may be viewed as a terminal illness or as a rich inheritance. Some endure, and some enjoy their later years. Some look back with regret, while others reflect upon their lives with gratitude. Through heartache or joy, life's experiences may bring a sense of defeat and disappointment or of contentment and fulfillment. One ninety-year-old woman wrote:

> I remember the pain, and I remember the joys,
> And I'm living and loving all over again.
> And I think of the years, all too few, gone too fast,
> And accept the stark fact that nothing will last. . . .

YOUTH

Older people may envy youth, but youth see things from a different perspective:

> You see youth as a joyous thing
> About whom love and laughter cling.
> You see youth as a joyous elf
> Who sings sweet songs to please himself.
> You see his laughing, sparkling eyes
> To take earth's wonders with surprise.
> You think him free from cares and woes
> And naught of fear you think he knows,
> You see him tall, naively bold.
> You see him thus, for you are old.
>
> But I, I see him otherwise
> An unknown fear within his eyes.
> He works and plays and never knows,
> Where he is called nor why he goes.
> Each youth sustains within his breast
> A vague and infinite unrest.
> He goes about in still alarm,
> With shrouded future at his arm,
> With longings that can find no tongue.
> I see him thus, for I am young.

And so it goes. The point is that life itself is full of the anguish and the adventure of adversity—for all of us. Life is not either good *or* bad. Life includes both good *and* bad. It always has and it always will.

Life is filled with paradoxical situations. One man was asked what the worst day of his life was. It was, he said, when he was thirteen years old and he had told his alcoholic father to leave, that the family would be better off without him. The father did leave, never to return. Then the man was asked, "What was the *best* day of your life?"

He thought for a moment before he replied: "The same day."

* * * *

We were placed on this earth to experience life, including adversities and afflictions. We might call adversity the common denominator of the mortal experience. It touches all people, and the faces of adversity are endless.

Some see it in the death of a child. Others experience it in seemingly endless days in a hospital, nursing home, or sick bed at home. Many see it in various forms of loss: employment that is terminated; children who stray; marriages that fail; estrangement from family or friends; property that is lost because of calamity or of the actions of others. Some might see adversity in unfulfilled hopes, dreams, or promises: the unfulfilled yearning for marriage, for children, or for personal goals.

But if life is going to be a first-class experience, then we must expect to have some first-class trials. How can there be refining fires without enduring some heat? And whether the heat of adversity consumes or purifies us depends on how willing we are to learn, how willing we are to look for God's purpose in it. Life can be a first-class experience only if we develop a patient faith in God and in his unfolding purpose for our lives.

The difficulties in life are to make us better, not bitter. They will soften our hearts or harden our hearts, depending upon how we view them. James Russell Lowell said, "Mishaps are like knives—they either serve us or cut us, as we grasp them by the blade or by the handle."

After a devastating hurricane in Florida that destroyed thousands of homes some time ago, a news report quoted two people who had lost their homes. In each case the homes were destroyed but family members were not injured. One man said that this tragedy had destroyed his faith: how could God allow this to happen? The second man said that the experience had strengthened his faith. God had been good to him, he said, because although the family's home and possessions were lost, their lives were spared and the home could be rebuilt. Each of us chooses how we will react when we experience adversity.

Marianne Williamson recalled speaking at the funeral of a young mother who had been brutally murdered. She said to the husband, "Michael, you will never be the same, we all know that. You have two choices: You will become harder or you will become softer. You will conclude from this that no one, including God, is ever to be trusted again, or you will allow your heartbreak to so soften you—you will allow your tears to so melt the walls that surround your heart—that you will become a man of rare depth and sensitivity."

Steve Dunn illustrates the difference that attitude can make: "When my great-great grandparents came to America from Sweden over one hundred years ago, they were faced with a long ocean voyage, a train trip from New York to Omaha, and then a trek by wagon to Salt Lake City. But when they boarded the train in New York, they discovered that they were to ride in stock cars that had been used to haul hogs to market—the cars were filthy and filled with hog lice. Grandmother accepted the inconvenience, but the humiliation was almost more than Grandfather could bear.

"Grandmother was expecting another child, and somewhere on the plains of Nebraska, a healthy baby was born. But a few days later, the three-year-old son contracted cholera. In the middle of the night, Grandfather went to a neighboring wagon to borrow a candle, but was told they couldn't spare one. This angered him, and he fumed as he sat in the dark with his son's limp, feverish body in his arms. The boy died that night.

"The next morning the wagon master said they would hold a short funeral service and bury the boy in a shallow grave, apologetically explaining that they were in dangerous Indian country and didn't have time to do anything more. But Grandfather couldn't accept this and insisted on staying behind and digging a grave deep enough so the animals wouldn't get the body.

"Throughout the day and into the night he worked, building a strong wood coffin and digging a grave five feet deep in the hard soil. Finally, exhausted and sobbing, he buried his son and then walked all night to catch up with the wagon train. He was heartbroken and he was mad—mad at the wagon master for not waiting to give his son a proper burial, and mad at God for allowing his son to die. When he arrived at his wagon and vented his feelings to his wife, she spoke to him tenderly.

"'Father, we have to make the best of it. The baby and I are all right and, thank the Lord, the rest of us are well. If we get to our journey's end without any more trouble, we must be very thankful to our Heavenly Father. We are not the only ones that are having sorrow and trouble on this trip.'

"This wasn't the end of their difficulties; they continued to suffer serious hardships and adversities throughout their lives. But although they both went through identical experiences, each was affected differently by them. Grandfather became withdrawn, cantankerous, and bitter. He stopped going to church and found fault with church leaders. He became caught up in his own miseries, and the light of Christ grew dimmer and dimmer in his life.

"On the other hand, Grandmother's faith increased. Each new problem seemed to make her stronger. She became an angel of mercy—filled with empathy, compassion, and charity. She was a light to those around her. Her family gravitated toward her and looked to her as their leader."

How we allow our afflictions to affect us, whether we give up or endure, whether we become bitter or compassionate, is our choice.

CHAPTER THREE

The Things that Really Matter

IT WAS JANUARY 26, 2000, and North Carolina had just experienced the worst snow storm in recorded history. The people were unprepared to cope with it, and with 200,000 people without power, the governor declared a state of emergency. But this disaster came only four months after Hurricane Floyd caused flooding that had already devastated the state, resulting in six billion dollars worth of damage. "How much can you take?" the newscaster asked the governor.

"Well, we'll take as much as we're given," was his reply, adding, "but this is tough. Many people are still trying to get back into their homes after the hurricane." He then expressed gratitude for the help of the people of the nation who had already reached out, asking now for their faith and prayers in this latest disaster. "But we'll get through it," he ended.

Immediately following the interview with the governor, a commercial aired. An attractive woman in her thirties explained earnestly: "Age was catching up to me. I was getting furrows on my forehead and crows' feet around my eyes, and I didn't like it." She then told of the skin-enhancing product that solved her dilemma.

The contrast in the relative size of the two trials was astounding, even ludicrous. I thought it an excellent illustration of the things that really matter.

＊ ＊ ＊ ＊

When Evan (our second miracle baby, born when I was 44 years old) was only four months old and Merrie Anne was three, I had a frightening experience that caused me to recognize more fully the things I value most. From my journal comes this:

Yesterday was one of the worst days of my life. In the night, as I lay in bed, I experienced the tingling-numb sensation in my left leg that happens quite often these days. Before, I'd thought it interesting, but dismissed it. But _this_ time, I remembered an article I'd just read called "Three Months to Live," which told of a woman who had experienced a numbness in her left hand, then her arm, then her entire left side, then her face. They finally did a brain scan that revealed a brain tumor the size of an orange.

Now I was gripped with the fear that this sensation in my own left leg was also the symptom of a brain tumor. I would not be so paranoid were it not for the fact that I _did_ have to have a craniotomy to remove a brain tumor four years ago, and I'd never had the follow-up MRI to make sure it was still gone. . . .

I was assailed with all kinds of fearful thoughts. Of the financial ramifications and the fact that we had just dropped our health insurance three weeks earlier. Of the pain that I might experience before my demise: must I have a dramatic departure? I _hate_ pain.

But the worst thought that filled my heart with grief was of my children, of not being here to see them grow up, to love and enjoy them. Heavenly Father, why did you send these long-awaited, precious little children to me if I wasn't going to be able to stay long enough to raise them?

I awakened Micheal and we talked of many things; I was full of despair, of dread mixed with panic. Finally we went back to sleep.

The next day, Sunday, my heart was very heavy. I longed only to cuddle and cradle my two precious children. I thought of how valuable my time with them might be—how limited. When I looked into their faces, I smiled at them, because I wanted them to remember me smiling—but inside, my heart was weeping. It was one of the most difficult days of my life. . . .

Obviously, I didn't die. It was found that my body was in such poor condition structurally that it was restricting circulation: thus the sensation of numbness. But that frightening experience caused me to face my own mortality and to embrace my blessings with added joy. And the very next day, I could write: _Today was one of the happier days of my life._

In truth, none of us has any idea how long we have to live. We end up spending our time and energy and lives doing things that aren't all that important. We forget how precious life really is. "Whereas ye know not what shall be on the morrow. For what is your life? It is even a vapor, that appeareth for a little time, and then vanisheth away. For that ye ought to say, If the Lord will, we shall live, and do this, or that" (James 4:14,15).

Our priorities will determine what we seek in life. What we seek in life will determine our happiness and peace of mind. Our happiness and peace of mind will largely determine how well we cope with the trials and tribulations we will all have to face as we journey through life. Regardless of our circumstances, peace and joy come when we have a true perspective of what is really important in our lives. When we have our priorities straight, we become more concerned about life forever than life today.

Why must we be reminded? Why must a close proximity to death be required to keep us aware of why we're here? A woman dying of cancer said to me, "In the end, you realize that there are only two things that really matter: your relationship with the Savior, and your relationship with others in your life."

From a daughter's letter after the death of her mother: "Despite the fact that I know I am going to miss her terribly, I was able to let her go, knowing that she was at peace with the world and particularly at peace with herself. She finally came to understand how important she was to so many people. The last few weeks were both terrible and wonderful."

The daughter's letter ended with one of the last things her mother had said to her: "Love—that's all that's important—that's what it's all about. Nothing else matters."

Another woman facing her own death spoke of her new awareness: "To live is to love—nothing more and nothing less. I finally learned this."

Some of life's events cause us to change and broaden our perspective, as we are forced to recognize the things that really matter. Families who lose a loved one often express regrets such as, "Why weren't we closer when we had the chance?"

A mother who lost a seventeen-year-old son to brain cancer wrote: "Today, when I see parents impatient or tired or bored with their children, I wish I could say to them, 'But they are *alive*; think of the wonder of that!' Never have I felt the wonder and beauty of life so keenly as now in my grief that Johnny is not here to enjoy them. . . . Embrace your children with a little added rapture and a keener awareness of joy."

One month ago, my husband and I were traveling in heavy,

stop-and-go freeway traffic when the lane we were in momentarily stopped. A woman in a large van, looking over her shoulder while attempting to change lanes, did not see that our lane had stopped and rear-ended us going full speed, as evidenced by the fact that there were no skid marks. Our car was totalled. Our injuries were relatively minor: facial lacerations where my husband's face and glasses hit the steering wheel, and whiplash for us both.

We had purchased our heavily constructed, full-sized car only one month before. Had we been in our other car, a little tin-can hatchback, it might have been a different story. And I shudder to think of what might have happened had our two little children, now aged seven and four, been riding with us in the back seat in our smaller car, with only a flimsy seat, two feet of air space, and glass between them and a speeding van.

One minute we were living our ordinary lives, caught up in the small things of the day, and the next minute our lives might have been changed forever. Thinking of the tragedy that was avoided, I once again drew my children closer—in my arms and in my heart.

None of us likes to contemplate the possibility of losing a child to an early death. But even when they are with us until maturity, our time together is relatively short. We felt, when they were babies, that we would have them in our homes forever. But that forever is something like 216 months, and then they are never really ours again.

The adversity we experienced on the freeway became a blessing, for it gave me a clearer perspective, a better sense of the things that really matter. I began to be more involved in the lives of our children, thinking of the ever present possibility that each day could be their last—or mine. My relationship with our little children has changed in happy ways.

* * * *

Early one Saturday morning several years ago, we set out for a family outing. Not many miles from our home, we passed the scene of an accident on the opposite side of the freeway where a blue van had hit a metal pole. A helicopter, ambulance, and several police cars were at the scene.

It wasn't until the next day at church that we learned that the people involved in the accident were the Nelsons (names have been changed), members of our church, who, with their eight children, were en route back home to North Carolina after visiting relatives in Utah. The father and fourteen-year-old son had been killed, and all the rest of the family members except one were seriously injured and taken to three area hospitals.

For the next several weeks, our lives became entwined with theirs, as they were in our thoughts and prayers. Though visits to the hospitals were curtailed, the progress of the family members were reported regularly in church congregations throughout the area. Young children made cards and gifts for the Nelson children. Many tears were shed as we empathized with the plight of these "strangers" in our midst.

I had heard of the strength of this woman, Annette Nelson, the mother of the family, and for a long time I felt that I should meet her. It was six months later and 1500 miles away that I finally had the opportunity.

I must admit that the first thing one might gain from their experience is a clearer perspective of the things that really matter. One Saturday some weeks after the accident, I recall feeling very frustrated. I'd purchased a new sofa set, and we had given away our old set. For a week we'd been sitting on wooden chairs in the living room with the promise that on Saturday a truck would be obtained and we would go pick up the new sofa set. But on Saturday, the keys to the truck couldn't be found.

Besides that, our car had a problem where it might stall or refuse to start at any place or any time, and on that Saturday, I'd been stalled for sixteen minutes (I timed it) in a store's parking lot before it decided to start. I was really quite distressed as these types of frustrations mounted.

That evening I recorded the happenings of the day in my journal. When I was finished writing in it, I thought of calling for an update on the condition of the members of the Nelson family.

In addition to the father and fourteen-year-old son being killed, the mother was paralyzed from the chest down, with hope that one day she would have more complete use of her arms and hands. Trevor, seventeen, was the only one uninjured. Caroline, sixteen, had severe facial injuries which would require plastic surgery, as well as head trauma resulting in the loss of much of the use of her left leg and hand. Richard, twelve, suffered leg injuries so severe that it was still not known whether or not his legs could be saved. Jeremy, ten, was still in a coma, with only hope that he would one day come out of it. The twins, Mike and Mark, eight, were the least injured and were in casts and were now staying with their uncle in Illinois. And Melinda, six, whose foot was partially graveled away, had undergone reconstructive surgery—four times in four successive days.

I thought of my own major trials of that day: learning I would have to wait another two days to get my new sofa set, and being stalled in a parking lot for sixteen frustrating minutes. I compared them to the adversity of the Nelson family—and I was ashamed.

(As one person dryly commented when I shared the story of the Nelsons with her: "I'm thankful for the *little* things that keep *me* down!")

So often our trials are so minute, so trifling, of such little importance in the larger scheme of things. As feelings of stress mount, we might ask ourselves, "Will this really matter in eternity? Will it matter ten years from now, or next year? Will it even matter tomorrow?" Most things won't matter beyond the moment. But how we react to those small, yet numerous stressful situations *will* make a difference—in our relationships and forever.

When I visited Annette Nelson, she spoke about how her own perspective of the important things in life had changed so drastically because of the accident: "We are all so caught up in the temporal, earthly things—whether it is carting kids to baseball games or whether it is buying exactly the right piece of furniture or the right clothes or remodeling our homes. . . . How much our lives are focused on the material things instead of the spiritual things. But I have learned through this that material things mean nothing, absolutely nothing. Even when I start thinking about our new house that we plan to build (a custom home built to accommodate a wheelchair), it really means nothing. It is only a place for us to be until we can do the really important things."

The really important things. Twelve-year-old Richard Nelson was the most vocal of the children as we visited. He was making a list of wishes for his future. The list was long, and included "a dog, a BMW, and a wife. . ."

I smiled at him. "Richard, your list is so long. If you could have only one wish, what would it be?"

Richard became more thoughtful and then asked, "Could I have *two* wishes?"

"All right," I conceded. "Two wishes."

"I would wish to have my dad and Ryan back," he said quietly.

* * * *

Extreme adversity, such as the loss of a loved one, can bring about an abrupt, sharpened focus on the things we value most and can give us a clearer perspective of life and what we're here for. "How are you doing?" my cousin was asked as he climbed into the van for the ride to the cemetery after the funeral of another cousin's eighteen-year-old daughter.

His reply: "How am I doing? Not very well in the things that don't matter."

Yet it is often difficult to maintain that clear perspective amidst everyday frustrations. Lucille Johnson, lecturer and family counselor, related how one day as she showed an important guest through her home, she was mortified to look into her son's room and find it a shambles. Later that same evening, she expressed her embarrassment and her displeasure with her son at having the guest see his room in such disarray.

Her son put his arm around his mother and said to her sympathetically, "Mother, next time someone comes to you for counseling—someone who has just learned that they are terminally ill with cancer—or maybe a lady whose husband has just run off with another woman—or parents who don't know what to do because their kids are doing drugs—you just tell them this: 'You think *you've* got problems! You should see my Gary. He doesn't keep his room clean!'"

It may be difficult to follow heavenly traffic signs when you're traveling in earthly traffic jams. But if we can see the long-range plan, perhaps we will not be so frustrated by short-range challenges. With a broader view, it is easier to deal with the details. He who has a *why* to live can stand almost any *how*. But sometimes it is hard to see the picture when you're inside the frame. We need to have a more eternal perspective to enable us to see beyond the anguish to the adventure of adversity.

These are the things of eternity,
These are the things that are sure.

They light the path for the journey Home
Where good things will endure.
And I pray that my heart will always be
On the things of eternity.
          (Janice Kapp Perry)

One man who had recently lost his teenage son in a car accident said, "We now look at life and the experiences we endure here with an eternal perspective. We are able to cope with adversity and trial because we know why we are here and we know what will be the result of our endurance."

               * * * *

Marlene Mullarkey recounted how, through her own grief, she had gained such a perspective. One summer her grandmother passed away. Two weeks later, her father died suddenly of a heart attack. Then, a little over a month later, at the time her first child was to be born, a knot in the umbilical cord cut off his oxygen supply, robbing him of life. She described her agony and then, with time, a renewed faith.

"My despair was replaced by a feeling of peace and calm, and with it my perspective on life altered dramatically. Things that would have bothered me prior to that summer seemed unimportant. The urgency to do this or that no longer tugged at me. It was as if by accepting death I had caught a glimpse of eternity beyond mortal life. . . .

"I felt that time was not meant to be measured by a clock or a calendar; these things were merely tools to help us in our daily existence. Rather, time was meant to be marked by the significant events in our lives, both sad and happy. It is our lot to endure hardship when it comes and realize that this too shall pass. Waiting for the wounds to heal is, perhaps, the hardest part of all. What is significant is how well we succeed in enduring and what we learn from the experience.

"The good that we do, the love we give, and the things we learn through hardship mature and guide us through life. These are the things by which our time on earth should be measured, rather than by minutes, days, and years. . . ."

CHAPTER FOUR

To Teach Us

DO WE REALLY think we are here on earth just to watch other people hurt—to learn from *their* suffering and not our own? We came here to learn from our *own* experiences, painful as they may be. This learning process may appear to be unfair, as the innocents seem to suffer disproportionately. But if we are willing to let him, God can work all these things together for our own good.

The great tragedy of this life is not in suffering, but suffering in vain. It is only wasted if we learn nothing by it. Our richest source of understanding is our own experience. We learn a great deal from the things that we suffer. "One can learn more from ten days of agony than from ten years of contentment," observed Merle Shain. Even the Savior learned from suffering: "Though he were a Son, yet learned he obedience by the things which he suffered."

"Everything I have learned in all my years, has been through affliction, and not through happiness," reflected one person. Another declared, "I have tough days and good days. On the good days, I live. On the tough days, I learn." One plain fact of life is that we often think deeper and learn faster when we hurt. Looking back over my own life, it seems that I have learned the most when I felt the greatest pain.

> I walked a mile with Pleasure;
> She chattered all the way,
> But left me none the wiser
> For all she had to say.
> I walked a mile with Sorrow;
> Not a word said she,
> But oh, the things I learned from her
> When Sorrow walked with me!

You will forget the times of your distress, but you will never forget the lessons they taught you. Looking back on my own journey, I can see that it took some pretty hard knocks to dislodge some of the dross I carried with me. The experiences of my life humbled me, taught me, changed me. They gave me a clearer perspective and a new heart.

I remember one man recalling a time of deep trial in his life: "I learned some things through that heartbreak that I could never have learned any other way." Boyd K. Packer verbalized a similar feeling: "I have learned this from experience: life will teach us some things we didn't think we wanted to know. But these hard lessons can be the most valuable ones."

"And though the Lord give you the bread of adversity, and the water of affliction, yet thine eyes shall see thy teachers" (Isaiah 30:20). But sometimes the crust on the "bread of adversity" is so very hard!

The reward of suffering is experience. Abigail Van Buren said, "If we could sell our experiences for what they cost us, we would all be millionaires." How much is experience worth? Can a price tag be put on it?

C. S. Lewis offers a positive perspective: "What I like about experience is that it is such an honest thing. You may take any number of wrong turnings; but keep your eyes open and you will not be allowed to go very far before the warning signs appear. You may have deceived yourself, but experience is not trying to deceive you. The universe rings true whenever you fairly test it."

As has been said: "Good judgment comes from experience. Experience comes from bad judgment." Unfortunately in life, only some of us can learn from other people's mistakes. The rest of us have to be the other people.

One very important purpose of adversity is to teach us, to educate us. Adversity is, I believe, the primary teaching tool of a wise and loving Father in heaven. God could have organized this world in some other way. Perhaps he could have arranged to have some very fine videos to teach us about this life and the things of eternity. But apparently, He felt that the best way to learn is through our own experience, painful as it sometimes is.

"Life is like playing a violin solo in public and learning the instrument as one goes along," said Samuel Butler.

John Holt articulated a similar analogy: "Not many years ago I began to play the cello. Most people would say that what I am doing is 'learning to play' the cello. But these words carry into our minds the strange idea that there exists two very different processes: (1) learning to play the cello; and (2) playing the cello. They imply that I will do the first until I have completed it, at which point I will stop the first process and begin the second. In short, I will go on 'learning to play' until I have 'learned to play' and then I will begin to play. Of course this is nonsense. There are not two processes, but one. We learn to do something by doing it. There is no other way."

Could God prevent these "learning experiences"—these hurtful things that come to us? Of course he could. He is omnipotent, with all power to control our lives, save us pain, obstruct injustice, intercept all accidents, prevent sickness and discomfort of all kinds. But he will not.

How unwise would be a parent who, in his desire to protect his child from suffering, decided that he should keep that baby strapped in her swing or enclosed in her playpen in order to avoid the repeated pain and frustration that would inevitably be a part of her attempts to try walking. God knows that, in shielding His children from disappointment, heartache, temptations, sorrows, and suffering, he would also impede their progress, interfere with their growth, and obstruct their learning.

A wise man stated: "Every trial and experience you have passed through is necessary. There is not a single condition of life or one hour's experience but what is beneficial to all those who make it their study and aim to improve upon the experience they gain." I am convinced that everyone is exactly where he needs to be in order to learn the lessons he needs to learn.

I had a dear roommate in college who, when things were going badly for her, would say, "What is God trying to teach me through this experience?" Instead of asking "Why me? Why this? Why now?" we can ask, "What can I learn from this? How can I grow through this experience and become a better person?"

Orson Whitney maintained that "no pain that we suffer, no trial that we experience is wasted. It ministers to our education, to the development of such qualities as patience, faith, fortitude, and humility. All that we suffer and all that we endure, especially when we endure it patiently, builds up our characters, purifies our hearts, expands our souls, and makes us more tender and charitable, more worthy to be called the children of God. And it is through sorrow and suffering, toil and tribulation, that we gain the education that we came here to acquire."

* * * *

The world is not a playground; it is a schoolroom. Life is not a holiday, but an education. We have been sent away to "school" by loving Parents who miss us, who are eager to communicate with us, and who long for our return after we have obtained our education, gained experience living away from Home, and learned the things we were sent here to learn. God has provided a customized curriculum for each of us in order to teach us the things that we most need to know. Some graduate early, with honors. Sadly, some drop out. The rest of us are left to continue the process of learning and growing until we are notified of graduation and are able to return Home.

Just as in school we are given exams to test our knowledge of a subject and presented with problems to prove our competency in solving them, so are we also asked to participate in a similar manner in this "school of stress" called life.

One person quipped, however, that "experience is an interesting teacher. It gives the exam first and teaches the lesson after."

Another man observed: "Adversity gives us a test, grades us, checks our progress. Unless we had those tests, we wouldn't evaluate that often enough. Adversity not only builds our strength, it also shows our weaknesses."

Some may complain that the exams are too difficult, the problems too complex. But any good teacher knows that students must be given problems just beyond their comfortable grasp, problems that require some stretching—for that is how growth and learning are achieved. As one young man observed, "The Lord's class is not dismissed until the lesson is learned—and even then there is still homework."

If I have demonstrated a lack of skill in forgiving others, I may be signing up for a course in Remedial Forgiveness in which I attract situations that will provide many opportunities to learn the basic fundamentals. As long as forgiveness is something I need to learn, I will continue to attract opportunities to practice it.

If I feel quite competent in my knowledge of patience, my Counselor might offer me a course in Advanced Patience to develop my skills even further through practical work experience—on-the-job training.

If I feel extremely confident in my humility, my class schedule might include that subject under the Honors Program, where I can either demonstrate my competency or be brought low due to the extremely difficult course material included there (in which case, I may have to humble myself enough to ask for some special tutoring).

Trials are but lessons that we failed to learn, presented once again. Actually, it is our own stubbornness that determines how difficult our curriculum has to be. God loves us enough to do whatever it takes to win our loyalty and to purify our hearts. If we resist the lessons He provides, if we rebel and refuse to learn, the lesson is repeated—presented to us in various forms—until it is mastered. Then we can go on to the next lesson.

As a young man, Peter Jeppson was in a terrible automobile accident and was so severely burned that he was declared dead until a nurse, passing his covered body on the stretcher in the hallway of the hospital, noticed a movement when his arm flinched. He lived, spending a year as a full-time patient, and many more months in and out of the hospital where he underwent a series of 28 operations to reconstruct his facial features and correct injuries suffered in the accident. He has since married, had children, is a successful businessman, and lifts others by sharing his story.

Peter related the experience of finding himself a passenger on an airplane along with a man he greatly admired. The man asked him: if he had a choice, would he go through that incredible ordeal again. Peter opened his mouth to give the obvious answer but noticed that the man had turned his attention back to his paper, as though expecting Peter to take some time to reflect before giving an answer.

And so Peter contemplated the question. He reflected on all that had happened to him. He thought of all the blessings, the qualities of sensitivity and of patience that had been forced upon him through that experience. The question so perplexed him that he took a whole year to answer. Finally, he wrote a letter to the man with his response.

Yes, he *would* go through it again. That "tragedy" had been a blessing in his life. He had learned a great deal and gained qualities he might never have attained without it.

Kenneth Beesley observed: "What seems to be a tragedy and a cause for suffering may from an eternal perspective be a blessing and a cause for rejoicing. Sufferings have the potential of blessing man. They may strengthen us for future tasks. They can make us sensitive to the pains of others and more willing to sacrifice for others. They may help us appreciate Christ's atonement; they may help to purge our imperfections and to purify us."

> My thanks come easily when my fortunes rise
> And my will is king and all the world seems my estate.
> My thanks come easily such times, but wait . . .
> Today, let me reflect upon those thanks I owe
> But which I find express themselves less fluently.
>
> Today, let me remember to give thanks,
> Not only for the sunlight,
> But for those darker hours
> That teach me Fortitude.
>
> Let me profess, today, a grateful heart,
> Not merely for successes I may know,
> But as truly for those failures
> That teach Humility.
>
> Let me express my gratitude
> For all those petty, inner conflicts
> Which, once resolved, breed new Serenity . . .
> And for those small, distressing fears
> That have their ways of building Hope.
>
> Let me breathe appreciation
> For all those poignant slights
> That teach me Thoughtfulness,

The wrongs that teach me Fairness,
And for each violated trust
That leaves Loyalty as its lesson.

And let me not forget, today,
To whisper thanks for these:
The contempt that teaches Pity,
The tear that teaches Joy,
The pain that teaches Mercy
And the loneliness that teaches Love.

So, now . . .
Let me reflect upon these thanks I owe . . .
And let my thanks come easily today!
                                    (John Deer)

In his booklet, *Tragedy or Destiny?* Spencer W. Kimball stated: "Being human, we would expel from our lives physical pain and mental anguish and assure ourselves of continual ease and comfort, but if we were to close the doors upon sorrow and distress, we might be excluding our greatest friends and benefactors. Suffering can make saints of people as they learn patience, long-suffering, and self-mastery."

Kimball was, himself, the personification of those virtues. His personal secretary said of him, "He was no ordinary man. He has been the finest example of faith and courage and long-suffering and patience that I have ever known." Spencer Kimball spent his life in service to others, even through life-threatening physical afflictions including throat cancer and surgery, open-heart surgery, and brain surgeries.

At his death, another associate said of him, "As long as our memories function, we will be nourished and encouraged by the eloquence of the example of this man in overcoming—or coexisting with—adversity after adversity. His resilience was exemplary. His deft humor occupied the place which might have so easily been commandeered by self-pity. His selfless dedication, time and again, caused him to be up and about his Father's business, sometimes even before he was well. The examples are legendary and will be recounted for many years!"

Kimball's heart surgeon, Russell Nelson, was asked to be one of the speakers at his funeral. Kimball's wife said to him, "No one knew his heart better than you," and "You knew him at his worst moments."

Dr. Nelson disclosed, "As I watched him face his own trials, I witnessed the depth of his love for others as he frequently disappeared from his own hospital bed to bless the sick, even strangers. Whether their problems involved fever, cancer, or the heart, he could say in sympathy, 'I know how you feel.'"

* * * *

Mary Dawn Nuzman shared what she had learned and gained through adversity: "I started out in life weak and afraid. In grade school when we had to get those awful shots, I always fainted. Everyone in my class wanted to stand by me because they liked to see my eyes roll back in my head. Even when my children came along later, I fainted when one of them got hurt.

"As a young mother, my life was relatively free from real, serious trials. I had a good life. And then, suddenly, I was faced with a real change. After 18 years of companionship, I found myself alone with five children to raise. My children were young. I was not trained or prepared to support them. I felt so alone; I was so afraid. Every day I would sit in my room and cry. Then I wondered what other people did when they needed help. I decided to learn from them.

"First, I went to my parents where I was strengthened by their wisdom and the example of courage that they are to me. I remembered the things that they had taught me as a child. That we have a purpose here on earth, that we all agreed to come here to earthly life and to accept all its happiness and joy, as well as its grief, illness, and loss.

"My parents now told me that I could lose faith, place blame, or, even worse, sink into everlasting depression—or I could get hold of myself and make something of my life. It was my choice. And so I looked at my children who were looking to me for help, and I made my choice.

"Second, after my parents, I looked to my friends, many of whom had faced trials in their own lives. Could I do any less than they? Their trials were serious, yet they seemed to be growing by their experiences. I learned from them that we each deal with different aspects of life in individual and unique ways.

"And then, most important, I turned to my Heavenly Father for the strength I needed to grow spiritually. I prayed as I had never prayed before. I learned that we may not get the answer we want, but we *will* be lifted in spirit. We *will* have a sense of direction, and most important, we will feel God's love for us.

"And then I studied. I read every book I could get my hands on, it seemed. I learned from the scriptures that we need not suffer in this life alone. 'But if from thence thou shalt seek the Lord thy God, thou shalt find him, if thou seek him with all thy heart and with all thy soul. When thou art in tribulation and all these things are come upon thee, even in the latter days, if thou turn to the Lord thy God and shalt be obedient unto his voice, he will not forsake thee" (Deut. 4:29,30).

"Now we are faced with a new trial in our lives: that of seeing a cherished son nearly lose his life in a tragic accident [thrown from a horse] and being faced with a long and difficult recovery. And again I feel the need to gain strength. But the sources are the same: my family members who have been constantly at my side. My husband and his children who themselves are no strangers to grief. My daughter whose spirit is much more mature than mine. . . . I've gained strength from friends who have fasted and prayed and who daily express concern—friends who have known more heartache than I.

"I have learned that it is not the number or the size or the kinds of trials that we are called to face. It is the way in which we choose to face them—and what we become because of them. Those are the things that have eternal consequences."

Mary Dawn Nuzman's account was written twelve years ago and was included in the previous edition of this book. Two years after the account was written, her daughter "whose spirit is much more mature than mine" was killed in a car accident.

I spoke to Mary Dawn today. Despite continuing challenges, her tone is upbeat, her attitude positive, her spirit strong. There are good things happening in her life, happy things to look forward to. She is very different now than the "weak and afraid" person she described herself as being earlier in her life. Whatever the lessons she needed to learn, she seems to have learned them well. I learn from her.

Richard Bach asserted: "Learning is discovering what you already know. Doing is demonstrating that you know it. Teaching is reminding others that they know it just as well as you. We are all learners, doers, teachers."

CHAPTER FIVE
To Prove Us

WHILE VISITING WITH the Nelson family about adversity, I attempted to define for six-year-old Melinda the meaning of the word: "It's all the crummy things that happen to you in life."

But sixteen-year-old Caroline proceeded to give a much better definition, one with a more positive connotation than the one I had offered. She said simply, "It means opposition."

Friction or resistance are necessary forces, without which a person or vehicle couldn't move, or if already in motion, could not be stopped except by collision. Simple things like nails, screws, and bolts wouldn't stay in place; a cork wouldn't stay in a bottle; a light globe would drop from its socket; a lid wouldn't stay on a jar.

The law of friction or resistance that we think of as only applying to science seems to apply also in our personal lives. Unless we have something to struggle against, something to challenge us, something to oppose and to test us, something that would cause us to stretch further and reach higher, we probably wouldn't do it on our own—not when we're comfortable where we are. But when we're confronted with opposition, we tend to become stronger through overcoming. That is how we reach and stretch and grow and progress. There is no triumph without a battle, no victory without a conflict. Opposition is as much a part of God's plan as is deliverance. "You must meet with triumph and disaster and treat both of those impostors just the same," someone observed.

The path may be strewn with rocks that bruise our feet, but they only tend to toughen and strengthen our resolve. If we banish hardship, we banish hardihood; walking close behind calamity is courage.

Annette Nelson's final comments as we ended our visit were impressive. She said: "Things were so perfect in our family before the accident. Everything in our lives seemed to be going so well. In fact, the thought had occurred to me at one time that I might finish my life here and return to God, and he might say to me, 'Well, Annette, you did all right—but then, you didn't have any real problems, either.'"

She went on. "Often, when things are good and wonderful, you are not struggling to become better because things are so comfortable as they are. Before the accident we were probably complacent and we might have lacked motivation. Maybe we were taking things for granted. We were in a nice rut. Because things were easy, we weren't pushing ourselves to be better. 'I'm doing fine; why do I need to do more?'

"But now, since the accident, we have to be motivated just to survive. The things I have to work through right now are more defined. When everything is going well, you may actually be at a disadvantage, because we're here to do the best we can with what we've got. Maybe I wasn't doing my best before; maybe now I am."

Someone said, "Conflict is a necessary experience in life. Because of it we rise or fall, but without it we never rise at all."

When I am working with dough for dinner rolls, I admit that I have an unreasonable fear that if I punch the dough down after it has risen once, that it will never rise again and that the end product will be flat and dense. In reality, the opposite is true. It is punching the dough down and allowing it to rise again—and it *will* rise again—that creates dinner rolls that are light and appetizing.

God trusts us enough to punch us down. He has confidence in our buoyancy and resilience to rise again, to become better than we could otherwise have been—if we are willing to respond to the leavening of his love.

* * * *

According to B. H. Roberts, "Some of the lowliest walks of life, the paths which lead into the deepest valleys of sorrow and up to the most rugged steeps of adversity, are the ones which, if a man travel in, will best accomplish the object of his existence in this world . . . The conditions which place men where they may always walk on the unbroken plain of prosperity and seek for nothing but their own pleasure are not the best within the gift of

God. For in such circumstances men soon drop into a position analogous to the stagnant pool; while those who have to contend with difficulties, brave dangers, endure disappointments, struggle with sorrows, eat the bread of adversity and drink the water of affliction, develop a moral and spiritual strength, together with a purity of life and character, unknown to the heirs of ease and wealth and pleasure."

B. H. Roberts' words were not mere rhetoric; he spoke from his own experience. His use of words such as valleys, rugged, steeps, travel, plain, difficulties, and dangers are more than creative analogy. As a ten-year-old boy, he and his older sister crossed the plains of America in 1866, their mother having made the journey from England four years earlier. The journey was fraught with the anguish and adventure of adversity. Yet, he had such high expectations of his new home that when they reached their destination, he mistook a beautiful church for his new house. His family's humble cottage with its sod roof and dirt floor was a great disappointment.

But opposition made him strong. After serving on the general councils of his church at a relatively early age, he was elected to the United States Congress. He was a prolific writer of theology and history.

> For every hill I've had to climb,
> For every stone that bruised my feet,
> For all the blood and sweat and grime,
> For blinding storms and burning heat,
> My heart sings but a grateful song—
> These are the things that made me strong!
>
> For all the heartaches and the tears,
> For all the anguish and the pain,
> For gloomy days and fruitless years,
> And for the hopes that lived in vain,
> I do give thanks; for now I know
> These are the things that helped me grow!
>
> 'Tis not the softer things of life
> Which stimulate man's will to strive,

But bleak adversity and strife
Do most to keep man's will alive.
O'er rose-strewn paths the weaklings creep,
But brave hearts dare to climb steep!

(L. E. Thayer, *Friendly Obstacles*)

TO TEST AND TO PROVE US

One might wonder, since the Old Testament prophet Abraham was promised a great posterity, why God tested him by requesting that he sacrifice his only chance for posterity? Could it be that Abraham needed to learn something about Abraham? Abraham learned that his commitment to God was total and unconditional. And so he also learned that God could now bless him without reservation.

C. S. Lewis was severely tested at the early death of his beloved wife. He wrote: "You never know how much you really believe anything until its truth or falsehood becomes a matter of life and death to you. It is easy to say you believe a rope to be strong and sound as long as you are merely using it to tie a box. But suppose you had to hang by that rope over a precipice. Wouldn't you then first discover how much you really trusted it? Only a real risk tests the reality of a belief. Your view of eternal life will not be serious if nothing much is at stake. A man has to be knocked silly before he comes to his senses.

"I had been warned—indeed, I had warned myself. I knew we were promised sufferings. That was part of the program. We were even told, 'Blessed are they that mourn' and I accepted it. I've got nothing that I hadn't agreed to. So if my house collapsed at one blow, that is because it was a house of cards. The faith which took these things into account was not an adequate faith. If I had really cared, as I thought I did, about the sorrows of others in this world, then I should not have been so overwhelmed when my own sorrow came. I thought I trusted the rope until it mattered. . . ."

Trials can help us learn more about ourselves, about our allegiance and our strength of commitment to the values we espouse. Adversity is the test of principle. Without opposition and testing, our freedom of choice loses its meaning. Opposition, tribulation, afflictions, the refining fire are part of the eternal plan. Besides personal growth, adversity provides the opportunity for us to be proven trustworthy before God.

Job could say with confidence: "But he knoweth the way that I take: when he hath tried me, I shall come forth as gold. My foot hath held his steps, his way have I kept, and not declined" And later, "Til I die I will not remove mine integrity from me. My righteousness I hold fast, and will not let it go; my heart shall not reproach me so long as I live." May we say with the much tested Job, "Til I die I will not remove my integrity from me."

Character is best formed in the stormy billows of the world. A smooth sea never made a skillful mariner. How will courage, discipline, and perseverance ever flourish if we were never tested? Seneca observed: "The bravest sight in the world is to see a great man struggling against adversity."

Show me someone who has done something worthwhile and I will show you someone who has overcome adversity. If we study the lives of great men and women we find that invariably, greatness was developed, tested, and revealed through the darker periods of their lives. One of the largest tributaries of the river of greatness is the stream of adversity. J. C. Penney said, "I would never have amounted to anything were it not for adversity. I was forced to come up the hard way."

A Chinese proverb states: "A gem cannot be polished without friction, nor a man perfected without trials." No pressure, no diamonds. The finest steel has to go through the hottest fire. So it was with Job; so it is today. As was said of one good man: "He is a man of proven integrity who has been tempered by the refiner's fire."

When I was thirteen years old, I was told by a spiritual leader: "Because you have been blessed with so many talents and abilities, it might well be that your trials shall be a little extraordinary, for your Father in heaven wants you to return into His presence with your mettle having been completely proven . . . ."

In 1972, the first six months of marriage we lived in a very old house for which we paid rent of $60 per month. Although daylight could be seen through cracks in the walls, we felt fortunate to have found such a bargain in our college town in the middle of the school year. It even came with a wringer washing machine. In my youthful idealism, I could not have known what lay ahead in the trials that awaited me. I've been through the wringer enough now to know that I neither fade nor shrink. In fact, I hope that I have come out brighter.

A kind friend paid me a great compliment when she wrote: "You are a veteran soldier who has been through some hard and difficult battles, and have been victorious because your scars are a broken heart and a contrite spirit—a sure sign of those who truly love the Lord. . . ."

Yet, it is natural for us to flinch at the pain. One young woman expressed her feelings poignantly: "My head hurt; the pain had become most excruciating. I recall wanting all the questions pounding inside me to stop, wanting life to withhold so much pain and so many trials. I wondered why all I wanted in life seemed to be obtained only through periods of suffering. I wanted only for once to be able to enjoy a chapter of my life without the suffering, without the trials, without the worry, without the failures, without the hurt . . . I wondered how I could show the Lord that he could trust and have faith in me without having to test me. I wanted the blessings I desired most to come without trials."

* * * *

Nedra Redd, after recounting some of the major trials in her life culminating in life-threatening, emergency surgery for removal of a brain tumor, expressed her beliefs gained through her own experience. "I remember thinking when things were really hard that that just wasn't the way it was supposed to be. But it *is* the way it is supposed to be. There are times when we are to be tried and tested, you know. And along the way at proper intervals, our Father in Heaven provides the break times, the relief times, the special times when we know that we just couldn't be happier. . . . But it is not we who regulate the magnitude of our tests or determine the time of relief."

Ardith Kapp agrees: "The very hour one might expect relief may be the moment in which the Lord will take count of our endurance and our faithfulness."

> After the trial, we will be blessed,
> But this life is the test.
>   (Janice Kapp Perry)

CHAPTER SIX

Not to Impoverish, But to Enrich Us

ANN LANDERS WROTE, "No one knows why life must be so punishing to some of God's finest creatures. Perhaps it is true that everything has a price and we must sacrifice something precious to gain something else. The poets and philosophers say adversity, sorrow and pain give our lives an added dimension. Those who suffer deeply touch life at every point; they drain the cup to the dregs while others sip only the bubbles on top. Perhaps no man can touch the stars unless he has known the depths of despair—and fought his way back."

Kahlil Gibran shared his own feelings: "It is my fervent hope that my whole life on this earth will ever be tears and laughter. Tears that purify my heart and reveal to me the secret of life and its mystery, laughter that brings me closer to my fellowmen, tears with which I join the brokenhearted, laughter that symbolizes joy over my very existence."

Life is always difficult in proportion to its intensity and reality. I'm certain that we have all felt grief so intense, so all-consuming, that it wrenches our very heartstrings and we thought at the time that we could not bear it. A journal entry after a major disappointment reflects such a feeling: *Many weeks have passed. It seems as though the pain is duller and the remembrance of the horror dimmer. But then something happens and it hits me all over again. And there returns the emptiness and the ache in my heart. And I weep again at the sadness and the heartbreak. And my heart cries out for the hundredth time, "Will this hurt never end?"*

God polishes and refines us. He lets us know discouragement and failure. He allows us to experience illness and sorrow. All this is part of a refining process, and the effect of that process can become beautifully evident in our lives. Sometimes, however, it is so painful that we may be tempted to put up a wall to shut out the pain or to become calloused. But "the protective shield we put up against possible hurt also reduces our chances to be exposed to, and to enjoy, possible pleasure. In isolating ourselves from pain, we also isolate ourselves from joy."

Eda LeShan further noted: "Our natural inclination as parents is to try to protect children from pain. We have the mistaken notion that if a child is happy we are doing a good job; if a child is sad we are failing as parents. But giving children the message that happy is good and sad is terrible decreases their capacity to explore the full range of human experiences.

"Children need to understand that suffering, frustration and failure are not only inevitable but helpful. . . . Children need to experience such feelings as they grow up; it helps them to develop the patience, persistence and ability to cope that they'll need later on. There is nothing so terrible about failing and feeling pain; what hurts in the long run is not trying because of the fear of pain."

A father told of how painful it had been for him to tell six-year-old Lenny that his dog had been run over and killed. Worried about his son's reaction, he said, "I know this is a terrible shock; if you like we can go pick out a new dog right away."

The son, weeping for his dead dog, looked up at his father and said, "No, it's not time yet. I have to miss Benny first." About six months later Lenny told his father he was ready to look for a new dog.

"I realized later," his father said, "that Lenny enjoyed the second dog far more than he did Benny; something had been added, not taken away. We pay a price in pain, but in some strange way, it's worth it."

What could we know, except by its opposite? Who could count the days if there were no nights in between? Who could appreciate the light were it not for the darkness? How could we feel gratitude for health if we've never experienced illness? If we do not know hardship, we cannot enjoy ease. If we never tasted the bitter, we could not know the sweet. Death makes life more precious; frustration makes success more fulfilling; failure makes the next accomplishment more meaningful. For some reason, sleep, riches, and health, to be truly enjoyed, must be interrupted.

Wise men speak of it. Ben Franklin: "When the well's dry, we know the worth of water." Emerson: "When it is dark enough men see the stars." Carl Jung: "There are as many nights as days, and the one is just as long as the other in the year's course. Even a happy life cannot be without a measure of darkness, and the word 'happy' would lose its meaning if it were not balanced by sadness."

> All sunny skies would be too bright,
> All morning hours mean too much light,
> All laughing days too gay a strain;
> There must be clouds, and night, and rain,
> And shut-in days, to make us see
> The beauty of life's tapestry.

The hole that suffering carves in the soul will someday be the receptacle for our joy. Just as spring is born from winter's laboring pain, we all must die a bit before we're born again.

> It seems as you look back over things,
>   that all that you treasure dear
> Is somehow blent in a wondrous way
>   with a heart pang and a tear.
> Though many a day is a joyous one
>   when viewed by itself apart,
> The golden threads in the warp of life
>   are the sorrows that tug at your heart.
>   (Edgar A. Guest, *The Sorrow Tugs*)

Steven Cramer wrote, "There are many circumstances which seem so hopeless and devastating that it truly takes diligent searching to find God's purpose in them. Someday, on the other side of eternity, we will be able to look back over life's adversities and see divine purpose in them as they gave us experience, built character, and helped us learn how much we needed the Savior in our daily lives. . . . You can test this principle of divine purpose in adversity by tracing the pattern of your own experience. Examine a situation in your life which now brings you great joy. Trace it back through the genealogy of circumstance that preceded the present victory, and you will inevitably find that its roots lie in some challenge of the past, some weakness or difficulty which once gave you great sorrow."

* * * *

At a yard sale I purchased a framed piece of hand-lettered prose:

> Then a woman said, Speak to us of Joy and Sorrow.
> And he answered:
> Your joy is your sorrow unmasked.
> And the selfsame well from which your laughter rises
>   was oftentimes filled with your tears.
> And how else can it be?
> The deeper that sorrow carves into your being,
>   the more joy you can contain.
> Is not the cup that holds your wine the very
>   cup that was burned in the potter's oven?
> And is not the lute that soothes your spirit
>   the very wood that was hollowed with knives?
> When you are joyous, look deep into your heart
>   and you shall find it is only that which has
>   given you sorrow that is giving you joy.
> When you are sorrowful, look again in your heart,
> And you shall see that in truth you are
>   weeping for that which has been your delight.
> Some of you say, "Joy is greater than sorrow,"
> And others say, "Nay, sorrow is the greater."
> But I say unto you, they are inseparable.
> Together they come, and when one sits alone
>   with you at your board, remember that the other
>   is asleep upon your bed.
> Verily you are suspended like scales between
>   your sorrow and your joy.
> Only when you are empty
>   are you at standstill and balanced.
> When the treasure-keeper lifts you to weigh
>   his gold and his silver,

> needs must your joy or your sorrow
> rise or fall.

Henry Ward Beecher mused, "Affliction comes to all of us, not to make us sad, but sober; not to make us sorry, but to make us wise; not to make us despondent but by its darkness to refresh us as the night refreshes the day; not to impoverish but to enrich us."

> If all our life were one broad glare
> Of sunlight clear, unclouded:
> If all our path were smooth and fair
> by no soft gloom enshrouded;
> If all life's flowers were fully blown
> Without the sweet unfolding,
> And happiness were rudely thrown
> On hands too weak for holding—
> Should we not miss the twilight hours,
> The gentle haze and sadness?
> Should we not long for storms and showers
> To break the constant gladness?
>
> If none were sick and none were sad,
> What service could we render?
> I think if we were always glad
> We scarcely could be tender.
> Did our beloved never need
> Our patient ministration,
> Earth would grow cold and miss indeed
> Its sweetest consolation:
> If sorrow never claimed our heart
> And every wish were granted
> Patience would die, and hope depart—
> Life would be disenchanted.
>   (Albert Crowell, *The Joy of Incompleteness*)

Marian Liautaud learned that the purpose of adversity is not to impoverish, but to enrich us. She wrote of the devastation as well as the growth she experienced after losing their home and all their belongings in a fire: "We had no choice but to rent every single item necessary for a functioning home, from the beds we slept in to the spoons we ate with. I felt like a prisoner of circumstance, sentenced to live without ownership rights to anything. Gradually, as I learned to accept the situation we were in, it dawned on me anew: 'I don't have ownership rights to anything. Everything I have is because of God's grace—whether it's my next breath or our next paycheck. Since when is a comfortable lifestyle one of my inalienable rights?'

"Looking back, I see how the fire was the culmination of a process of prying my fingers loose from the 'things' I'd held on to so dearly. Like iron that's purified in the white heat of a furnace, God used the fire to reveal my tendency to find more security in the things of this world than in his promises to care for us. . . .

"I'm sure I haven't finished learning about letting go of things and becoming more attached to the Lord. But one thing I do know for certain. To lose was to gain. Outwardly, we have less. But what remains on the interior—the contents of my heart—is the security of knowing I have an indestructible home with God. This is one emotional attachment even fire can't destroy."

CHAPTER SEVEN

The Price We Pay for Our Blessings

JOB, A MAN whose life earned him an entire book in the Bible, ran the gamut of emotions during adversity. In the end, he could say that he had "heard of thee but now mine eye seeth thee." He recognized that through his trials, his relationship with God had become a personal one.

One man described an experience in which, during some of his darkest hours following the devastating breakup of his family, he went alone into the hills and poured out his heart. He wept and prayed, reminding God that he wasn't Job. Years later, however, he reported his circumstances to be much better than they had been before the adversity came. Though he had lost much, he had gained more. And just as with Job, "So the Lord blessed the latter end of Job more than his beginning."

Other scriptures also teach us that adversity is the price we pay for our blessings. James reminds us, "Behold, we count them happy which endure." Paul agreed: "For I reckon that the sufferings of this present time are not worthy to be compared with the glory which shall be revealed in us."

With the proper perspective, the human soul can mature through trial and suffering. Such things can have a refining influence, can soften hearts and open eyes to a new under-standing—and that refinement is a type of *compensation* for the problems encountered. The rewards can have a profound and lasting effect upon life.

> Ye fearful Saints, fresh courage take;
> The clouds ye so much dread

Are big with mercy and shall break
In blessings on your head.

His purposes shall ripen fast,
Unfolding every hour;
The bud may have a bitter taste,
But sweet will be the flower.
(William Cowper, *God Moves in a Mysterious Way*)

Linda Rutzen wrote of the blessings that resulted from her trial. She recalled the year of treatments that followed her being diagnosed with Hodgkin's Disease, a cancer of the lymphatic system. "Staring at my mortality, I began to realize how shallow and unproven my perceptions of my Creator were. Most profoundly came the understanding that certain dimensions of God's love and character are assessable only through suffering. I came to know that we cannot fully understand the concept of an intimate Creator, of Immanuel—God with us—until we've felt God beside us during distressing times, and eternal changes are made in the hidden regions of the heart. . . . I realized that only in my brokenness could I find a new intimacy with Him."

Wrote a girl whose sister had almost lost her life in an accident in which her leg was severed, she was comatose for some time and then had to relearn the alphabet: "There is, I think, a bittersweet success that has come of all the pain. Though the tragedy was not a path any of us would have chosen, and the events that followed forced us all to travel through our own individual nightmares; we all surfaced as stronger, more compassionate and far more sensitive human beings. I know that the same situation that twisted and tormented me also left me with an inner strength."

Of her sister, she reported: "She is now a special education teacher, and her great compassion has won her many children's hearts and many awards. She married three years ago and recently gave birth to a healthy little girl named Margot."

Leisel McBride spoke of their "rubella child," born blind, deaf, and so severely brain damaged that he had to be placed in an institution. She described how, after his birth, she had hurt so badly and felt so alone. Her husband coped with his own grief by turning inward, and she interpreted that to mean that he didn't care. "And so, I began to turn to Him who knows me best. I begged Him to help me through each day. I began getting up earlier each day, praying fervently and reading the scriptures. And because of that, I became what I am today. That painful, difficult experience turned into a great blessing."

Difficulty is one of the prices we pay for our blessings. A problem does not exist without a gift in its hands. Helen Keller said of her own life: "I thank God for my handicaps, for through them, I have found myself, my work, and my God."

Nancy Petersen, a spiritually sensitive woman, revealed her understanding of this truth in a comforting letter written to ease my own pain after divorce: "Some of the most marvelous women I have had the privilege of knowing have struggled—in unknown ways—to save a difficult marriage. Somehow the experience has tested them to limits much greater than imagined. Two of my fondest friends have divorced and, in time, remarried—to outstanding men who have really cherished them for the truly caring women they are. Both now delight in the opportunity to give of themselves to their spouses in a manner that is appreciated, received, and added upon.

"Sometimes our most difficult times are also our best times, simply because we humble ourselves and draw as close as possible to our Heavenly Father. We need strength and guidance and comfort. All of a sudden scripture study is more meaningful and sincere, as also are prayers, church attendance, etc. It's the time in our life we recognize as difficult, yet wonderfully rewarded with overwhelming spiritual experiences, as we prepare and allow ourselves to be taught and assisted from on high. Over and over we realize and relearn vividly that we are children of divine parentage who will always love us, just as we will always love and cherish our own children.

"Realize you are experiencing a refiner's fire and after the trial come the blessings. Keep up your positive attitude and approach to life. All will work out, although the transition period will not seem to be the greatest at all times. Yet, really it is, since the growth experienced can be the greatest!"

As one person said, "Every adversity carries with it the seed of a greater benefit, if we'll only look for it."

So often our trials are "blessings in disguise"—although I must say that I sometimes wish my blessings didn't come in such disguises!

I contemplated the blessings that have followed some of my own trials. Whenever I think of the saying, "Only through exquisite pain is beauty born," I'm back in the labor room of the hospital seriously begging to die. I will spare you the details—but the blessing that came as a result of that never-to-be-forgotten and never-to-be-repeated experience is a delightful, loving, cherished little boy named Evan.

My heightened gratitude, particularly for the blessings of good health, for the beauty of nature, for husband and children, and for friends and neighbors came as a result of my experience six months ago, recovering from double major abdominal surgery.

My pain-filled first marriage brought me greater understanding and allowed me to write some articles that became a booklet that was distributed for years to women who came to the local shelter for women in crisis. Eventually, it also allowed me to rejoice in the greatest blessing of my life: being now married to a wonderful man whose love is constant and unconditional.

When my family of origin cut me off nine years ago, it was, emotionally, the most difficult experience of my life. But that forced me to turn from them to my Father in heaven as the source of my strength and security and sense of self. That experience changed my life and ultimately brought about my writing two books: *Forgiveness: The Healing Gift We Give Ourselves* and *His Law Is Love* that have, I'm told, changed the lives of many others, as well.

Adversity is the price we pay for our blessings.

I think of the story of my grandparents, as told in a composite account by their children (compiled by Elena Larsen): "Many, many years have passed since the young William David Harris met the even younger Alice Fewkes, walking home from church on a hot and dusty country road. . . . Had they been able to foresee the trials, illnesses, hurts and struggles that would accompany their marriage and the bearing of fifteen children—they would have started out anyway, just as they did—because they would have also been able to foresee the tremendous blessings and joy that would be the result of their union.

"Pa and Ma experienced rough times in the early years. Pa was sometimes ill and unable to work. Dust storms destroyed our crops. Sometimes Pa had to go off the farm for work. There were times of having no shoes, of inadequate shelter. (We ate with blankets wrapped around us.) There were times when Pa had tears in his eyes when the Church brought food to us. I suppose that Ma and Pa became terribly discouraged at those times. One Christmas when things were still quite unsettled and we were without much in the line of material wealth, one of the little girls was asked what she wanted for Christmas. She replied that she wanted a piece of cheese.

"Some years later, we had become more prosperous, in a modest way. But we had to leave our lovely home in Burley and move to Eagle into a 50-year-old, hastily built house that needed a lot of work done on it. No electricity, no bathroom, no running water. Pa fixed it up into a comfortable home. Moving, however, was a real shake-up for us. . . .

"We had our full share of illnesses and accidents. Mother lived through fifteen pregnancies for which she deserves a medal for persistence and bravery. Dad suffered typhoid fever, broken bones, ulcers, and finally, cancer.

"All of us suffered severe diseases when we were small, and sometimes we were all sick at the same time. Once six of us had the measles together. Some of us had accidents with animals or machinery. Whatever the cause, there were times when we were so terribly ill, and Mother was always there nursing us so tenderly and loving us so much. I remember the tenderness that Father also demonstrated. He, too, shouldered his share of the caring for his sick children. I never realized how hard it must have been on Mother and Father. So many long days—and even longer nights—with so little sleep, and with so many other things to do all at the same time. So very many of us to worry about. . . .

"We knew death; he visited us several times. [Two boys passed away as infants, the father died of cancer when the youngest child was six, and three years later, that youngest boy was kicked in the head by a horse and died.] And we would all have to come to grips with one of life's hardest lessons all over again. Giving up a loved one is difficult, but from our parents' example we learned to have faith that Heavenly Father's will had been done and that life does go on."

My mother was the thirteenth of those fifteen children. She is one of the three children still living, now 84 years old. Life *did* go on, and today these two who endured so much, who struggled with such adversity, and who had to be so strong—have posterity numbering well over 2,000—strong, good, capable people who contribute to society rather than detract from it—a great, immeasurable force for good.

* * * *

One wise leader said, "Whenever the Lord has a great blessing for one of his children, he puts that son or daughter in the way to make a great sacrifice." I am convinced that, if we endure it well, no suffering that we undergo will ultimately remain uncompensated.

We are promised that God "shall consecrate thine afflictions for thy gain." In Romans 8 we read, "And we know that all things work together for good to them that love God, to them who are called according to his purpose."

> Little one, remember when I took
> > the five brown pennies from your hand,
> > and in their place I put a gleaming silver dime?
> To my surprise, you cried with rage—
> > replacing five with one could not be fair!
>
> I smiled, then, at childish reckoning . . .
> > until I thought how often our Father takes away
> > the copper blessings from my hand
> > and in their place He puts more precious ones.
> Yet, angrily, I count myself defrauded by the gift.
> I have not understood Eternal reckoning.
> > > (Jean Chapin Seifert, *Coins*)

CHAPTER EIGHT
In Memory of Sarah Jane

In Memory of Sarah Jane
By Mary Jane Hawkes

ONCE THE QUESTION had been raised, our doctor friend left me alone with my new daughter to see for myself. He had mentioned a few of the signs: low placement of ears, flat nose, stubby hands and fingers, large cleft between big toe and little toes, umbilical hernia, simian crease in hands, mongolian fold in eyes.

She was so tiny and new. I had laughed at her birth and said she looked "just like a baby chimpanzee," not beautiful, but funny adorable. I had expected her to be different from her three small brothers.

It was late evening, and no one bothered me. No nurses came. I examined her from head to toe and found some of the signs to be possible. She was so little it was hard to tell. But even then, without clinical verification, I sensed it was true. Our little girl was mongoloid, born, as I was later to know, with Down's Syndrome.

Cuddled there together in a darkened hospital room, I felt we faced a menacing world. I carried the memory of a shallow conclusion formed years before that the greatest gift a man could possess is a brilliant mind, the greatest curse, a dull one. I had actually expressed it: "Give me a child with a physical handicap, never a mental."

My experience was limited. From elementary school, I remembered two small brothers who said very little and clung to each other on the playground. None of us played with them, and none of us seemed to know where they had gone. There was a foster child placed with a family in our neighborhood, a little girl who watched us enter the chapel each Sunday with slow gaze and heavy tongue. These were nightmares as I applied them to our tiny daughter.

Of my little Sarah I asked overwhelming questions. "What kind of person will you be? What will people do to you? What will your dreams and heartaches be? Will we be able to teach you?"

My husband and I asked the age-old questions: "Why was little Sarah born this way?" "What did we do wrong?" In its ancient phrasing, "Who did sin, this man or his parents, that he was born blind?" (John 9:2)

Now, as we look back on Sarah Jane's short four and a half years of life, we have found at least partial answers to these questions.

In answer to the first question, "What kind of person will you be?" our doctor assured us that she would be loveable. The best possible thing, he said, would be to take her home and love her. That was a good beginning.

We read books and visited a center for developmental disabilities. We received regular visits from our county health nurses. Our most comforting resources, however, were other parents of handicapped children. One woman touched me: "My little daughter was born following three healthy boys. She is the light of my life." I clung to that.

As we learned, we taught others. We decided to share Sarah with all who were interested. The Sunday Sarah received her name and blessing, Glen announced to the congregation that she had a unique mission in life and that we were not sure yet what it would be. Everyone was warm and interested. Some families in the neighborhood made a special project of Sarah. They visited and brought little gifts. They always spoke to her. Certain she was among friends, she developed a bright response and ready smile.

I had feared most the answer to my second question: "What will people do to you?" From the beginning, we discovered that this answer depended largely on us. Sharing Sarah openly helped a great deal. I had dreaded the natural, open questions of children, not knowing in advance what I should say. Simple answers proved the solution to simple problems. What people did to Sarah was to care for her, to learn from her, and to love her.

The answer to my question, "What will your dreams and

heartaches be?" is much more difficult. We can only guess. Sarah was just beginning to want to do much more than we were ready to allow her when she passed away. We had much evidence that she was full to overflowing with talent, desires, and capabilities that wanted expression.

From infancy she was responsive to music. She loved it. When my piano students played, however badly, she quieted and listened or bounced her rocker rhythmically. When my trio sang, she clapped and shouted, "Wow!" When the stereo played especially stirring music, she danced, changing her body movements to harmonize with mood and tempo. She had favorites among my piano pieces. Whenever I played a particularly lively Schubert number, she would come running, climb onto the piano bench, and beat time with me on the high keys. It became a kind of ritual with us, our duet.

We sensed in her celebrations a gigantic spirit. Whenever anything delighted her, she used all her resources to say so. When Grandma and Grandpa came or our friends stood at the door, she greeted them with a big "Hiya!" She danced and laughed and hugged and kissed.

When we had spaghetti for dinner, she clapped and hollered, stamped her feet, and passed her dish for more. Dogs, cats, horses, birds, and bumpy roads made her lift her arms and squeal and laugh. If she had found any more means for expression, we feel she would have used them.

Sarah had a special sense for peace and happiness. Discord distressed her. If the baby cried, she said, "Oh, bee," and pulled me to him, or pushed his head toward me, knowing milk would quiet him. If a visiting cousin were minus a toy and crying, she would snatch one from her brother and offer his toy as a solution.

Quite by accident, we discovered her fierce desire to accomplish household tasks, though it was not always apparent. Sarah helped to keep us all tidy. Thoroughly smeared with spaghetti, she often demanded that we attend to the escaped pea or the spilled milk before she would continue eating. When she and her younger brother Ben were seated at their own small table, she assumed responsibility for him, mopping his face, the table, the floor, running for napkins and Kleenex, and pronouncing it finished with a big "There!"

Decidedly different from her five brothers, Sarah expressed a deep femininity. Any hat, shoes, or dress sent her trotting to the mirror, where she cocked her head and turned slowly, acting pretty. Her favorite decoration was a large, lacy doily made by my deceased grandmother, my treasure. Sarah discovered it no matter where it was. With the doily on her head, she walked a little straighter, regally peering up through the lace to see for herself just how pretty she looked.

She sensed my cotton balls were for her as well as for me. I found her seated before the mirror one morning, breakfast jam on her face, chin elevated just a little, sticking cotton balls wherever they'd stay and feeling especially beautiful. She loved to comb her daddy's hair, cranking his head this way and that by the chin and standing back to admire, as though she had a particular design in mind.

Like any little girl, she loved to mother. Her brother Ben was the victim of most of this. She dressed him in his coat, often upside down, and helped him escape from the house to play. Three weeks after Sarah was gone, Ben was still searching the house for "Tah-tah," his once constant companion.

Somewhat like her father, Sarah enjoyed ritual. She was upset if not always allowed to zip her sleeper. No matter how prolonged her bedtime antics, she settled to sleep in the same position, placing her two little hands in her daddy's big ones.

Some of her rituals demanded all her strength at times, but Sarah evidenced a Spartan power to endure. Just three days before her heart stopped for the last time, we watched her pull herself up the ladder at the park to do gown the slippery slide five times.

With breath and energy failing, Sarah often woke suddenly in the night. Religiously, she would cross the room, turn off her humidifier, and then turn on the light before stumbling to her daddy's bedside. Occasionally, these duties accomplished, she would collapse on the floor and whimper before she could reach him, but she refused to take shortcuts.

Once, following six days of intravenous treatment and liquid diet in the hospital, she was placed on a total fast for tests but allowed to go home. She woke in the morning and, as usual, stumbled to the cupboard for dishes, then stumbled on to set the table before requesting the breakfast we couldn't give. She was faithful to duty, uncomplaining.

The answer to our question, "Will we be able to teach you?" is simple. Yes. Sarah learned everything we consciously tried to teach and much that we didn't. Our big problem was assuming she could not learn. Teachers outside our home accomplished things with her we would not have tried. With her own stubborn insistence, she often taught us she could do more. She even learned several words on her own. Yes, we could teach her.

Sarah's short life broadened our view, expanded our hearts. Her life has been of value, all of it. To us she has been, not a partial person, but so whole we were constantly conscious of Spirit. She reminded us of the frailty of this life and of her need and ours for fulfillment in the eternities. During her time with us, we found ourselves thinking and speaking of her as "our bright spot, our little sunshine, the light of our lives."

So at last, to the age-old question in its ancient phrasing, "Who did sin, this man or his parents?" (Why was Sarah born this way? What did we do wrong?)—the answer is the Master's: "Jesus answered, Neither hath this man sinned, nor his parents, but that the works of God should be made manifest in him" (John 9:3).

The works of God have been manifest in Sarah Jane. In her sweet influence and innocent suffering, she has made again the sacrifice, "the just for the unjust." She has caused great longing in us to be reunited with her. If we accomplish this, she will have helped to bring to pass our Eternal Life as well as her own. Then the works of God will finally be manifest in her glorious resurrection.

CHAPTER NINE

I've Been There;
Take My Hand

Help me up, my friend. Dust me off. Feed me warmth.
You are comfort. Let me lean on you until I can stand
alone. I will then stand a little taller, and you will be
proud to have a friend such as me.

(from *How to Survive the Loss of a Love*)

I HAVE BECOME acquainted with several families who had
"mongoloid" children. A familiar thread seemed to weave itself
through all their stories. First came the initial shock and the pain
of learning of their baby's condition. Then later, after they had
had some time to adjust—usually with the support of other
parents—and to gain some experience of their own, came a
common desire to reach out to others in similar circumstances.
One mother of a Down's Syndrome child, Shirley Chase, shared
their story.

"My beautiful little daughter had all her fingers and
toes—there seemed to be nothing wrong with her—except she was
limp. And there was something a little strange about her eyes. A
terrible, overwhelming fear enveloped me when I was informed
that she was Downs, and I felt like my world had been turned
upside down. I loved the baby even more, but I was filled with
frightening questions and worries.

"The doctor sent a wonderful family to help us. Mary Jane
and Glen Hawkes [see previous chapter] brought their three little
boys and their darling little four-year-old Down's Syndrome girl to
visit us. Seeing how cute their little girl was and their cheerful,
positive attitude did a lot to lift our spirits and helped to dispel
some of the negative feelings.

"Time passed but we were still weighed down by worry, fear, pity, and guilt. We loved our baby and we wouldn't have given her up or traded her for any other baby. But we longed so for her to be normal. When I told Mary Jane Hawkes about the things I was worried about—whether she would be healthy or die young; whether she would be able to learn; whether people would be unkind to her; whether we would be able to discipline her; whether our other children would be affected in a negative way; who would care for her if we should die first; etc., etc., she had said to me: 'Oh, don't do that. Worry is such a waste of energy. It makes you face every problem twice—and some you would never have to. And worse, it will rob you of the pleasure you can receive from Denille. Some of those problems are inevitable. But you won't have to face all of them. Wait to worry until you know which ones you have to worry about.'"

Shirley Chase continued the story, recording the difficult and the joyous experiences with little Denille Marie—her happy, affectionate spirit, the love shared with her other brothers and sisters. And then she recounted the events surrounding her unexpected death after a minor, low-risk surgery.

"I thought our hearts would break. They let us go in and hold her one more time and say good-bye. Our little sunshine was gone. The Lord had let us enjoy her for almost four years, and now He had called her home. . . . Even though my heart still aches and I long so to have her, I thank my Heavenly Father for this blessing."

When I wrote to thank Shirley Chase and to ask permission to share her story with others, she replied, "Please *do* use it whenever and wherever you think it might help someone. That was my purpose in writing it." Then she added this thought regarding adversity:

"This experience was like climbing a steep, rugged mountain. It looked so hard, even impossible at first, but we just kept praying and trying and when we reached the top, the view was magnificent. From that day on, we thanked the Lord every day for giving us that mountain to climb. Now we're climbing another one because of her death. It's more difficult than the first one. But we know we can make it because we did it once. And we know when we finally reach the top, the view will be just as magnificent.

We want to help everybody else climb their mountains—at least to get started."

Shirley Chase collected stories and experiences of other families who have had Down's Syndrome children, hoping to strengthen others encountering the same type of bewildering event. Among her stories, I found this excerpt from another mother:

"After the birth of our Down's Syndrome baby, I regained my physical strength much faster than my emotional strength. I had daily crying spells, and at nights, it was even worse. I woke up with the same old piercing pain, and I could not stop crying. This recurring experience turned my nights into nightmares, and I felt that I was doomed to have this literal heart-breaking pain for the rest of my life. In desperation, after two weeks of sleepless, agonizing nights, I asked Tom one morning if he could pray for me . . . . He plead with the Lord to help me find peace of mind and an acceptance of our situation. That very same day we received a letter from a woman named Shirley Chase which began: 'Dear Mr. And Mrs. Welch, you don't know me. Your Aunt Verda lives in our neighborhood. She walked home from church with me this morning and happened to mention that you have a new Down's Syndrome baby. Congratulations! We have one, too. Our little girl is eight months old now. Her name is Denille.

"'I imagine you are going through the same emotional upheaval we did when our baby was newborn. I hope this letter will help to assure you that things will get better. In fact, you will go from despair on one end of the emotional scale to great joy on the other end. Anyway, *we* have. . . .'

"This letter was an answer to prayer. Immediately the pain left me, and from that time to now, never have I experienced this excruciating pain again. I have never since cried nor felt this heartbreaking feeling because of our Holly."

And so we see that Mary Jane Hawkes, having drawn on the support of other parents and using her own experience, reached out to Shirley Chase, who, strengthened by Mary Jane's encouragement and experience, passed her own along to the Welches—and on and on, as the links of compassion are joined together in bonds of caring and love. Going through adversity ourselves can help us gain empathy for others in their distress and suffering. We remember our own, and we want to reach out and to help them.

> Are you troubled, burdened, blue?
>   Take my hand.
> I've been troubled, burdened, too;
>   I understand.
> Where you've fallen, once I fell—
> Oh, I know these pitfalls well.
> Let me help the clouds dispel—
>   Take my hand.
> Others helped when I was weak,
>   Took my hand.
> Helped me face toward the peak,
> Helped me stand.
> What they did, now let me do—
> Pass that kindness on to you.
> Some day you'll help others, too.
>   Take my hand.
>   (Helen Lowry Marshall, *Take My Hand*)
>   * * * *

My own greatest desire in life was to have twelve children. My mother had been one of fifteen children; I was one of eight. Our infertility studies began when we had been married only 14 months. How can I describe the frustration? Only those who desire children and cannot bear them can, perhaps, appreciate the heights of hope and the depths of despair through the anxious years as, month after month, hopes are raised and then dashed. We went through ten years of infertility studies with seven different doctors.

And so, when I finally became pregnant after eleven and a half years of marriage, our joy knew no bounds. We had adopted three children already. But this was our child of promise, the baby we had prayed and yearned for, given up hope for, and then rejoiced for. And it was such a warm and wonderful feeling to know that my very own baby was tucked in my very own body, all safe and secure.

Then, at a routine visit to the doctor, that rapid little

heartbeat previously listened to with such gladness, could no longer be detected.

Leaving the examining room after having the ultrasound that confirmed the doctor's fears, I walked through the waiting room past the other expectant mothers, out to the car where the diaper changing table I'd picked up on my way to the doctor's appointment still lay on the back seat.

In those first dark days, I felt surrounded by love, offered freely by those who cared deeply. Dear people, who refused to let us bear the loss alone, called or showed up on our doorstep simply to express their sorrow and their support and sometimes just to cry with me. I had not known how much we were loved.

Some days later, labor was induced in the hospital. I thought I was handling it rather well emotionally. But the days that followed were the darkest days of my life up to that point.

In my saner moments, I tried to remind myself that I had much to be grateful for, and had other positive thoughts. But the sense of loss and failure as well as the drastic hormonal change combined to give me such feelings of despair that everything seemed black; I felt no joy or purpose in living any longer. I cried almost constantly during the days and part of the nights. Sometimes the pain was so great I thought I could not bear it.

Everything was a painful reminder: pregnant women, little babies, my maternity clothes, my un-maternity clothes, the things we'd purchased in preparation for the baby, plans that would have to be altered or laid aside or that simply didn't matter anymore.

How my heart ached! I thought of the pain of the labor, yet of how happy I would be to go through it every day until April 24 if it would bring my baby back. During those dark, seemingly endless days, I also felt isolated from my husband who reacted to the loss in ways that were very painful to me. I felt so alone.

Then I received a letter from a new friend, Colleen Bernhard. A beautifully comforting letter which said in part: "Cheryl, what's up? What's Father 'pulling on you' now? My 'heck!' He's sure handing you tough stuff to handle! It's a good thing we *know* He loves us, huh? We *do* know, don't we? But why does it have to hurt so bad, so deep, so long, so *alone* right now? What a blow! What a *hard* thing to face. How much you've wanted this baby.

My heart aches for you. Now—what is Father intending to be learned?"

Her letter continued. "It must be very rough—this almost having—then 'snatching' away. May I share with you my knowledge that Father loves us. And there is not *one single* experience in life that we will not be so deeply thankful for in the end that we will fall on His neck and the first thing we'll feel to thank Him for will be the roughest times of all: 'Oh, and Father. Thank you so much for *that* experience. I learned so much. That one blow struck more dross away than any other.'

"So, dear Cheryl—learn, feel, experience, hurt, weep, heal—and out of the valley of the shadow of death bring back a journal, an account of what it was like in there. And write, write, write. You have a great work to do and have already spread enlightenment and strength. . . ."

I was so touched that this mother of eleven could show such understanding and compassion and would take the time (at 4:00 a.m.) to share her insights and her heart with me.

I had thought that having a miscarriage was something other women seemed to be able to "take in stride" and that I was the only one suffering so intensely. Therefore, I felt even more of a failure for not being better able to cope with my feelings.

But then women started opening up their hearts and hurts to me, sharing their own experiences of having also lost a baby or having had a stillborn child. One neighbor, a teacher, drew me into her classroom where she taught when I went to pick up my daughter after school one day. She wept as she recalled and shared her experience of 20 years before. "It was our first baby, and I was in the hospital ready to deliver. But that was also the day President Kennedy was assassinated, and apparently the nurses were watching the television closer than the baby monitor and weren't aware of fetal distress until it was too late." Though the heartbeat had been heard just moments before, she gave birth to a stillborn baby girl.

I would never have imagined that this vibrant, happy woman, now so involved in the lives of her eight children, could have experienced such a thing. But I believed her when she gave me counsel about how to deal with the grief.

Another said to me, "I still miss the two little spirits of the babies I lost. I guess I always will. But time will ease the pain for you; it *does* get better," she promised. I was comforted.

Another friend, one who had lost five babies, said that she had been depressed all winter after she lost a baby. It wasn't until she saw the first flowers in the springtime that something happened inside and she knew that she could make it, that everything would be all right again.

One young woman related how she had returned home from the hospital and closed the door of the nursery that had been prepared for their baby. It would be six months before she could open it again.

Another, in recalling her own experience with a miscarriage, said to me, "I had forgotten that pain, but talking with you brings it back to me, and it makes me want to reach out and help you get through it. Oh, if only I could remove you from this sorrow! If only I could give you a piece of *time* so that this pain could have dimmed for you!"

After that conversation, I recorded in my journal: *It was so immeasurably comforting to me that I cannot describe it. I felt enfolded by her love. I truly felt that she understood how I feel; and she assured me that one day I would be happy again. I felt her total love and empathy; I felt her lift me from despair to hope. What a wonderful gift to bestow on someone! I feel so much better!*

And so, the one thing that helped me more than any other through that dark time—the thing I clung to—was the realization that these sensitive women were now normal people who could talk and laugh and sing and function, living life fully again. I saw that they, too, had suffered intense sorrow and grief. To know that others had been through a similar kind of pain and had survived, gave me hope that one day, I, too, would be able to laugh again. Finally, I wrote: *Now I know that I, too, can make it through and survive. Because others have been there before me and have offered me a hand as I floundered. Because of their compassion and the healing power of love, I know that the pain of today will fade into the promise of tomorrow. And one day I will be able to sing again—perhaps even a lullaby.*

P. S. April came, and with it the due date of the baby that would not be born. Again, I felt overwhelmed with renewed grief.

Then the unexpected phone call came: "Would you be interested in adopting a baby boy born two weeks ago?"

Two weeks later, David was in my arms. A beautiful little boy, David was truly a gift from God to fill my empty arms.

Chapter Ten

Bring Back a Journal

Good morning, yesterday.
You wake up, and time has slipped away,
And suddenly it's hard to find
The memories you left behind.
Remember, do you remember
The laughter and the tears,
The shadows of misty yesteryears,
The good times and the bad you've seen
And all the others in between
Remember, do you remember the times of your life?

Reach back for the joy and the sorrow;
Put them away in your mind,
For memories are times that you borrow
To spend when you get to tomorrow.
Here comes the setting sun.
The seasons are passing, one by one.
So gather moments while you may;
Collect the dreams you dream today.
Remember, will you remember the times of your life?
(Paul Anka, *The Times of Your Life*)

I AM CONVINCED that one of the greatest means of assisting us in maintaining perspective through the adversity in our lives is to keep a personal journal. I love what one person wrote: "The process of enduring and recording life-changing trauma leaves a chronicle of strength—and often what we refer to as a memoir is actually the story of one person's survival. Our life-writing is a passage through grief to knowledge."

Peggy Claude-Pierre expressed her feelings about her journal during a most difficult time as she battled for the life of her anorexic daughter: "My journal became my best friend. It was my only sanity. It cherished my fear and pain yet nurtured my logic. Without its comfort, I would not have survived. It heard me and forgave me everything. In it I set out a long-term plan for how we would get through the next six to eight months. They were the roughest of my life."

I began my own journal when I was just turning twelve years old. It was a cheap little item, received for Christmas that year. The strap and locking clasp broke off long before they had filled their purpose. The binding is long since gone; a thick rubber band now holds the thing together. Though an almost pocket-sized affair to begin with, in characteristically frugal fashion, I divided the small pages horizontally so that it would serve me for two years rather than the one year originally intended.

Now, 37 years later, my full-sized, hardcover journals fill two bookcase shelves. Volume #61 currently rests beside me.

Perhaps the first sad event of my life recorded in that original little diary was the death of our beloved Christmas puppy, Lady, a very intelligent German shepherd, who had contracted distemper.

Lady has been getting worse. Mom called the Kindness Hospital and they said that there was no hope. Mom and Dad are going downtown to buy a drug which will put her painlessly to sleep. They're going to buy her some meat for her last meal. She will be glad to get out of her misery. We'll bury her in a wooden box . . . .

It is difficult to read the entry now, 37 years later—not only because the writing is small and in pencil, but also because the page is wrinkled and discolored from having been held close to my face in order to catch the falling tears that I wanted to preserve, as well.

Also recorded during that year was the never-to-be-forgotten event of November 22, 1963, as written from the perspective of a twelve-year-old: *President Kennedy was assassinated!! We heard about his death over the intercom during the noon dance! He was shot in the head! Everyone was so stunned at first that we didn't really realize it at first. Most of the girls cried during 4th period. Poor Mrs. Kennedy! She held his bleeding head during the drive to the hospital and it was all so horrible! The killing happened in Dallas, Texas. L. Johnson now president.*

A journal may have great value to posterity someday, but I

believe that the greatest value of a journal is for yourself. There is something therapeutic about writing your feelings, even your frustrations and negative thoughts. One girl, on a bad day, wrote *PHOOEY* in letters 15 spaces high, in her journal. It helped, she said.

I recall the words in the letter from my friend at the time my heart was broken after my miscarriage: "So dear Cheryl—learn, feel, experience, hurt, weep, heal—and out of the valley of the shadow of death bring back a journal, an account of what it was like in there. And write, write, write. . . . Be honest though—hurt and face that you hurt. . . . And learn that you might teach." How could she have known that my journal was my constant companion during those darkest of days?

I think of my journal as a dear friend. It means comfort and security to me. My journal listens to me, oh, so patiently. When I go deep inside myself to find just the right words to match the unrepeatable emotions of the moment, there will sometimes be long, reflective pauses. People are not generally good at waiting. The page will wait; it has nothing better to do.

My journal listens quietly, reflectively, never judging, never criticizing, never saying "I told you so." Unlike some of the humans I have shared my life with, my journal has never once said an unkind word to me.

I feel safe to reveal my true self to my journal, my friend. It will take the good and the bad of me. My journal always sees things the way I do, yet at the same time, it also has tremendous insights and, if asked, it can gently remind me of the lessons of life that I have learned in the past. We've shared so many, many memories together. We've shared secrets. We've shared private victories and defeats.

It has seen me at my highest, and it has seen me at my lowest, and it has been there, steadfast, through it all. When I stumble or flounder, it can remind me quietly and gently, that things are never as bad as they seem. I've had my journal in happy times and in sad. There will be more of both. As I keep it, it will remind me that better times follow the bad.

* * * *

In the challenges of the "here and now" it helps to remember the promises and blessings of the "there and then." When we count our blessings on paper, our gratitude grows. Happy memories are handles to pull you out of the bottom of the barrel.

Keep a journal. If you do, every year you will be happier that you started when you did. It is comforting to have recorded evidence of where the years went. A birth certificate proves that you were born, but a journal proves that you lived. As we read, we laugh again or weep anew. Either way, life is much richer.

Material blessings are not the "things" we need to pass on to our children. We need to pass on to them spiritual insights from our own experiences and growth. I think of my grandmother who died when I was just learning to walk. While her memory has been kept alive through her many descendants and family reunions, how I would love to have been able to know her as a person. To have known her feelings, the longings of her heart, the love she felt for her family, the pain she knew in losing a child, and how she coped with all the adversities in her life. But I can only guess her feelings. She never kept a journal; she never wrote her thoughts. (Perhaps, with fifteen children, we needn't wonder why.)

My sister expressed a wish that our own mother had kept a journal so that we could see how she went through the things that we were experiencing when she was our age. And I thought, "She was *our* age? My own mother was once the same age I am right now?" The thought came as a little shock to me, since I had always thought of her as being 34 years older than I would ever be. I, too, wish she had kept a journal; what great value it could be to us as we struggle.

A good friend said to me, "I want my posterity to see that being a mother and having children is not easy but that we can overcome. I want them to know that it's not all good times, that there are frustrating times and depressions but that I can rise above them and conquer the things that hold me back." I could not have known that a short time later my friend would be dead from a brain hemorrhage one week after giving birth to her sixth child.

Life is so fragile; none of us knows how long we'll be here. We assume our stay will be long and that we will always be here in person to influence our children and grandchildren with our lives and with the insights we have gained through experience. In reality, none of us has any guarantee to a long life. But our influence can still be felt, on and on, through recording our inner thoughts and strivings on paper. A life is never finished when it can be picked up and read again in the written word.

> Write a name, a woman's name.
> She was born. What time? What place?
> Read her journal, feel her spirit.
> I can see her face. . . .
> Oh, Grandmama, what are these things?
> Proof you breathed one short space?
> Tiny photos, bent, but ageless,
> Lovely tattered lace.
> I will be as you someday;
> Lift the pen, what does it tell?
> Words on paper saying softly,
> Love life; live it well.
>
> (Laurie A. Huffman, *I Can See Her Face*)

* * * *

In addition to journals, there are countless inspirational biographies that can strengthen and teach us and provide examples to follow. We are inspired and encouraged in facing our own trials as we learn of others who overcame obstacles in their own lives. We learn that the lives of great men and women were often beset with extreme deprivations, misfortunes, and heartaches. Such stories give us new perspectives on our own difficulties as well as renewed gratitude for the blessings we often take for granted.

I wept as I read of William Horsley who, as an eleven-year-old boy in 1855, was sent from England to America and across the plains with the promise that his mother and brothers would follow when his mother had earned their fare. He was alone, living with first one family and then another, sometimes treated well, and sometimes not. "Thoughts of Mother, brothers and home now began to crowd thick and fast on my lonely little heart, and many a night my pillow was wet with tears as visions of the happy fireside and well-filled table of the days long past floated through my mind. I had grown thin for want of food; my clothing had become nothing but rags; my feet had been bare for months, and I must indeed have been a pitiable sight. . . . Very often we went hungry. I well remember one day, as I was digging over the potato patch to see if I could find some potatoes that had been overlooked and lain all winter, when I heard someone calling me. I looked up and saw a neighbor, who was motioning for me to go to her. To my great surprise and unspeakable joy, she gave me two large slices of bread and some meat! None but those who have suffered the gnawing pangs of hunger can realize how delicious was the taste of that food. It was the most thankfully received of any present I was ever given."

Recently, I learned the incredible stories of two men, each of whom, as little boys, were cruelly treated, even tortured, by a parent. Yet their resilient spirits allowed them to overcome the horror of their childhoods, as they each refused to let a tragic past get in the way of a bright future. One even expressed gratitude—that his experiences made him stronger and more able to embrace the "splendor of life." Seeing their happy, healthy attitudes now was inspiring to me.

Becoming aware of the obstacles overcome by men and women of accomplishment, past and present, can spur us on to greater achievement as we are motivated in our own decision to reject defeat. As someone said, "If, for awhile, the harder you try, the harder it gets—take heart. So it has been with the best people who ever lived."

We can learn from their examples.

CHAPTER ELEVEN

The Way Down
Is the Way Up

HUMILITY IS DEFINED as "the state of being humble and free from pride." Pride has been called "the universal sin." It adversely affects all of us at various times and in various degrees. Pride is a damning sin in the true sense of that word, because it limits or stops our progress. C. S. Lewis said, "A proud man cannot know God. A proud man is always looking down." The proud are not easily taught. They won't change their minds to accept truths, because to do so would imply that they have been wrong.

The antidote for pride is humility, meekness, submissiveness. Humility is a knowledge of what we would be without Him, and a realization of what we can be *with* Him. Humility has been called "the solid foundation of all the virtues." The scriptures tell us that the Lord "resisteth the proud, and giveth grace to the humble."

In *The Life of Christ*, Farrer wrote of "spiritual humility. Just as in earthly society the pushing, intrusive, self-conceited man must be prepared for many a strong rebuff, and will find himself often compelled to give place to modest merit, so in the eternal world, 'whosoever exalteth himself shall be abased, and he that humbleth himself shall be exalted.' Pride, exclusiveness, self-glorification, have no place in the kingdom of God. Humility is the only passport which can obtain for us an entrance there.

> Humble we must be, if to heaven we go;
> High is the roof there, but the gate is low."

Sometimes, however, we may be confused in our thinking and allow discouragement to become a substitute for humility. Yet true humility is the opposite of hopelessness and despair; it is inward strength gained as we learn to trust God.

When you downgrade yourself, don't call it humility. Call it a lack of confidence due to the denial of the power of God in your life.

My favorite line in *Anne of Green Gables* is when Marilla says, "To despair is to turn your back on God."

The bad times in our lives—when we experience misfortunes, unexpected disasters, illness, when we lose opportunities or are passed over or unappreciated, when we feel unhappy and alone—can become a turning point in our lives, for these experiences can destroy the results of our personal pride. These blows can "strike away the dross" and help us become meek and lowly in heart.

To be humble is to be teachable. Thus, the way down is actually the way up. "I didn't know I'd have to be torn down before I could be built up," said one.

One woman reported, "I am finally learning how to give up. I truly have issues with wanting to be in control of my life and situations I find myself in. I am learning slowly, though, to let go and let God. I am at a point in my life where I have given up. At first, those words scared me. Since then, though, I have come to realize that this kind of 'giving up' is literally giving the problem *UP*—as an upward motion to my Lord. I am learning how to turn things over to Him, put things in His hands. I am learning to trust that He can do and will do whatever is needed according to His wisdom and power. I just have to give up the controls."

"It is a fearful thing to fall into the hands of the living God" (Hebrews 10:31), but this woman is learning that God gives the very best to those who leave the choice to Him. Instead of asking, Why me?, humility bespeaks the quiet acceptance of what is. No judgment, no anger or bitterness, no hostility or resentment, but a quiet willingness to go with it rather than fight it.

Spiritual progress becomes possible when we are willing to submit to every test without faltering. When we become meek, humble, submissive, patient, and teachable—then it is that the spirit of God can work its lifting, refining influence in our lives. Why does the Lord chasten those he loves? Because they may be the only ones willing to learn.

A spiritual leader, Ezra Taft Benson, identified ten good

things that come as we, in humility, surrender to God: "Men and women who turn their lives over to God will find out that he can make a lot more out of their lives than they can. He will deepen their joys, expand their vision, quicken their minds, strengthen their muscles, lift their spirits, multiply their blessings, increase their opportunities, comfort their souls, raise up friends, and pour out peace. Whoever will lose his life to God will find he has eternal life."

God will have a humble people. We can choose to be humble ourselves by loving God, submitting our will to His, and putting Him first in our lives. Or, if we fail to choose it on our own, adversity may compel us to be humble. "My divorce planted me firmly on my knees," remarked one man.

A wise old preacher once wrote, "No life on this earth finds the real, deep springs of communion with the Almighty until it has met adversity and, by that adversity, has been forced to a point that it is broken, utterly helpless before God."

A woman who had cancer spoke of how adversity had helped her gain humility: "Accepting help from others softens the stiff pride in one who has always been incapable of accepting help in any form. What a humbling experience is that of learning to be a gracious receiver."

Another spoke of the difficulties experienced in being unemployed and financially bereft for a time: "We did suffer a lot, in a way. But what we learned most was humility, of trust in the Lord, of the great love of others who helped us. Was that such a terrible thing? No."

After one man shared with me the story of his past—including an abusive, alcoholic father, physical afflictions, and a broken marriage, I asked him, "What have you gained through your trials? When you come through a hard time still in one piece, don't you feel stronger? Don't you feel proud of yourself? Don't you say to yourself, 'I did it!'?"

His reply surprised me. "No," he responded thoughtfully. "What the trials have helped me learn is how dependent I am upon the Lord."

The Apostle Peter encourages us: "Humble yourselves therefore under the mighty hand of God, that he may exalt you in due time: Casting all your care upon him for he careth for you."

Sometimes we must break our hearts before we can pray from them. It is then that we can pray not to change God, but to change ourselves. Our prayers, more frequent and fervent, reflect a contrite spirit. Being in agony, we will pray more earnestly (even as we remember that cries of agony are not the same as cries of despair). Stooping in anguish, we may then stand up in humility.

A woman wrote of her great-grandmother: "Her character was shaped by the chisel of experience. Now when I behold her portrait, I see a gentle spirit of refinement, with head held high because it was so often bowed."

One great leader said, "I have sought the Lord in my own extremities and learned for myself that my soul has made its greatest growth as I have been driven to my knees by adversity and affliction."

Someone advised, "If your troubles are deep-seated and long-standing, try kneeling." And another: "When the outlook is not good, try the uplook." God will mend a broken heart if we are willing to give him all the pieces.

My dear friend, Leah Jane Brower, wrote of her own humbling through the adversity of battling with her son a severe chemical depression. A year later, he would take his own life.

> Control and being responsible
> Have always been my motto
> Raise predictably good children
> And be a predictably good mother.
> Contribute, persevere, and lengthen your stride.
> Be an example.
> Though others might stumble
> And falter, and fall
> Surely, I and mine would not—
> For so much time and love and focus
> Had been devoted to my precious, celestial stewardships.
> And with the seeds planted and oh, so carefully nurtured
> The law of the harvest would surely be fulfilled.
> But then it came.
> That unwelcome, uninvited apparition
> That hurled my world
> From sweet predictability

Into devastating darkness.
And then came the humbling
And the digestion
And the realization
That life brings falls
Even to those who are careful and responsible.
And so I stand, stripped of pride,
Humbled, now, enough
To start again, not from scratch
But from the increased height
That wisdom, earned from disaster, can somehow bring.
And so this Humbling, this difficult Humbling
Has become a dear friend
That allows for weakness and falls
Yet still embraces
And, in the end,
Brings greater strength.
(Leah Jane Brower, *The Humbling*)

Humbling experiences become invitations for us to learn life anew. A successful life is one of change, progression, growth. Some transformations come uninvited. Sometimes it takes wrenching of the soul to open our minds to new ways of thinking. Internal earthquakes may jar us into re-examining our beliefs. In the process, old feelings and realities are crushed, as awareness moves us toward change. Personal upheaval may bring about growth, a change of heart that begins with a willing mind—even a willingness to *change* one's mind.

Stephen E. Robinson wrote: "If a yardstick that is too long or too short is always used to measure *itself* when it is checked, the error will never be detected. We live daily with the bloody noses that result from the way things *really* are being different from the way we *suppose* them to be. If we don't maintain a certain humility, and therefore a certain caution, about our ability to reason correctly and thereby to control our own fate, life will wound us dearly. And we are most at risk when we are most sure of ourselves."

Life is a long lesson in humility. The original script for my life that I had created in my days of prideful self-sufficiency was shredded. After a second divorce, I embarked on the journey of a lifetime, beginning with the greatest darkness I had ever known and culminating in the greatest joy ever experienced—a personalized journey that would change my life forever. . . .

CHAPTER TWELVE

A Change in Direction

THE NEW YEAR and the new decade of 1990 began with a deep depression, something I had never experienced before. It was dreadful. Even the darkness and despair I experienced in my marriages did not compare.

I remember in the depths of my depression kneeling by my bed and crying out in anguish, pleading with Heavenly Father to help me, and finally praying, "I can't do it alone anymore. . . ."

But it took that depression, that spiritual pain, that soul-wrenching realization of my need for help, to move from self-sufficiency to self-surrender. Life had humbled me, and my heart was now open, because it had been broken. It took that redemptive turbulence for me to seek the light with desperate intensity, with all the energy of my soul, as I hungered and thirsted for truth.

The fact that my life didn't seem to be going well led me to examine my cherished, lifelong beliefs about how to live it. My experiences and my questioning resulted in a revolutionary change in the way I viewed life, a thorough upheaval in my perceptions about human relationships. My life will never be the same.

* * * *

Sometimes the medicine bottle carries the words, "Shake well before using." There are times when God must do the same with us. And sometimes we turn to God when our foundations are shaking only to find out that it is God who is shaking them.

Pain is God's megaphone. Like it or not, adversity is often the means by which God gets our attention, brings us to our knees, and opens our hearts to the need for repentance. Repentance means, simply, a change of direction.

We are frightened of change. We cherish the familiar. Change plunges us into emotional free-fall. But our pain and desperation accelerate the process of finding our spirits. You cannot grow spiritually without making choices that stretch you.

Let's face it, "Some people have to be out on a limb before they'll turn over a new leaf." Challenges often precede changes. Yet, as Anatole France notes, "all changes, even the most longed for, have their melancholy; for what we leave behind us is a part of ourselves. We must die to one life before we can enter into another!"

Jeffrey Holland spoke encouragingly when he said, "Repentance is not a negative word. It is, following faith, the most encouraging word in the Christian vocabulary. Repentance is simply the scriptural invitation for growth and improvement and progress and renewal.

"You can change anything you want to change and you can do it very quickly. It is a mistake to think that repentance takes years and years of struggle. It takes exactly as long to repent as it takes you to say, "I'll change"—and mean it. Of course there will be problems to work out and restitutions to make. You may well spend the rest of your life proving your repentance by its permanence. But change, growth, renewal, repentance can come for you immediately and instantaneously."

Sometimes the change is subtle, sometimes a stunning turnaround. Some moments in our lives are so decisive that they have been referred to as "hinge points." Such a moment was experienced by Alfred Nobel, as reported by Rabbi Harold Kushner: "There is a story behind the establishing of the Nobel Prizes, the supreme awards for achievement in the arts and sciences. Alfred Nobel, a Swedish chemist, made a fortune by inventing more powerful explosives and licensing the formula to governments to make weapons.

"One day Nobel's brother died, and one newspaper by accident printed an obituary notice for Alfred instead. It identified him as the inventor of dynamite and the man who made a fortune by enabling armies to achieve new levels of mass destruction. Nobel had the unique opportunity to read his own obituary in his lifetime and to see what he would be remembered for. He was shocked to think that this was what his life would add up to, to be remembered as a merchant of death and destruction.

"He took his fortune and used it to establish the awards for accomplishments in various fields which would benefit humanity [including the Nobel Peace Prize], and it is for that, not for his explosives, that he is remembered today." With Nobel's abrupt realization of a need for change, for repentance, he gave the last part of his life a new direction.

Yesterday with its triumphs and tragedies need not define us, for each new day contains the promise of a fresh, new start. No matter what your past has been, your future lies before you, spotless and untouched. The only reason to look back is to see how far you've come. And then turn your face forward to a future filled with promise. Many of the insights of the saint stem from his experience as a sinner.

Christ offered us a wonderful invitation: "Return unto me, and repent of your sins, and be converted, that I may heal you." The Hebrew word for repentance means to "turn back to him"—to leave unhappiness, sorrow, regret, and despair behind and turn back to your Father's family, where you can find happiness, joy, and acceptance. Remember that the mistakes we make in life are not so important as the lessons we draw from them. As someone quipped, "If you don't learn from your mistakes, what's the use of making them?"

Carrying the burden of unrepented sin is like waging a civil war within yourself. You can't do wrong and feel right about it. We all have enough adversity in our lives without also carrying the weight of unrepented sin. As one man asserted, "He who fights himself the least has the most strength for the outside battles." Another said, "A man can stand a lot as long as he can stand himself."

Surely we are punished by our sins and their consequences. But even so, this kind of adversity which we bring upon ourselves is still the primary teaching tool of a wise and loving Father in heaven. Because of His great love and desire for our ultimate happiness, its purpose is to bring us to repentance. The scriptures tell us that "wickedness never was happiness." Even our weaknesses may be viewed as a gift to open our eyes.

"As many as I love, I rebuke and chasten: be zealous, therefore, and repent" (Revelations 3:19).

The storms of life will surely create tumult and beat upon us, but the basis of real happiness does not lie in trying to subdue the storms outside us, but in giving up the sins we carry within us.

Indeed, without the storms we might have thought that happiness lay in our own ability to control people and external events around us. Instead, the storms propel us to God, to the peaceable things, to joy in our lives. Out of every crisis comes the chance to be reborn. As one phrased it, "Tragedies serve as an express elevator to Spirit."

"Peace I leave with you, my peace I give unto you: not as the world giveth, give I unto you. Let not your heart be troubled, neither let it be afraid" (John 14:27).

Allan Burgess in his book *Be of Good Cheer* stated: "We know the peace Jesus offers as tranquility of the soul, or inner peace. It is mighty and powerful. It is indestructible and immune to the actions of others. It can endure all calamity, every disaster, all manner of turmoil. It enables individuals to rise above whatever tumult surrounds them.

"Consider the great power of this peace that Jesus offers us. It can resist any and every problem that arises through our daily living. When we place our trust in the Savior and strive to follow in his footsteps, his peace can help us through every negative situation that we face. This peace can transcend feelings of hate, bitterness, discouragement, disappointment, loneliness, fear, and all other feelings that keep us from enjoying life and hoping for a better future.

"Sometimes we seem afraid to commit our all, thinking we may have to give up something we really want, but in most cases God asks us to give up only those things that are stumbling blocks to our happiness. Just as the Savior put God's will ahead of his in the Garden of Gethsemane, we too can do the same, and eventually share with Christ and God all that they have."

Lloyd Newell, voice for the Mormon Tabernacle Choir, offers these words of encouragement: "Although we may get discouraged from time to time and—if only for a moment—believe that we cannot change or improve, we must quickly separate ourselves from our failures and remember that failure is an *event*, never a person. God did not make any failures. Instead, He created changing, growing, developing sons and daughters who can become more like Him.

"We, with the Psalmist, can say, 'In thee, O Lord, do I hope.'

This precious perspective will strengthen our hope as life's lessons refine and define us."

As we endure adversity, we must be careful that our cries of complaint do not drown out the voice within—that voice that whispers the need for change that will bring us peace.

Leave behind the extra baggage. Empty yourself of everything you no longer need. The pathway to peace, happiness, and freedom is the only pathway where littering is permissible, even encouraged. Leave behind the debris, drop it, let it go. Make space for your emerging spirit.

CHAPTER THIRTEEN

The Trial of Your Faith

WE FIND IN the bitter chill of adversity the true test of our faith. It is a faith which triumphs over conditions merely physical and external. Independent of circumstances, it is grounded upon our knowledge that God loves us and that he will keep his promises to us.

We speak of God's unconditional love for us. But what of our love for him? Is our love of and faith in God conditioned upon his blessing us according to *our* wishes and according to *our* schedule? Do we, in essence, say to him, "This is your work, as I have outlined it for you"?

We must continue in faith and trust God unconditionally, regardless of what happens to us. I am inspired by the account of Shadrach, Meshach, and Abednego, about to be thrown into a furnace of sevenfold heat for obeying God rather than the king. Even when their *fate* was uncertain, their *faith* remained certain. "If it be so, our God whom we serve is able to deliver us from the burning fiery furnace, and he will deliver us out of thine hand, O king. *But if not*, be it known that we will not serve thy gods, nor worship the golden image which thou hast set up." Even if God chose not to deliver them, their obedience and their faith would remain unshaken. (see Daniel 3:17,18)

And what of us? What of *our* tests of faith? Ezra Taft Benson declared, "It is a great blessing to have an inner peace, to have an assurance, to have a spirit of serenity and inward calm during times of strife and struggle, during times of sorrow and reverses. It is soul-satisfying to know that God is at the helm, that He is mindful of His children and that we can with full confidence place our trust in Him."

Steve Young, legendary quarterback for the San Francisco 49ers and two-time league MVP, verbalized his own faith: "Center your life on God. I've been able to put everything in perspective the last couple of years. Now when something comes in and hits me, it doesn't go all the way to the center. I think that's because my life is not centered on what others think of me. I have something else at the center of my life. Don't waste your time worshipping sports heroes, rock stars, movie idols, or CEO's. Please, just worship God, your Heavenly Father.

"Turn to him in faith; let him take you by the hand and lead you through this life. He will not let you down. I have come to understand that life's whole process is a walk in faith. It is faith that prepares you for that next experience. It is faith that makes you understand clearly that there is something to learn from every experience. And faith reassures you that there is life beyond your current activity."

We must each be filled with a deep-rooted, immovable conviction of the love and goodness and mercy of the Lord. It must be impressed on each of our souls so deeply that nothing can separate us from the knowledge of the love of God. His promises never fail. We can, with assurance, trust him, regardless of the storms that may assault us.

> And when the tempest rages high
> I feel no arm around me thrust,
> But every storm goes rolling by
> When I repose in him my trust.
> (Theodore E. Curtis, *Come unto Him*)

Faith connects the soul to God. We must learn to know and trust God, just as we have to know and trust a friend in order to have a relationship with him. The scriptures assure us that "*all things* work together for good to them that love God."

God's love for us is unconditional, unchanging, eternal. It is *our* love for God that remains to be proven. Separation from God is self-imposed. Faith is a "submissive hope," and hope cannot be taken from you; you must surrender it.

During a difficult time in my life, I felt comforted and renewed to read Peter's words: "That *the trial of your faith*, being much more precious than of gold that perisheth, *though it be tried with fire* might be found unto praise and honor and glory at the appearing of Jesus Christ: Whom having not seen, ye love; in whom, though now ye see him not, yet believing, *ye rejoice with joy unspeakable* and full of glory: Receiving the end of your faith, even the salvation of your souls." I realized that even through our trials—even though our faith be tried with fire—we can still rejoice with joy unspeakable.

Just as coping with tribulation *requires* faith, so can adversity serve to *strengthen* our faith. How?

> If all the days were fair
>   and every dream came true
> There'd be no need for prayer
>   of faith to guide us through.
> If every day brought mirth
>   to mortals as they plod
> If heaven could be on earth
>   there'd be no need for God.
> 'Tis when the storms assail
>   and when we're sorely tried,
> When all resources fail
>   then God is at our side.
> Through darkness and through pain
>   when other aid has flown
> And all our strength seems vain,
>   He makes His presence known.
> And so from hearts that grieve
>   from anguish and despair,
> Come courage to achieve
>   and faith to conquer care.
>   (Edgar A. Guest, *Burdens*)

Adversity and trial can drive the roots of faith deep in order to tap the reservoir of spiritual strength that comes from such experiences. And when we do not receive a witness at the time of the trial of our faith, then our faith either strengthens or slackens—for the winds of tribulation which blow out some men's candles of commitment, only fan the fires of faith in others.

Those who know the path to God can find it in the dark. One

woman expressed her faith during trouble in this way: "I would rather walk with God in the dark than alone in the light."

> Lead kindly Light, amid the encircling gloom;
>   Lead thou me on!
> The night is dark, and I am far from home;
>   Lead thou me on!
> Keep thou my feet; I do not ask to see
>   the distant scene. One step enough for me.
>   (John Henry Newman, *Lead, Kindly Light*)

We are promised in Isaiah: "I will bring the blind by a way that they knew not; I will lead them in paths that they have not known: I will make darkness light before them, and crooked things straight. These things will I do unto them, and not forsake them." God permits difficulties to enter our lives in order to strengthen our faith in him.

> God never would send you the darkness
>   If He thought you could bear the light;
> But you would not cling to His guiding hand,
>   If the way were always bright;
> And you would not care to walk by faith
>   Could you always walk by sight.

One man, in recalling the major difficulties and setbacks that had occurred in his life, spoke of what he had gained: "I have learned that there is someone, under all circumstances, who I can trust. Someone who I never have to doubt or worry that He loves me. My Father is there; I *know* that He listens, and I know that He cares. And I *do* know Him."

A scripture that has given comfort to those wading through the uncertainties of life is found in Proverbs 3:5: "Trust in the Lord with all thine heart; and lean not unto thine own understanding. In all thy ways acknowledge him, and he shall direct thy paths."

Chieko Okazaki was eloquent in the expression of her faith in relation to adversity: "We have taken upon ourselves the name of Jesus and the way of the disciple. Our way will also lead to gardens of anguished prayer, to crosses, to tombs. At those times, we, like the apostles, must endure in faith and love. We must endure despite our pain, *with* our pain, in the depths of our pain, until the moment of the resurrection in us when we understand the greater purpose in the cross and the tomb. I testify to you that those moments of understanding and acceptance will come."

I met Gary Gillham on a sunny Saturday morning just a few days after his wife's funeral. She was the second young wife he had lost to cancer, leaving him now with six motherless children.

The story of his life is one of faith as well as sorrow. As we became acquainted that first day, I asked him what he had learned from his experiences. "I have learned to trust in the Lord," he said simply. As we became friends, Gary shared with me some of his earlier writings from the time of his first wife's illness and death:

"March 12: I wonder how much more of the strain of her sickness I can take. There have been times when I felt like pulling my hair out or knocking my head against a block wall. Yet I am reminded of the comment that God knows us and who we are and were and what we can become, but He has given us trials so that *we* can find out who we are, were, and what we can become.

"June 12: Thirty-three years ago I was in a hospital, unknowingly, to be sure. A tiny infant, newly born, naive to what the future years would bring. Joy and grief. Heartache and fulfillment. Understanding and prejudice. Success and failure. . . .

"July 8 [the day after his wife's death]: It all seems like a bad dream. It's hard to believe that she is gone now, but we are taking this nightmare more easily. The Lord is strengthening us in this trial of trials.

"[Two days later] she looked so peaceful and serene. Before the family came in to see her, the two little children were brought in to see their mommy. It's hard to tell what went through their little minds, but they seemed to take it fairly well. Each of them put a flower in her hands. . . . Who but the Lord understands how much they comprehend? Who but the Lord understands at all?"

And now Gary Gillham could say, "I have learned to trust in the Lord."

* * * *

Peace comes to those who trust in God. Marvin J. Ashton said, "When sorrow, tragedy, and heartbreaks occur in our lives,

wouldn't it be comforting if when the whisperings of God say 'Do
you know why this has happened to you?' we could have the
peace of mind to answer, 'No, but you do.'"

Abraham Lincoln is credited with saying that all that he *did*
know about God led him to trust God for all those things that he
did *not* know.

Faith will not miraculously change our circumstances from
deepest gloom to brightest light. It will, however, give us an inner
light, a strength that will help us meet the good days with
gratitude and the bad days with trust and determination until a
new dawn offers relief.

An ancient prophet testified, "For I do know that whosoever
shall put their trust in God shall be supported in their trials, and
their troubles, and their afflictions, and shall be lifted up at the
last day."

Carla Perry, the mother of eight children, wrote of her
struggle after becoming incapacitated from a back injury. "I
wanted to run and scream to escape from the limitations of my
body and be the mother my children had always had." Yet, her
adversity actually strengthened her faith until she could say, "As
the months have crept by, I have watched growing within my soul
a new patience and a better understanding of the purpose of why
I'm on this earth. It is amazing to me that the body can be so
limited and yet the spirit can soar.

"My Heavenly Father has blessed me so richly with peace and
joy. I have learned that the answers to the difficult questions of
life: Why me? Why this? Why now? may not be answered in this
life, but I have learned to reach my hand out to my Heavenly
Father in faith, knowing that I can trust in His deep love and can
be blessed with His peace."

> I will not doubt, I will not fear;
> God's love and strength are always near.
> His promised gift helps me to find
> An inner strength and peace of mind.
> I give the Father willingly
> My trust, my prayers, humility.
> His Spirit guides; his love assures
> That fear departs when faith endures.
> (Naomi W. Randall, *When Faith Endures*)

CHAPTER FOURTEEN
Learn to Wait

WE MUST HAVE faith in God's timing as well as in his existence. "It is good that a man should both hope and quietly wait for the salvation of the Lord" (Lam. 3:26).

Said Neal A. Maxwell: "Patience is tied very closely to faith in our Heavenly Father. Actually, when we are unduly impatient, we are suggesting that we know what is best—better than does God. Or at least, we are asserting that our timetable is better than his."

The Apostle Paul relates a faithful hope to patience: "For we are saved by hope: but hope that is seen is not hope: for what a man seeth, why doth he yet hope for? But if we hope for that we see not, then we do with patience wait for it" (Romans 8:24,25).

Some years ago, when I suggested to my friend that perhaps the reason for both of us being childless at that time was to teach us patience, she stamped her foot and said, "Yes, but I already learned that lesson!"

Sometimes what we are doing is right enough, but we simply need to be patient and persistent in it. One woman who heard me speak on reaching goals, called me the next day, very excited, saying she had tried my suggestions and they really worked. She had even made a sign for her refrigerator, a message to herself: "I *will* persevere—for at least a week!"

Paul speaks of life and how we must "run with patience the race that is set before us" (Heb. 12:1). We must "endure to the end" of this marathon race. Patience is obedience prolonged. When we are impatient, we are too self-centered. Just as patience is akin to faith, so are selfishness and impatience companions. Patience and humility are also close friends.

A religious leader promised, "No pang that is suffered by man or woman upon the earth will be without its compensating effect if it be met with patience."

Learn to wait—Life's hardest lesson
Conned, perchance, through blinding tears;
While the heart throbs sadly echo
To the tread of passing years.

Learn to wait—hope's slow fruition;
Faint not, though the way seems long;
There is joy in each condition;
Hearts through suffering may grow strong.

Thus a soul untouched by sorrow
Aims not at a higher state;
Joy seeks not a brighter morrow;
Only sad hearts learn to wait.

A hymn titled *Unanswered Yet?* speaks of adversity in relation to patience and the eternal perspective:

Unanswered yet?
The prayer your lips have pleaded
In agony of heart these many years?
Does faith begin to fail, is hope departing,
And think you all in vain those falling tears?
Say not the Father hath not heard your prayer;
You shall have your desire, sometime, somewhere.
(Ophelia G. Adams)

"How poor are they that have not patience; what wound did ever heal but by degrees?"

Richard L. Evans observed: "Some things we have to leave to time. And if we have faith enough, and patience enough, time will work many wonders. It will soften many sorrows. It will heal many wounds—wounds of the flesh, of the heart, of the mind, and of the spirit. It will right many wrongs. And even if in our time we don't find all the answers, immortal man can have faith in the limitless future—if we do each day what can and should be done, and leave to time what time alone can do."

Often, we may be too close to a problem to see it clearly.

When we experience a crisis it is as though we hold a magnifying glass up to it, and to ourselves, to try to understand what is happening. Magnifying not only enlarges things, it also distorts them out of proportion.

A child held a pebble up to his eye and said, "Look, Dad, this rock is as big as the moon." Sometimes, while we are in them, our adversities block our vision. We lose perspective. They seem overwhelming, "as big as the moon."

Mary Lou Carney wrote: "When we built our house twenty years ago, my husband Gary placed a huge rock at the end of our driveway. The kids would climb on it while they waited for the elementary school bus. The rock towered over the tiny shrubs and bright pansies I planted at its base. Recently, a friend who hadn't visited me in several years stopped by. 'What happened to that big rock you used to have at the end of the driveway?' she asked.

"'Oh, it's still there—only now the shrubs are bigger than it is,' I replied.

"She walked to the window and looked down the driveway. 'It used to be a lot bigger,' she said."

Mary Lou thought back on the trials in her life that had seemed overwhelming at the time. Now, with the perspective of time, she could see that patience and prayer and appropriate action had made them seem smaller.

Distance in time or events allows perspective. What seems true by lamplight is not always true by sunlight.

Edward Pusey stated: "We have need of patience with ourselves and with others—for the greatest things and for the least—for disappointments as to the weather, or the breaking of a heart; in the weariness of the body, or the wearing of the soul; in everyday wants, or in the aching of sickness or the decay of age; in disappointment, bereavement, losses, injuries, reproaches; in heaviness of the heart or in sickness and delayed hopes. In all these things, from childhood's little troubles to the martyr's sufferings, patience is the grace of God, whereby we endure for the love of God."

Henry Ward Beecher's words deserve pondering. "The moment an ill can be patiently borne, it is disarmed of its poison, though not of its pain."

* * * *

Janice Perry used her hands a great deal. Not only was she doing typing for college students and professors as she had done for the previous fifteen years, but she had also recently become serious about writing music. It was in the spring of 1979 that she noted in her journal the troubling fact that she couldn't use her index finger on her left hand and needed to go to a doctor.

The entire hand grew progressively worse and Janice soon had to give up typing. Her hand curled into an awkward position, and it became painful to play the piano, too. Mistakes became frequent, and she had to give up playing in public first, and then in private, as well.

She had to learn to write her songs mentally. During this time she was writing a cantata, *The Savior of the World,* about His miracles. Since she needed the use of that hand in order to be more effective in using her talents to serve the Lord, she had great faith that He could work a miracle and heal her, as well.

Janice went to forty different medical specialists, but none could provide a cure or even give a conclusive diagnosis.

In the sixth year of her affliction, she went to see Dr. Iliff Jeffrey, an osteopath. Dr. Jeffrey was seventy years old and blind. He performed physical therapy to relieve the cramps in her arm. "As I complained to him, I suddenly was struck with the irony of my complaining to a man who had been totally blind since childhood."

Janice told him one day about her awareness of the irony and then asked for his help: "It doesn't look like my hand is going to get better, so maybe you could teach me about how to deal with a handicap."

Dr. Jeffrey began to teach her the things he had learned from his own experience. About believing in the Lord's timing. About how we can, through our trials, learn more patience, become more sincere in our prayers. He urged her to remember and dwell on the things she *could* do rather than the things she couldn't. He pointed out that she had obviously developed a different, yet effective, way to write music, since she was still writing it. He voiced his faith that someday there *would* be a time of healing—either in this life or the next—if we endure well.

"He taught me how to have peace of mind in spite of my problem. He inspired me so, that I wanted to write something to honor him for the way that he dealt with his own severe test."

And so, *The Test* came to be written. The first verse was for Dr. Jeffrey. The second was written about Janice's feelings about her own situation as well as others she had witnessed. The third verse was written for family members who had lost a loved one yet were able to continue to live their lives productively and joyfully despite their loss.

> Tell me, friend, why are you blind?
> Why doesn't He who worked the miracles
>   send light into your eyes?
> Tell me, friend, if you understand,
> Why doesn't He with power to raise the dead
>   just make you whole again?
> It would be so easy for Him—
>   I watch you, and, in sorrow, question why.
> Then you, my friend, in perfect faith reply:
>
> [*Refrain*]: Didn't He say He sent us to be tested?
> Didn't He say the way would not be sure?
> But didn't He say we could live with Him
>   forevermore, well and whole,
> If we but patiently endure?
> After the trial, we will be blessed,
> But this life is the test.
>
> Tell me, friend, I see your pain,
> Why, when you pray in faith for healing,
>   does the crippling thorn remain?
> Help me see, if you understand,
> Why doesn't He who healed the lame man
>   come with healing in His wings?
> It would be so easy for Him—
> I watch you, and, in sorrow, question why.
> Then you, my friend, in perfect faith reply:
>
> [*Refrain*]: Didn't He say He sent us to be tested?
> Didn't He say the way would not be sure?
> But didn't He say we could live with Him

forevermore, well and whole,
If we but patiently endure?
After the trial, we will be blessed,
But this life is the test.

Tell me, Love, why must you die?
Why must your loved ones stand with empty arms
    and ask the question, "Why?"
Help me know so I can go on,
How, when your love and faith sustained me,
    can the precious gift be gone?
From the depths of sorrow I cry.
Though pains of grief within my soul arise,
The whisperings of the spirit still my cries:

[*Refrain*]: Didn't He say He sent us to be tested?
Didn't He say the way would not be sure?
But didn't He say we could live with Him
    forevermore, well and whole,
If we but patiently endure?
After the trial, we will be blessed,
But this life is the test.

Janice continued to write songs, composing them in her mind. She is, perhaps, one of the most prolific songwriters ever. (The literal meaning of *prolific* is "creating many products of the mind.") As of the year 2000, Janice Kapp Perry has produced forty albums. She has written over 750 songs, many of them well-loved and widely sung.

P.S. When I spoke with Janice Perry in order to update her story, she told me that despite the various challenges she has faced in the intervening years, life, to her, is incredibly sweet. I inquired as to the current condition of her hand, whether "the crippling thorn remained." She replied that it did, but "I never think about it anymore. How could I think about something for over twenty years?" She had chosen to patiently co-exist with her adversity.

Some trials can be overcome, and some must be patiently endured. Janice's response reminded me of Helen Keller's remark:

"I seldom think about my limitations, and they never make me sad."

Both statements reminded me of a newspaper interview with Kurt Bestor, Emmy winner and composer of over thirty film scores and numerous television themes. The question was asked, "What challenges have you faced in your life? Have you had health problems in your family?"

His response: "While I have no personal health problems, both of my daughters were born with the birth defect spina bifida. Kristen (now 19) uses a wheelchair, and Erika (now 12) walks with braces. We're all used to it by now, but it seems to be of great interest to everyone else. It certainly helps our family to focus on what's truly important."

* * * *

There are many things to be endured: illness, injustice, insensitivity, poverty, aloneness, being misunderstood and misrepresented. The list is endless.

Patient endurance is not the same as controlled impatience, not the same as resignation. "Endurance is more than pacing up and down within the cell of our circumstance." It is not only acceptance of our situation, but improving upon it, as well. It requires pressing forward even when we are weary or wary as we await our longed-for relief.

Often we need the process of time to come to our spiritual senses. Twigs are *bent* into shape rather than snapped into shape. Without patient and meek endurance, we will see less, hear less, feel less, and learn less. Qualities of spirit and character require time and endurance for their full development.

Once again, we consider a quality that is *needed* to face adversity—and once again, adversity helps us to *attain* that same quality: patience.

Paul spoke of this quality and its relationship to adversity when he said: "We glory in tribulations also: knowing that tribulation worketh patience; And patience, experience; and experience, hope"(Romans 5:3).

CHAPTER FIFTEEN
Make Me Brave

IT TAKES COURAGE to face adversity, to reject defeat, to overcome discouragement. Discouragement is not the absence of ability; it is the absence of courage. Victor Hugo wrote: "Have courage for the great sorrows of life and patience for the small ones, and when you have laboriously accomplished your daily task, go to sleep in peace. God is awake."

In Joshua we read, "Be strong and of good courage; be not afraid, neither be thou dismayed: for the Lord thy God is with thee whithersoever thou goest."

Phyllis Hansen wrote of adversity and courage after her twenty-eight-year marriage ended: "Life is full of surprising and puzzling turns in the road. Sometimes the knocks are so very hard. I have grieved over the broken marriage as for the dead. My heart aches for my husband. But through it all I have felt the comforting love of our Heavenly Father and know that his arm is around me. Believe me, this has taken more raw courage and faith than anything I've ever done before!"

Six months later, she wrote: "Every new experience carries with it certain risks that are so frightening at the time. But the courage it has taken has built confidence and calmness and a greater ability to trust that I am not alone and need not be so fearful.

"Today [in a church meeting] virtually everyone who spoke told of how difficult this year had been but each expressed how much he/she had grown because of the struggles and how their testimonies of the Savior had been strengthened. I can add my resounding *amen*. It's part of the eternal plan and always a personal challenge for each."

Another person offered advice from experience: "Surviving grief is the hardest work you'll ever do. It takes incredible courage. It is purging and healthy to cry."

God, make me brave for life:
Oh, braver than this.
Let me straighten after pain,
As a tree straightens after the rain,
Shining and lovely again.

God, make me brave,
Life brings such blinding things.
Help me to keep my sight;
Help me to see aright.
That out of dark comes light.

It may (or may not) be comforting to know that "that which doesn't kill me makes me stronger."

Well-known attorney Morton L. Janklow fought to live and learned about courage in the process. He was found to have a rare fungus in his lungs, considered to be incurable. He lost 80 pounds in three months because of the drug he was given. He made the first complete recovery in medical history.

"My brush with death put things in perspective for me," he said. "Who can scare me? If a client threatens to leave my firm, what does that mean in the context of my whole life? Something else: I came to the conclusion that the payoff in this world is in courage, the capacity and willingness to take risks. Survival has to do with a lust for living. The people who confront death the best, in my opinion, are the people who confront life the best."

Just as physical strength is measured by what one can carry, so may spiritual strength be measured by what one can bear.

George Herbert stated it powerfully: "You may search all the ages for a person who has no problems. You may look through the streets of heaven, asking each one how he came there, and you will look in vain everywhere for a man morally and spiritually strong, whose strength did not come to him in struggle. There is no exception anywhere. Every true strength is gained in struggle."

Phillips Brooks added: "When a man conquers his adversaries and his difficulties it is not as if he never had encountered them.

Their power is in all his future life. They are not only events in his past history, they are elements in all his present character. His body carries with it not only the record, but the power of all it has passed through. He is stronger by the strength of trial."

The Apostle Paul wrote: "Therefore I take pleasure in infirmities, in reproaches, in necessities, in persecutions, in distress for Christ's sake: for when I am weak, then am I strong" (2 Cor. 12:10).

> Whenever we are troubled
> And when everything goes wrong,
> It is just God working in us
> To make our spirits strong.

Isaiah tells us, "He giveth power to the faint; and to them that have no might he increaseth strength." And in the book of Samuel: "God is my strength and power: and he maketh my way perfect."

Because they are so painful, we do not go seeking for those "growing experiences," no matter how promising their potential for making us strong! No one would ever have crossed the ocean if he could have gotten off the ship in a storm. There are times when we believe we must be strong as an example for others even when we feel like giving up ourselves. This, too, takes courage. And sometimes people make it through a crisis together by each assuming that the other is handling it better than he is.

* * * *

It is not the miracles that strengthen our faith—the tangible, seeable evidence of God's concern for us. Ah, no—it is the trial of our faith that makes us stronger. The stretching, the reaching, the groping, the grasping, the asking, the begging, the weeping.

The Israelites had been led out of the power of the greatest empire in the world at that time. They had been personal witnesses to plagues that afflicted the Egyptians but left Israel untouched. They had with their own hands smeared blood on the doorways of their homes and then heard the cries of the Egyptians as their firstborn fell. They had walked between towering walls of water that divided at the command of Moses, then watched as those walls collapsed on the armies of the pharaoh. They ate bread that miraculously appeared each morning, drank water gushing from a rock, felt Sinai quake, and saw it glow with fire.

What people in all of history had greater witness that God was with them and would use his unsurpassable power in their behalf? They had so much and were promised so much more. Then came the choice. In one foolish, blind, faithless choice this generation of Israel lost it all.

It was time to possess the promised land. But the people were weak and discouraged; they cried that it would have been better for them never to have left Egypt. A movement was started to reject Moses and choose a leader who would take them back to Egypt. Israel lost the privilege of immediately entering the promised land, and for the next thirty-eight years they were to wander in the harsh wilderness of Sinai—until all above the age of twenty who had repudiated the power of the Lord were to die in the wilderness.

Ah, no—it is not the visible, tangible evidence of God that strengthens us spiritually. It is the trial, the testing, of that faith. In order for faith to grow stronger, it must be exercised.

* * * *

Ernest Hemingway observed: "The world breaks everyone and afterward some are strong at the broken places." Does suffering really make our spirits strong? Can adversity help us gain strength? Yes—perhaps in the same way that storms make oaks take deeper root.

> The tree that never had to fight
> For sun and sky and air and light,
> That stood out in the open plain
> And always got its share of rain,
> Never became a forest king,
> But lived and died a scrubby thing.

> Good timber does not grow with ease;
> The stronger the winds the tougher the trees.
> The further the sky the greater the length
> The more the storms the more the strength,
> By sun and cold and rain and snow
> In "trees or man" good timbers grow.
>   (Douglas Malloch, *Trees and Man*)

On the same theme, Carol Lynn Pearson wrote a piece called
Short Roots:

> The tree at the church next door to me
> Turned up its roots and died.
> They had tried to brace its leaning,
> But it lowered and lowered,
> And then there it lay—
> Leaves in grass and matted roots in air,
> Like a loafer on a summer day.
>
> "Look there," said the gardener,
> "Short roots—all the growth went up—
> Big branches—short roots."
> "How come?" I asked.
> "Too much water.
> This tree had it too good.
> It never had to hunt for drink."
>
> Especially in thirsty times,
> My memory steps outside,
> And looks at the tree at the church next door to me
> That turned up its roots and died.

An interesting book titled *Cradles of Eminence* records the
results of a study of the childhoods of 400 famous people, people
eminent in many different walks of life, from comedians to
politicians to scientists. Interestingly, almost none of the eminent
came from calm, loving, stable homes; most came from troubled
homes. Some of the children reacted to great physical handicaps
in various ways. Almost all of them had to overcome obstacles of
one kind or another.

The book states: "There is no way of determining whether the
400 had fewer or more environmental handicaps than did most
persons in their times and in their communities. It is fairly
evident, however, that almost any conceivable handicap has been
successfully overcome by some eminent person. In many instances
the handicaps are considered by those who experience them to
have been motivating factors in their achievements."

Can adversity make us stronger? Rather than praying for lighter burdens, perhaps we should pray for stronger backs. History rests on the shoulders of those who accepted the challenge of difficulties and drove through to victory in spite of everything.

CHAPTER SIXTEEN
Empathy through Experience

EMPATHY IS THE measure of our love for another human being. The word *compassion* comes from a Latin word meaning "to suffer with." We need to feel with one another, to mourn together, to not be afraid to love and hold one another. Most often, we gain that empathy through our own experience.

> Who never mourned hath never known
> What treasures grief reveals,
> The sympathies that humanize,
> The tenderness that heals.

How many people are there in the helping professions who initially chose their careers because they had watched a loved one suffer? How many support groups were organized by people who had either witnessed, been affected by, or experienced those things themselves? Alcoholics Anonymous was founded by a recovering alcoholic; HOPE (Helping Orphans and Parents Everywhere) was begun by parents who had already adopted children and hoped to help others going through the procedure; Up with Down's is a support group for parents with Down's Syndrome children; MADD (Mothers Against Drunk Drivers) had its start through the efforts of a mother whose child was killed by a drunk driver, to name just a few. A support group for parents dealing with the grief of losing a child to death was not organized by a social worker, but by a mother whose eight-year-old son had died in a drowning accident.

A wonderful book titled *The Courage to Give: Inspiring Stories of People Who Triumphed Over Tragedy to Make a Difference in the World* contains numerous accounts of people who turned their own misfortunes and heartbreaks into programs or organizations to benefit others in similar circumstances.

It seems that those who are most zealous in their battle against smoking and the tobacco industry are those who lost someone close to them to lung cancer or some other tobacco-related condition. Patrick Reynolds of the R. J. Reynolds Tobacco Company dynasty is a classic example. He watched his father die from smoking. Though he inherited a substantial amount of stock, he divested himself of the stock and began to wage a campaign against smoking. He has spoken before a Congressional subcommittee, urging the limiting of advertising and banning false advertising by the tobacco industry.

The Kennedy family organized the Special Olympics in order to give handicapped young people the opportunity to participate in competitive sports and feel the thrill of achievement. The Kennedys had a mentally retarded daughter/sister of their own.

Alexander Graham Bell had a deep interest in the problems of the deaf all through his life, even before he married. (Bell's wife had been left deaf by scarlet fever when she was four.) He once told his family he would rather be remembered as a teacher of the deaf than as the inventor of the telephone.

When the French government awarded Bell the Volta Prize of 50,000 francs in 1880 for his invention of the telephone, he used the money to help establish the Volta Laboratory for research, invention, and work for the deaf. Ten years later, he founded and financed the American Association to promote the Teaching of Speech to the Deaf.

It was to Bell that Helen Keller's father took his six-year-old daughter. "Yes, I think she can be taught. You must contact the director of the Perkins Institute in Boston. Mention my name. I am sure he can find a teacher for Helen."

Through the Perkins Institute they found a 20-year-old woman already experienced in overcoming obstacles. She herself had almost been blinded by a disease, but operations had partially restored her sight. She had obtained an education and learned how to teach the blind. She had within her a tremendous force and drive toward success. Her name was Anne Sullivan.

Helen Keller herself is an outstanding example of a person who experienced adversity but rose above her disabilities to become internationally famous, helping handicapped people to live fuller lives.

After college she became concerned with the conditions of the blind and the deaf-blind. She became active in different organizations; she appeared before legislatures, gave lectures, and wrote books and articles. Her books have been translated into more than 50 languages.

She worked for bettering conditions for the blind in underdeveloped and war-ravaged countries, lecturing in their behalf in more than 25 nations. During World War II, Helen Keller worked with soldiers who had been blinded in the war. Wherever she went, Helen Keller brought new courage to blind people.

Would Helen Keller have achieved so much and made such a great contribution to others with disabilities had she not experienced her own? Likely not.

* * * *

At 27, Deborah Wolfe was the youngest woman ever to be crowned Mrs. America when she won the title in 1984. But she points out that her life had been a soap opera, growing up in a broken home with all kinds of tragedies stalking her life. She neither smoked nor drank at the time she tried to take her own life with drugs at the age of 19. Many questions had haunted Debbie throughout her life. "Who am I? Where did I come from? What is my purpose in life?"

Some time later, a doctor she was working for asked her to research why the health statistics of Mormons are so much better than the national average. Before she was through with her study, she had gone through 16 Mormon missionaries and felt she had found the answers to her questions. She and her husband joined the LDS Church.

Debbie had many concerns, one of which was drugs and drunken driving, not only because her husband Kim was a police officer, but because of her brothers. Her stepbrother was in an automobile accident as a result of mixing drugs and alcohol. He is now a quadriplegic. "He was always very macho—liked to ski and race cars," she said. "Now his bones have been fused and he is confined to bed—can't even use a wheelchair." A second stepbrother was on probation for drug abuse; it was she and her husband who turned him in.

Deborah has been involved in MADD (Mothers Against

Drunk Drivers). She also became involved in other ways, speaking at youth homes, schools, firesides, and even to inmates, telling them that there is a better life. She knows.

* * * *

Another example of empathy through experience is provided by a letter from a woman who had suffered a horrifying chemical depression during her last pregnancy. She wrote: "My friend is going through a terrible, deep depression. It tears at my heart to see her suffering so. No one knows how bad you suffer while in the depths of depression—unless you've been through it. I wish I could make her all well, take the pain and suffering away. But all I can do is try to give her hope that she will be well again.

"When you are like that, you think you will *always* be like that. And it is terribly frightening. I have written her several letters, talked with her on the phone, and gone to visit her a few times. It is very draining for me to be with her. It hurts to see someone you love go through such misery. Oh, what a nightmare it is . . . . But because I have been through it myself before, I can help her and others. I can give her the understanding and the hope that she needs so desperately. . . ."

In her next letter to me, she reported that her friend seemed to be doing a little better. Then she added, "There is another lady in our neighborhood who is in deep depression—and I mean *deep*. She reminds me so much of myself, and how I reacted when I was in the worst of my depression. I have gone to visit her lots of times, given her things to read, written her notes or letters of encouragement. I am grateful that I got over it. I am so thankful that I'm the one who can put my arms around someone else and try to give them a tiny glimmer of hope.

"I caught myself thinking the other night, for the very first time, 'I'm glad I went through the worst kind of depression so I can understand and help others,' and then I felt shocked to have even had such a thought. I would not want to go through that again for anything, nor have I ever been glad. But I have come to a realization that no matter how terrible our trials are, they are for some purpose."

* * * *

Rae Jean York was a young teenager, a new bride, and thrilled as she floated out of the obstetrician's office that autumn day in

1951. She stopped to buy a maternity blouse on her way home.

Weeks later, Rae Jean became violently ill one day. It was discovered that she had a rare and malicious disease called Hydatidiform Mole Chorioneorthelioma. Associated with pregnancy, this form of cancer spreads from the uterus to the other organs of the body via the bloodstream. There were no known survivors of the disease; it would be 25 years before there would be another.

After an incredible ordeal, Rae Jean did survive, though her fetus did not. She now does volunteer work with the American Cancer Society. She enjoys meeting people, helping them on a one-to-one basis to "fight the dragon" as she calls the battle against cancer. She also has given many speeches to terminally ill people as well as to groups of young women, with whom she shares her story.

"I am grateful now that I had that experience. I don't regret it at all. That ordeal molded me into what I am today: hopefully, more caring and sympathetic. I feel that one of the reasons that my Father in heaven gave me this extension of life is for just what I am doing now: for me to be able to reach out to others who are struggling. Perhaps this is my assignment in life. To me, it is gratifying and humbling, pleasing and rewarding.

"I love to do what I can. I have real empathy for these people, because I've actually been there and know what they're going through. Some of us are asked to bear more than others. But people want to know that they are not alone or unique—that other people are going through ordeals—that we're all going down the road together."

So it was that Rae Jean York and Ora Pate Stewart, a prolific writer, collaborated on a book about Rae Jean's experiences called *I Will Wait Til Spring*. And from where did Ora Pate Stewart's sensitivity in her writing come? Was she born with this ability—or is it a sensitivity born of experience?

Perhaps she treated the subject of Rae Jean York's cancer so well because she is no stranger to cancer herself. At the time I spoke with her, I learned that she had already lost six of her own brothers and sisters to cancer, five of them within a two-year period. And she had just learned, a week prior to our interview, that yet another brother had the disease. She, herself, had had seven surgeries for cancer.

And perhaps Ora Pate Stewart's song, *To a Child*, has touched and lifted the hearts of so many (I had heard it sung at a baby's funeral) because it flowed from a depth of feeling—for she has been there, too. Her sixth child was a little girl, born prematurely and with a heart defect; she lived only 17 hours. Her works reflect the sensitivity of a heart grown tender through aching.

P.S. Ora Pate Stewart passed away since the printing of the previous edition of this book.

* * * *

A former religion instructor, now family therapist and counselor, told of how he had been forced to obtain a broader outlook and deeper empathy and understanding of people who have divorced after his own divorce: "It's a little different perspective from this side. . . . I remember before, being asked to address a group of single adults, many of whom were divorced. On more than one occasion, as I was making a presentation, I remember looking over the group and thinking something like, 'Boy, I can see why *these* people are here.' Labeling, judgmental kinds of things. Then I became one of those people. I got a chance to mingle with them as one of them, and I gained a whole different perspective.

"I saw the issues of their lives, not so much as defects, but as problems they were struggling with. The first time I addressed single adults after my divorce, it was as to a whole different group of people. I don't advocate having an experience like that in order to learn. But I am able to do the work that I do more effectively because of what I have learned."

* * * *

When one man was asked whether or not he was planning to go deer hunting, he smiled. "No," he said. "I was in Viet Nam. I know what it feels like to be shot at." Here was a man with the capacity to translate his own life experiences into feelings of empathy and compassion for God's other creatures.

From the story *The Ugly Duckling*, we glean this choice example of empathy from experience: "From the day he hatched, the duckling knew he was ugly. Everybody said so, even his mother. He did not look a bit like his brothers and sisters, who were fluffy and yellow. He was much larger, and gray, and clumsy. In the barnyard, everybody made fun of him. Even his own brothers and sisters chased him and pecked him."

After the ugly duckling had become a full-grown, beautiful swan and had learned his true identity, he recalled his earlier days of pain and rejection: "He lifted his head and cried out with joy, 'I will never be proud or mean, because I can never forget what happened to me when I was an ugly duckling!'"

One man made this observation: "If you know anything, you obtain that knowledge by experience. If you have been hungry, you can feel for those who are hungry when you are full. We might as well talk to a person about colors who is born blind, as to talk to a person of no experience what they feel and of the sympathy they cherish for being through afflictions they have never suffered."

Some time after a young man lost his hand in an accident with a hydraulic press, he could say, "Today as I look back, I see the challenge of adversity as something upon which to build. Of course, I cannot say the experience was pleasant; it was horrible. However, I hope I have used this adversity in a positive way. When I see others in trouble, in pain, when real adversity is knocking, I have an opportunity not only to feel something of what they feel, but perhaps I can help them because they can see that I have challenges of my own."

In the Book of Exodus, the Israelites were reminded of the empathy they should have gained through their own experience: "Also thou shalt not oppress a stranger: for ye know the heart of a stranger, seeing ye were strangers in the land of Egypt." And again in Deuteronomy 10:19: "Love ye therefore the stranger: for ye were strangers in the land of Egypt."

Whenever we went out to eat with a certain young man in our family, he made sure that we treated the waitress especially well, reminding us of how low her base salary is, how she depends on tips to make up for it, how frustrating it must be for her when we change our orders—again. It is because he was a waiter himself once, and that experience gave him empathy in that regard.

It is true that one doesn't necessarily have to experience every specific trial firsthand in order to feel empathy in that particular area. One can gain an empathetic heart that reaches to all areas of life. The kindest, most compassionate nurse who attended me in the miscarriage of my only pregnancy in twelve years of marriage was reticent to disclose the fact that there were at home seven children of her own under the age of eleven.

One woman gained her empathy vicariously rather than through actual experience. One night she dreamed that her husband was kissing another woman. She was so distraught that it took her husband the rest of the night to calm her down. "I won't have to experience that to know the real, incredible pain that wives who are so betrayed must feel," she said.

Oftentimes the empathy comes through witnessing someone close experience a particular trial. When I was newly divorced, I observed that many of those who demonstrated the most empathy for my situation—even strangers—shared the fact that someone very close to them had experienced something similar; thus came their gentle understanding.

Barbara Smith shares this: "I took a little granddaughter to the hospital to have some foot braces checked. I was pained that she had to wear those heavy braces. As I waited for the doctor, many women with crippled children came to empathize and sympathize with me over her condition.

"Then my heart really ached, because while I knew that her correction would be full and complete soon, I could see that their children might never know full health and activity. I now know of the great compassion of those women. They had developed their tender compassion for others because of problems."

One of those who shared my grief after my miscarriage was my friend, Eileen Pead. Perhaps Eileen's understanding came from her own widely varied experiences with motherhood. She had become pregnant shortly after marriage and had given birth to a baby daughter who had lived only one day. She knew the pain of losing a child. Then, for seven years after that, she had been unable to conceive; she knew the ache of wanting and not having.

She and her husband had then adopted a baby girl, a risky, private adoption. She knew the emotional anxiety associated with adoption, considering it the most difficult of all her experiences associated with motherhood.

Then she began having biological children—several, in fact, in rapid succession; she knew of those challenges. Her pregnancies became increasingly difficult; she gained even more experience.

Now she was concerned for my emotional state following my miscarriage. "How are you doing?" she asked when I appeared at church the day after coming home from the hospital.

"Fine," I replied. "Just fine." But my eyes betrayed me.

"Liar," she said, putting her arms around me. Eileen came to visit me. She listened. She knew. She had gained empathy through experience.

I had thought that Eileen had experienced every possible sacrifice associated with motherhood. I was wrong. I would not have imagined that thirteen months later she would be dead, having lost her own life one week after giving birth to her sixth child. She is one who graduated early, with honors. At her funeral, some of her little children spoke, telling what a good mother she had been, of how they had felt her love. Her husband was the main speaker. Then they all sang *Families Can Be Together Forever*.

CHAPTER SEVENTEEN

Worry, Stress, Fear, and Discouragement

WORRY

THERE IS THE story of a philosophical clock which fell to meditation. It thought about its future as it was placed on the shelf for the first time. It reasoned that it had to tick twice each second, 120 times each minute, 7200 times each hour, and 172,800 every 24 hours. This meant 63,072,000 times every year. And in ten years, it would have to tick 630,720,000 times.

The clock became so wound up at the thought of so much work, that it collapsed from nervous exhaustion. When it was revived by the clock maker, it realized in a moment of insight that all it had to do was to tick one tick at a time. So it began to tick again, and continued to tick for 100 years, becoming a cherished grandfather clock.

Edward Everett Hale advised, "Never bear more than one kind of trouble at a time. Some people bear three—all they have had, all they have now, and all they expect to have." No man sank under the burden of the day. It is when tomorrow's burden is added to the burden of today that the weight becomes more than one can bear.

In a work titled *Today,* an unknown author wrote: "There are two days in every week about which we should not worry, two days which should be kept from fear and apprehension. One of these days is Yesterday with its mistakes and cares, its faults and blunders, its aches and pains. Yesterday has passed forever beyond our control. All the money in the world cannot bring back Yesterday. We cannot erase a single word we said. Yesterday is gone.

"The other day we should not worry about is Tomorrow with

its possible adversities, its burdens, its large promise, and poor performance. Tomorrow is also beyond our immediate control. Tomorrow's sun will rise, either in splendor or behind a mask of clouds—but it *will* rise. Until it does, we have no stake in Tomorrow, for it is yet unborn.

"This leaves only one day—Today. Any person can fight the battles of just one day. It is only when you and I add the burdens of those two awful eternities—Yesterday and Tomorrow—that we break down. It is not the experience of Today that drives us mad. It is remorse or bitterness for something which happened Yesterday and the dread of what will happen Tomorrow."

Worry is pulling tomorrow's cloud over today's sunshine. Someone has mathematically calculated that forty percent of our worries will never materialize; thirty percent deal with old decisions that cannot be changed; twelve percent focus on criticism that is mostly untrue; ten percent deal with our health, which only worsens when we worry; and only eight percent are legitimate. The point is that life does present real problems that can be better met head-on when we eliminate useless and senseless worry. Worry never robs tomorrow of its sorrow; it only saps today of its strength.

Mark Twain said of worry: "I am an old man and have known a great many troubles, but most of them have never happened."

The misfortunes that are most difficult are those that never come. Worry is the interest you pay on the trouble you borrow. We draw conclusions from multiplying unknowns by improbables to get imponderables.

> Take yesterday's worries and sort them all out
> And you'll wonder whatever you worried about.
> Look back at the cares that once furrowed your brow,
> I fancy you'll smile at most of them now.
> They seemed terrible then, but they really were not,
> For once out of the woods, all the fears were forgot.

It takes a real storm in the average person's life to make him realize how much worrying he has done over the squalls.

Worry can be debilitating. It is a thin stream of fear trickling through the mind, cutting a channel into which all our other thoughts are drained. One method recommended for dealing with debilitating worry over a particular situation is to think, "What is the worst thing that could happen in these circumstances?" When that has been determined, face and accept that possibility—and then see if there is something constructive that can be done to improve upon that potential outcome.

> For every problem under the sun,
> There is an answer or there is none.
> If there is one, then try to find it.
> If there is none, then never mind it.

There are two kinds of things you should never worry about: those you have control over—and those you don't. Alcoholics Anonymous says it in the familiar words of their serenity prayer:

> God grant me the serenity
> To accept the things I cannot change—
> Courage to change the things I can
> And wisdom to know the difference.

STRESS

According to Jean Kerr: "If you can keep your head about you when all about you are losing theirs, it's just possible you haven't grasped the situation." My own personal method of dealing with stress is this: When in trouble, when in doubt, run in circles, scream and shout. I say, "*Anyone* can plan, but it takes a real manager to leap from crisis to crisis."

The character denoting crisis in the Chinese language is a combination of the symbols for danger and opportunity. We see the danger all too well, but we often miss the opportunity. Someone suggested, "When a crisis erupts, we should take a moment, pray, breathe deeply, relax, write down all possible options, talk them over with a person we respect, think about our ability to cope with the worst possible outcome, and keep the faith. After all, that's our best weapon.

Also, many of what we perceive to be crises are not crises at all. The problem may have been going on for months or even years, and only becomes a crises when we find out about it.

"Grace under pressure" is demonstrated when we endure well the stresses of our lives. Often it is the relatively small things, the daily frustrations added together that cause the most stress. In looking back with the perspective of time, they may even become humorous. At the time, however, they are not. In my journal is recorded an example:

I went to the BYU Bookstore to purchase the nine BYU T-shirts that I'd been asked to get for family and friends back in Missouri. That was a real experience. I parked the car and lugged heavy thirteen-month-old Allison [our adopted Korean-born daughter] clear through the parking lot to the Wilkinson Center to the Bookstore and downstairs. Holding her in one arm while I tried to select T-shirts and check sizes, etc., was impossible. Sitting her down, she would stay about two seconds, and when I looked again she would be gone and I'd have to find her in places like their storage room or somewhere else—going up the stairs, laid out flat on the stairs with my keys and checkbook by her side, or being carried by a clerk, who was asking all the Oriental people in the store if she belonged to them. (Boy, did she look surprised when I claimed her!)

Finally, all nine shirts were selected. But when I went to make out the check, he sent me upstairs to do it. After carrying Allison upstairs, I learned that since I didn't have a check guarantee card, they wouldn't cash it. Back downstairs to tell him to hold the T-shirts while I went to get cash. Which I did, driving to downtown Provo.

It was very hot, but Allison was tired, so she had fallen asleep in the car by the time we returned. Back through the Wilkinson center upstairs to the Bookstore, downstairs again to claim my nine T-shirts, with cash in wallet. But another clerk had unknowingly put them all back onto the various racks again! I was so dismayed, I could have cried, after all that time I'd spent choosing them and chasing Allison before.

Back to the car to get the list of T-shirt sizes again. Carried Allison upstairs, through the Wilkinson Center to the Bookstore and downstairs again. When I got there, I plunked her down on the counter and said, "This time, you watch her. I don't have another hour to chase her and choose the shirts again." The young man stammered, "Will she fall off?" I said, "No, but you may want to move all your papers off the counter."

I hurried and was able to find the T-shirts more rapidly this time, as I listened to the clerks talking to thirteen-month-old Allison and to each other ("Do you think she speaks English?") When I took the shirts to the counter, they'd given her a little blue BYU football to play with and she was being as good as could be. The shirts in a sack, we headed back to the car. Whew! Whew!

In recalling the frustrations of that experience, two thoughts come to my mind: (1) I must have had more energy back then, eighteen years ago, and (2) didn't we have a baby stroller? Some stress we bring on ourselves by our lack of planning or forethought.

A young wife I know was feeling the strain of poor health, going through a difficult pregnancy, caring for three small children, living in a two-bedroom apartment in a fourplex, and dealing with the stress of a less than adequate income.

One day she felt she couldn't handle the pressures any longer, and she went out onto the front deck shared by another apartment—and *screamed*. Soon other apartment doors opened, both upstairs and downstairs, and tenants looked all around for the source of the shrill cry.

The next day, feeling more able to cope with life, the woman apologized to her neighbor for having lost control. "Oh, was that *you?*" the neighbor asked, surprised. "I thought you were just out on the deck looking to see where the noise was coming from, just like the rest of us!"

"Don't hurry. Don't worry. You're only here for a short visit. Be sure to stop and smell the flowers," advised one person. Today let go of all expectations. God may have a surprise for you.

Relax. Turn your melodrama into a mellow drama. Life isn't an emergency. Don't worry about small things. Discard negative, insecure thinking. In the absence of your judgment, everything would be fine. If you are in the habit of being uptight whenever life isn't quite right, allowing your thinking to snowball in response to adversity, then your life will be a reflection of this practice, and frustration will be the result.

As Benjamin Franklin observed: "Our limited perspective, our hopes and fears become our measure of life, and when circumstances don't fit our ideas, they become our difficulties." It is our own unmet expectations that create our suffering. We spend our lives wanting things to be a certain way, and when they're not, we fight and we resist and we suffer. You have to see that your own uptightness is largely of your own creation. It's composed of the way you have set up your life and the way you react to it. You have created a chain of pain.

The book, *Don't Sweat the Small Stuff (And It's All Small Stuff)* contains good advice. Go with the flow. Everything—the good and bad, pleasure and pain, approval and disapproval, achievements and mistakes, fame and shame—all come and go.

Every experience you have ever had is over. Every thought you've ever had, started and finished. Every emotion and mood you've experienced has been replaced by another. You've been happy, sad, jealous, depressed, angry, in love, shy, proud, and every other conceivable human feeling. Unhappiness is the result of struggling against the natural flow of experience.

Life is just one thing after another. One present moment followed by another present moment. When something is happening that we enjoy, know that while it's wonderful to experience the happiness it brings, it will eventually be replaced by something else, a different type of moment. If that's okay with you, you'll feel peace even when the moment changes. And if you're experiencing some type of pain or displeasure, know that this, too, shall pass.

The happiest person on earth isn't *always* happy. Both positive and negative feelings come and go. In due time, you will be happy again. It's no big deal. Relax. Be graceful and calm. Don't fight them. They will pass away. The trick is to be grateful for your good moods and graceful in your low moods, not taking them too seriously.

Practice ignoring your negative thoughts. It's only a thought! It can't hurt you without your consent. You can give the thought significance and let it create inner turmoil for you. Or you can dismiss the thought. A more peaceful feeling is only a moment away.

FEAR

Fear is the antithesis of faith. Where doubt and worry are, faith does not exist. They can't exist in one person together. It is pretty difficult to look down and up at the same time. "For God hath not given us the spirit of fear; but of power, and of love, and of a sound mind" (II Tim. 1:7). If you worry, why pray? If you pray, why worry? Corrie ten Boom said, "Any concern too small to be made into a prayer is too small to be made into a burden."

Did you ever consider that when we are fearful, we may simply be demonstrating a lack of faith in God's ability to help us with our problems? It is as though we are saying, in effect, "I don't think God can handle this one. This is too big for both of us." Wouldn't it be easier for us to carry our burdens if we could develop faith enough to cast our care upon our Father in heaven, knowing of his love and concern for us? "I will trust, and not be afraid; for the Lord Jehovah is my strength and my song."

The Lord understands our fears. The scriptures tell us 85 times in the Bible not to be afraid. Why does fear seem to be a part of life? Perhaps God's greatest hope is that through our fears we might turn to Him. The uncertainties of life can help remind us of our dependence on Him for our security. But we must *choose* to take our fears to Him, *choose* to trust Him, and *choose* to allow Him to direct us.

The worst fear is the fear of the unknown. "Identify, define, and resolve" is a helpful process in working through situations. Keep it simple. Only do today what you can do today. Grab your fear of the future and ask, "What can I do about this right now?"

Challenge your fears and the fear loses its power. Eleanor Roosevelt said, "You gain strength, courage, and confidence by every experience in which you stop to look fear in the face." Ralph Waldo Emerson put it this way: "He has not learned the first lesson of life who does not every day surmount a fear."

You need not let fear control you. Say to yourself: "I'm safe. It's only change."

"Then shalt thou walk in thy way safely, and thy foot shall not stumble. When thou liest down, thou shalt not be afraid: yea, thou shalt lie down, and thy sleep shall be sweet. Be not afraid of sudden fear, for the Lord shall be thy confidence" (Proverbs 3:22-26). Sometimes the Lord calms the storm. Sometimes he lets the storm rage and calms His child.

> Do your duty and do your best;
> Unto God leave the rest.

DISCOURAGEMENT

> Your legs are only tired
> Because the road goes up.

All of us may become discouraged at times. Emma Lou Thayne wrote, "We have the right to be sad now and then, to have a depression with dignity, the hope that things will be better. Because surely these worst of times can become the best of times." She spoke of a discouragement linked to a hope that things would be better. But there is a kind of debilitating discouragement—a negative way of thinking that, rather than help us face our problems, can cripple us emotionally. Our setbacks give way to helplessness, and helplessness becomes despair. This depression is a loss of hope.

When the Lord chastises us, we feel encouraged and ready to try again. But when Satan discourages us, we feel like giving up. Thus, adversity is a tool used by two master craftsmen: by the Lord to lift us up, and by the devil to bring us down.

Trouble isn't necessarily connected with discouragement—discouragement has a germ of its own. But this small germ will work and it will grow and it will spread. A negative, cynical outlook can become a habit, a way of living and thinking. It takes a toll on our spirit, eroding our happiness and the happiness of others.

The ultimate purpose of the adversary—Satan—is to disrupt, disturb, and destroy. He wants us to feel unhappy, depressed, confused, frustrated, heavy, full of darkness, mind-muddled, empty, hollow, cold inside, fearful, and discouraged. When we are feeling these things, then we can know who it is that is influencing our thinking. These are far different emotions than the feeling I get from the scripture which says, "Fear not, let your hearts be comforted; yea, rejoice evermore, and in everything give thanks."

Thought is *cause*—experience is *effect* of those thoughts. If you don't like the effects in your life, you have to change the nature of your thinking. Many things are not truly awful unless you think they are. Catastrophizing is a leading cause of stress and discouragement.

Wrote Peggy Claude-Pierre: "Learning how to be objective,

how to see the good of life rather than what is not wonderful will help the journey. I clearly remember one of my first lessons. One hot summer day when I was a child, I had fallen off my bike; a very sweaty woman had hugged me; and I had lost my silver locket in the stream *all in the same day*. I was crying when a wise man I knew stopped to ask me what was the matter.

"I answered, 'Not one, but three bad things happened to me today, and I don't know that I can bear it.'

"'Bear it! Three things! Only three?' he asked incredulously, shaking his head. 'Here, wipe your tears, and when twelve things happen in your day that aren't pleasing to you, come to me and cry.'

"Twelve bad things have never happened to me in one day. No day has ever been that bad, and that was a long time ago, several lifetimes, I think. Life is, finally, only pertinent in our translation of it."

CHAPTER EIGHTEEN
Hold On!

A WOMAN REPORTED experiencing a series of trials that had caused her faith to waver: "It seemed that everywhere we turned there was a closed door. I remember kneeling by my bed one day to pray. I told the Lord, 'If I were a person of means, and my children had urgent needs, I would gladly help them.' Imagine! I was accusing God of child neglect! And saying that I had more compassion than He had shown! There was probably more self-pity than faith in my prayers that day."

The woman's difficulties and accompanying stresses and strains continued to mount. Then one night, she had a blowout on the freeway. She was vulnerable; this was the "straw that broke the camel's back." She didn't even know how to change a flat tire.

"I had pulled off the freeway near a merging lane. Before the dust had time to settle, a young man from the merging lane and an older Spanish man from the main freeway flow stopped simultaneously. In a matter of minutes the tire was changed. I thanked them both profusely and they went their ways, never knowing, I'm sure, just what their act of kindness meant to me.

"As I drove on down the freeway, it hit me. God was there all the time! He had not turned His face from me! There was some reason why He wanted us to have this whole drawn-out experience. It might take awhile to find out just what this reason was, but in the meantime I would trust His wisdom.

"By this time the tears were pouring from my eyes and I had difficulty seeing where to drive. I remembered an illustration about the mother eagle teaching her young to fly. First she would tear up the nest to make it uncomfortable for him. Then pushing him out into the air, she would hover nearby, gliding under him when he faltered, and catching him on her strong wings. I felt God's soft, but strong wings beneath me that night on the freeway. Somehow I knew that whatever happened, God was in control, and He would help us to cope with it. And He did."

Sometimes we're not sure what is happening to us, or why. But we *can* know that God loves us. There will be times in our lives when that must be the bottom line. We must know that God's love reaches before this world and beyond it. We must be so grounded in the love of God that nothing—no trial on earth—can shake us. We don't understand what's happening to us, but we *do* know that God loves us, and to know that, for the moment, is enough.

Yet, there will also be times when we feel totally, utterly alone. Indeed, an echo of the suffering Christ may fill our own hearts: "My God, my God, why hast thou forsaken me?"

Sanford T. Whitman offers comfort: "The greatest suffering that Jesus endured was the apparent withdrawal of His Father's presence in Gethsemane and on the cross. When you come to the days of silence, never forget that your very aloneness means you are high on God's mountain."

> In golden youth when seems the earth
> A summer-land of singing mirth,
> When souls are glad and hearts are light,
> And not a shadow lurks in sight,
> We do not know it, but there lies
> Somewhere veiled 'neath evening skies
> A garden which we all must see—
> The garden of Gethsemane. . . .
>
> Down shadowy lanes, across strange streams
> Bridged over by our broken dreams;
> Behind the misty caps of years,
> Beyond the great salt fount of tears,
> The garden lies. Strive as you may,
> You cannot miss it in your way.
> All paths that have been, or shall be
> Pass somewhere through Gethsemane.
>
> All those who journey, soon or late,
> Must pass within the garden's gate
> Must kneel alone in darkness there,

And battle with some fierce despair.
God pity those who cannot say:
"Not mine but thine;" who only pray:
"Let this cup pass," and cannot see
The purpose in Gethsemane.
                    (Ella Wheeler Wilcox, *Gethsemane*)

Surely we are never really alone, though we may feel like it at times. We are promised that we will not be forsaken, that our prayers will be heard. One person wrote: "Only one thing really held me together—the long and close relationship I'd had with Heavenly Father for so many years. I absolutely knew He was still there for us and that after our dark night of testing the sun would come out again. And it did."

The unwavering faith, eternal perspective, and the love of God are expressed poignantly in Paul's epistle to the Romans: "If God be for us, who can be against us? He that spared not his own Son, but delivered him up for us all, how shall he not with him also freely give us all things? Who shall separate us from the love of Christ? Shall tribulation, or distress, or persecution, or famine, or nakedness, or peril, or sword? For I am persuaded, that neither death, nor life, nor angels, nor principalities, nor powers, nor things present, nor things to come, nor height, nor depth, nor any other creature, shall be able to separate us from the love of God, which is in Christ Jesus our Lord."

Paradoxically, the very things that try to separate us from God have the potential also of drawing us closer to Him.

Someone said, "Adversity is no excuse for losing faith or giving up. On the contrary, there are many historical examples where faith has been intensified in direct proportion to the intensity of affliction. When the storms of adversity begin to howl, the Lord's people react by wrapping their faith, like a warm mantle, more tightly around them."

Some people who experience difficulties become bitter and question God's love, drifting away from commitments they have made. Feeling hopeless and helpless is to deny the power of God. He who loses hope may then part with anything. There will always be some shadows. There will always be some regrets. They are part of learning from experience. We cannot—we *must* not—lose faith.

Viktor Frankl, from his experiences in Jewish prison camps, observed that "the prisoner who had lost faith in the future—his future—was doomed. With his loss of belief in the future, he also lost his spiritual hold; he let himself decline and became subject to mental and physical decay."

Our Father in heaven knows and loves His children. One man quoted to me the scripture found in Hebrews 12:6: "For whom the Lord loveth he chasteneth," and then added, "Back in my bad days, that was good to hear."

God hath not promised skies always blue,
Flower-strewn pathways all our lives through;
God hath not promised sun without rain,
Joy without sorrow, peace without pain.

But God hath promised strength for the day,
Rest for the labor, light for the way,
Grace for the trials, help from above,
Unfailing sympathy, undying love.
(Annie Johnson Flint, *What God Hath Promised*)

Nothing is too hard if it has a visible end. The more difficult test comes when the end is not in sight, when no light can be seen at the end of the tunnel. One of the most important things to remember when problems and discouragements mount, can be summed up in two words: "Hold on!"

The message of this moment is so clear
And as certain as the rising of the sun;
If your world is filled with darkness, doubt, and fear,
Just hold on, hold on; the light will come.

Everyone who's ever tried and failed
Stands much taller when the victory's won.
And those who've been in darkness for awhile
Kneel much longer when the light has come.

It's a message every one of us must learn
That the answers never come without a fight.

That the answers never come without a fight.
And when it seems you've struggled far too long,
Just hold on, hold on; there will be light.
                    (Michael McLean, *Hold On*)

"The depth of darkness to which you can descend and still live is an exact measure of the height to which you can aspire to reach," said Laurens Van du Post. Graceful endurance includes hanging on for one moment more. It is when all virtues at the testing point take the form of courage. And then, after we have passed breaking points without breaking, our virtues take the form of endurance.

Job's wife, in his extremity, told him to "curse God and die." During the Great Depression, there were people who had lost everything, who did just that, jumping out of windows to their deaths. Not only had they lost their fortunes, they had also lost their faith. They had lost hope.

Yet, in *How to Survive the Loss of a Love*, we read: "Suicide is silly. It's leaving the world series ten minutes into the first inning just because your favorite hitter struck out. It's walking out of the opera during the overture just because the conductor dropped his baton. It's . . . Well, you get the picture. In this play called life, aren't you even a *little* curious about what might happen next?" Perhaps that is the adventure of adversity.

I have found that, often, when things seem the most bleak, something very good is just around the corner. Harriet Beecher Stowe said, "When you get into a tight place and everything goes against you, till it seems as though you could not hold on a minute longer, never give up then, for that is just the place and the time that the tide will turn." Longfellow agreed: "The lowest ebb is the turn of the tide." Joseph Campbell stated, "The dark night of the soul comes just before revelation. When everything is lost, and all seems darkness, then comes the new life and all that is needed."

We must hold on. Peter Jeppson, burned so badly in his car accident that he was given no chance to live, recalled: "As I arrived at the hospital, the young doctor who was attending me did what he could. But I had expanded so much, almost twice as big, like a blister, that it was very difficult to tell if I was lying on my back or my stomach. And with all that, he tried to find some life signs and couldn't. He declared me legally dead. He covered me with a sheet and took me back down to the entrance to the emergency care center. And there I was left on a cot. A nurse walked by. She was beside the cot when my arm flinched under the sheet. She became quite alarmed. They marshaled all their resources and took me back up to Intensive Care.

"I could hear them talking. I heard the doctor say to my mother, 'I don't know how he has made it this long. There's no chance that he'll live.' When I heard him say this, I became so angry I wanted to get up and hit the doctor. I'll never forget that feeling. . . . I remember thinking as I was slipping into a coma that I felt like I was dying. As I was slipping away I was so mad at the doctor that I said inside myself, 'I'll prove to you I'm not going to die. I'll hang on.'

"The pain was so severe that I made a commitment to myself that before I gave up I would count to ten. I would see if I could make it to ten before I died. I'd get to five or six and feel myself slipping, and I'd say, 'I've got to get to ten.' That happened many, many times. . . ."

* * * *

Satan wants us to feel unequal to the challenges we face. On the other hand, if we turn to God, He will lead us through our darkest hours.

Christ was not a quitter. As he hung on the cross, the words that passed his lips were, "It is finished." He endured to the end. And so must we.

Enduring is demonstrated in the determination never to yield in the struggle. We may need to say to ourselves constantly: "I will not give in to my failings, regardless of how often I lose my footing and slip backward on the path of progress. I will get up and move on. I will not quit."

Susan Evans McCloud expressed determination when she wrote: "Sometimes it's not easy; I stumble and fall. Sometimes I don't know if I'm climbing at all. Sometimes I get blinded by the wind and the rain, the fear and the pain. But I'll climb each mountain, no matter how high, one step at a time, 'cause I'm not letting go."

There may be times that we feel as though we simply cannot do it; we just don't feel we have the strength it takes to endure. It's during those hard times that you really get to know yourself. You are forced to look closer at yourself to find the hidden reserves of strength it takes to overcome adversity. Pain helps you to unfold yourself, to discover the treasures of spiritual wealth you did not know existed within you. Wrote Kent Potter in his poem, *Beyond*:

Incredible it is
That as we approach our boundaries
Our boundaries disappear,
That there, in the mists
Where we thought capacity ceased,
We find ourselves beginning.

We,
Capable, Beyond
all thought of only
Coping.
And here, only here
Pushed beyond ourselves, can we find
Ourselves.

Oh,
That we could
Remember always our divinity,
Reaching beyond our stretch
of sinew
Into cool faith
Beyond.

CHAPTER NINETEEN
The Cure for Self-Pity

ALTHOUGH TRIALS COME to all of us, it may seem at times that we are singled out. Or we see the prosperity of the wicked and the adversity of the righteous, and we feel violated by the injustices of life. Sometimes we may feel as though we or our loved ones are being unfairly punished. But we cannot afford to indulge ourselves in the dubious luxury of self-pity. Greatness is measured by how well we respond to the happenings in life that seem to be totally unfair, unreasonable, and undeserved.

Henry Ward Beecher opined: "Rebellion against your handicaps gets you nowhere. Self-pity gets you nowhere. One must have the adventurous daring to accept oneself as a bundle of possibilities and undertake the most interesting game in the world—making the most of one's best."

We cannot soar as long as we wallow in negativism and self-pity. We must bear our crosses with dignity and determination. The cross is easier to carry if we keep moving and avoid the sag of self-pity. Indeed, someone said, "Hell is being frozen in self-pity."

(In all fairness, I must say, however, that self-pity is the best kind—because you always know that it's sincere.)

One woman, suffering from a terminal illness, learned that "self-pity is a cancer in itself, just eating away at one's spirit until the strong, optimistic person that once was is no longer distinguishable."

If a life is filled with pain, that is the size of the person's life. But if he chooses to go on, to enlarge his life with other good things—while the size of the original pain may not diminish, at least it will be smaller in proportion to his life as a whole. Someone suggested we stop "awfulizing." An *awfulizer* is a person who is a terminal pessimist. When you cut your finger, you didn't lose your whole leg. Learn to respond intelligently, not emotionally.

* * * *

Anne G. Osborne wrote an article entitled, *The Ecstasy of the Agony—How to Be Single and Sane at the Same Time*. In it she stated, "I have found that a sure cure for depression—one might also say loneliness—is to realize someone out there needs me."

> Art thou lonely, O my brother?
> Share thy little with another!
> Stretch a hand to one unfriended,
> And thy loneliness is ended.
>   (John Oxenham)

Greg Fullmer, who served as student body president at Brigham Young University before becoming student body president at Harvard Law School, discovered early the grand secret of looking beyond one's self to lift others: "I wasn't the most athletic kid in school, I wasn't the most intelligent, and I certainly wasn't the best looking, so I decided I'd try to be the friendliest. *One way to feel good about yourself is to make other people feel good about themselves.*"

Rinda Sudweeks shared a similar discovery from her childhood: "As a girl I had lots of freckles and thought I was homely. I came from a big family, and my mother couldn't stand to see us sit and study but would set us to work instead. I decided, 'I am not pretty, and I'm not a really good student—but I can be happy.' When you get out of school nobody remembers what your grades were anyway, but they will remember how happy you were." This delightful and lively woman spent her life in joyful service to others. "Sometimes a stranger comes up to me and says, 'You are the happiest looking person I have ever seen.'"

* * * *

The greatest cure for self-pity is to look outward to others, to do something for someone else. It breaks the stranglehold of your moodiness and brings a feeling of strength. "The only door out of the dungeon of self is the love of one's neighbor," wrote George MacDonald. Serving others will not only take your mind away from your own problems, but it will provide you with increased self-esteem, for service replaces self-pity with self-esteem. Remember, if you can help someone else, you can't be a bad person.

I recall the counsel of a brother who first expressed sympathy for the pain I was experiencing at the time and then said, "Cherrie, you must quit hurting for yourself and start hurting for others. It's okay to hurt, but don't turn within. Lose yourself in others' needs. Share the pain of others; forget your own pain. You only find yourself happy when you've paid it no mind, while seeing to the happiness of others. . . ."

Louise Lake could have indulged in self-pity. She had contracted polio when she was 30 and had spent 25 years in a wheelchair. Yet, she said of her life: "When the rains have come splashing down upon me, I have lifted my face to the heavens. I have forgotten the rain, but I have not forgotten the rainbow." Young people often found their way to her door to share their joys and hopes and sorrows, and she could say, "We have rejoiced together over the goodness of our Heavenly Father." Teaching and touching the lives and hearts of others brought her great joy, despite her own pain.

Turning outward and paying attention to other people's problems is often the best medicine for fighting our own searing stress. In ministering to others, we heal ourselves. Barbara Winder shared this story: An elderly widow struggled with the pain of arthritis. When she came to live with her daughter, the mother retreated into her own uncomfortable world. She had to be assisted up and down the steps as she went in and out the door.

Hoping to give her mother a positive experience, the daughter suggested that her mother might read to a blind neighbor. Reluctantly, the suffering widow agreed. Moaning faintly at the effort, the widow allowed her daughter to help her down the steps. Then she hobbled up the street to make the dutiful visit.

An hour passed. Two hours. At last, her family saw her returning, coming happily down the street. Amazingly she came up the steps and into the house without assistance. "Well," she told her daughter, "I sure did her a lot of good."

Rosalie Rebollo Pratt had been a successful concertizing harpist who had to abandon her profession after battling for several years a rare form of arthritis that had attacked her fingers, robbing them of their dexterity and leaving instead excruciating pain.

"I went through a period when I was terribly, terribly bitter," explained Rosalie. "I had recorded two albums and I had concerts lined up. Everything had to be canceled and I felt extremely sorry for myself."

It was in that frame of mind that she went with a friend to visit a school for the mentally and physically handicapped. "I was so consumed with myself that I really wasn't interested," she explained. "But as I watched those children, I began to realize that their difficulties—tremendous physical and developmental problems—were enormous compared to mine."

While she listened to the children's attempts to make music, she examined her own swollen hands and began to manipulate a finger that was hurting rather badly. A small child with cerebral palsy approached her, took her finger and said sympathetically, "I know. Mine hurts, too, and it doesn't work either."

"In that instant my outlook changed. I was so embarrassed, so ashamed. This little girl, who had accepted a fate far worse than mine, made me suddenly see that sitting around feeling sorry for myself was an immense waste of time."

She admitted to herself that music had been her life and asked, "What can I do to be useful? How can I do something that is just as meaningful and to which I can give just as much energy as my concert tours?"

She found her answer: "It became so clear to me that my contribution would be to take my music skills and apply them to children with handicaps," she said. Although she became an internationally known music educator, awarded fellowships, degrees, and international honors, her greatest sense of accomplishment, she said, comes from her work on behalf of children.

"I realize that my life is so much richer than it was when I played the harp," she said. "I have turned away from being a very self-centered person—which I was—into what I hope is someone who is able to perceive the pain and need of so many others in the world. I wouldn't return to my former life even if it were possible. The longing is simply no longer there."

* * * *

When you find yourself feeling dejected, despondent, disheartened, or depressed, look around you and find somebody who is in a worse plight than you are. Susan Zugg wrote: "Several years ago I was a single parent facing life alone as my college-age son was preparing to move out on his own. I would say to my friends, 'I'm sure I could handle anything if I only had someone to share my life with.'

"One evening as I was walking and feeling lonely, I met a neighbor coming out of the hospital after visiting his wife who was in the last stages of cancer. I stopped to ask how she was doing, and he said to me, 'We were just saying that a person can handle anything if they only have good health.'

"I decided right there that I would be happy in my present circumstances. Since then I have practiced every day to be a positive and happy person."

When you get involved with others and *their* problems, suddenly yours don't seem so overwhelming. Helping someone in need enables you to see your own problems with a better perspective.

No act of compassion is ever futile or wasted. It can be as simple as listening to another's frustrations, or offering encouragement and hope—perhaps just a smile.

> They might not need me; but they might.
> I'll let my head be just in sight;
> A smile as small as mine might be
> Precisely their necessity.
> (Emily Dickinson)

We need to defrost the ice around our hearts. There are people out there who are hurting and would welcome an understanding friend. Giving of yourself blesses both of you. It is the best gift of all because it comes back in so many ways. Those happy people who have learned the secret of service express the belief that *they* are the ones who benefit the most. Someone to love, something to do, something to look forward to: these are the secrets of a happy life.

Elva Cowley, wife of Matthew Cowley, felt her world had shattered when her husband died suddenly in his sleep. Though she had always loved the outdoors, after his death the sky seemed dim to her, even on a sunny day. She would look at people and wonder how they could walk down the street smiling. She wept and grieved for months.

Then she accepted a position as a receptionist at the Primary Children's Hospital. She began to look outward, beyond her own suffering, as she compared her sorrow with the trials of others. That turning outward was a turning point for her, the beginning of finding joy in life again.

> Nothing to live for? Soul, that cannot be,
> Though when hearts break, the world seems emptiness;
> But unto thee I bring in thy distress
> A message, born of love and sympathy,
> And it may prove, O soul, the golden key
> To all things beautiful and good, and bless
> Thy life which looks to thee so comfortless!
> This is the word: "Someone hath need of thee."
> (Emma C. Dowd)

I was suffering from Mother's Day blues. Mother's Day had always been difficult for me, since I had never been able to bear children. We did eventually adopt children, but the two younger ones who were with me since the divorce were too young to be aware of my need to be recognized on this day.

Even so, I thought of how this Mother's Day, the first I would "celebrate" alone, was better than the previous year's when the day was spent enduring the bitter criticism of my husband as he repeatedly told me what a failure I was in this most important calling in life.

I was feeling pretty sorry for myself over all, throwing my own private pity party. I invited all kinds of negative thoughts and entertained them all.

The next day at work I asked a friend how his day had been. Tears came to his eyes as he replied that this Mother's Day was difficult for him, as his own mother had just recently passed away. Suddenly I felt ashamed of myself. I had been so self-centered, so caught up in my own pain, that I had forgotten that others also had "cause to mourn." I began also to think of the many great blessings I *did* have, rather than the ones I did not.

* * * *

Ann Landers wrote of the cure for self-pity: "Time is a healer, but those who help time by using it wisely and well make a more rapid adjustment. Grief, in part, is self-pity turned inside out. The widow who wails, 'He was everything to me. How can I go on without him?' is crying for herself, not for him. The mourner who refuses to let go of his grief eventually isolates himself from his friends. The world may stop for a few hours, or perhaps a few days, to hold a hand or to wipe away a tear, but friends and relatives have problems of their own. Life goes on—and those who refuse to go on with it are left alone to wallow in their misery.

"The best prescription for a broken heart is activity. The most useful kind of activity involves doing something to help others. I have told thousands of despondent people, 'Enough of this breast-beating. No matter how bad things are with you, there is someone who is worse off—and you can help him.'"

Some years ago a young husband came to me one evening asking for help for his wife, who was in the depths of despair. We two couples were very good friends, our husbands sharing a love for basketball, we wives sharing an unfulfilled longing for children.

Linda had recently become convinced that she was finally pregnant. The day came that they planned to make their announcement. But this must be a special announcement, because they had had to wait so long. Linda baked and decorated cookies in the shape of a baby rattle to be delivered to family and friends. But on that very day, she became utterly, crushingly aware that she was not pregnant after all. "Please see if you can go cheer her up," pleaded her husband.

Rather than attempting to take in a cheerful spirit and hope that she could pick up on it, I decided to use a different approach. I would take my own problems to her and give her the opportunity of forgetting herself in order to lift *my* spirits.

My husband and I had had a darling little two-year-old foster boy, a victim of child abuse. He had stayed with us for over five months before being returned to his parents, who were supposedly rehabilitated. How we had loved him!

Now, since he had been discovered near death this time, he had been removed from their home once again, placed in another foster home, and Family Services was seeking termination of parental rights.

Fear and anxiety filled my mind. Would the judge rule that he should be adoptable? Would we be the ones to have him? Surely *everyone* would want to adopt him, he was such a special little boy. My concern was so great, our yearning for him so strong.

I shared my own anguish with my friend. Linda forgot her own disappointment in a desire to sooth and encourage me in my heartache and apprehension. She forgot herself and lifted me. When I left, her own spirit was positive again, and she was ready to go on with renewed courage and strength.

It is a wonderful thing: when we forget ourselves in serving others, our own growth is assured, as well. The cure for self-pity in our own adversity is to look to the needs of others, for in ministering to others, we heal ourselves. And what are we here for, if not to make life less difficult for each other?

CHAPTER TWENTY

To Choose One's Own Way

SOME ADVERSITY IS inescapable; there are many things we cannot control. What we *can* control, however, is our attitude toward this uninvited guest. Perhaps we can learn to enjoy the excitement of uncertainty. If we can't avoid the anguish, at least we can experience the adventure of adversity.

I remember one time, as a single mother, experiencing a number of "catastrophes," all at the same time. The clutch went out on my little car and would cost $172 to be replaced. (When you pay $525 for a car, you wouldn't expect it to have any problems, would you?)

Additionally, my garage flooded, soaking all the boxes that were sitting on the floor. Moreover, I had noticed red streaks running up my arm from a superficial wound from someone's fingernail in a basketball game a few days before, and I was taking an antibiotic for blood poisoning.

My babysitter had just informed me that she would no longer be able to care for my children while I worked. Furthermore, I knew that my very job was in jeopardy because of a corporate budget crunch. (Since I'd been the last to come, I feared I would be the first to go.)

With all these problems added together, I recall thinking, as though it were a new revelation, "Hey, this life is not fun!" But perhaps a better, more adventurous statement in my self-talk might have been: "I can't *wait* to see what happens next!"

As one person said, "I believe in a life before this life. And I believe in a life *after* this life. It's *this* life I can't believe!"

* * * *

Attitude makes all the difference. A parable is told of a farmer who owned an old mule. The mule fell into the farmer's well one day and the farmer, upon hearing the mule braying, rushed over to see what had happened. After carefully assessing the situation, the farmer decided that neither the mule nor the well was worth the trouble of saving. Instead, he called his neighbors together, told them what had happened, and enlisted their help in hauling dirt to bury the old mule and put him out of his misery.

When the mule realized what was happening, he became hysterical. But, as the farmer and his neighbors continued shoveling and the dirt hit his back, a thought struck him. It suddenly dawned on him that every time a shovel load of dirt landed on his back, he could shake it off and step up.

So, this he did blow after blow. Shake it off and step up, shake it off and step up, shake it off and step up, over and over. Finally the mule, battered, dirty, and exhausted, stepped triumphantly over the wall of the well.

We, too, will receive blows in life that could bury us. But the manner in which we face our adversity will be all-important in determining the outcome.

Viktor E. Frankl, in *Man's Search for Meaning* recounts his own experiences as a Jewish prisoner in Nazi concentration camps. One sentence from his book has been quoted countless times: "Everything can be taken from a man but one thing; the last of the human freedoms—to choose one's attitude in any given set of circumstances, to choose one's own way."

Frankl's father, mother, brother, and wife perished in the gas ovens. The Nazis destroyed not only millions of lives, but attempted to remove every vestige of human dignity from those who lived. Yet he could say: "The way in which a man accepts his fate and all the suffering it entails, the way in which he takes up his cross, gives him ample opportunity—even under the most difficult circumstances—to add a deeper meaning to his life. He may remain brave, dignified, and unselfish. Or in the bitter fight for self-preservation he may forget his human dignity and become no more than an animal. Here lies the chance for a man either to make use of or to forego the opportunities of attaining the values that a difficult situation may afford him. And this decides whether he is worthy of his sufferings or not.

"Often it is just such an exceptionally difficult external

situation which gives man the opportunity to grow spiritually beyond himself. In reality, there was an opportunity and a challenge. One could make a victory of those experiences, turning life into an inner triumph, or one could ignore the challenge and simply vegetate, as did a majority of the prisoners. Life for such people became meaningless.

"Man is *not* fully conditioned and determined; he determines himself whether to give in to conditions or stand up to them. In other words, man is ultimately self-determining. Man does not simply exist, but always decides what his existence will be, what he will become in the next moment."

Truman G. Madsen shares his insights: "The miracle is that suffering can have totally opposite effects, depending on how we respond to it. I know a man who has received 3,200 blood transfusions. He is a hemophiliac, hospitalized with inner bleeding every three weeks. He copes with pain with an expression on his face that would convince a child he was praying. He can inspire a depressed soul, whether in the hospital or out. He has not known a day or a night in fifteen years without pain—and I don't mean low-level aches like stiff muscles, pleasant pains. I mean the hydraulic pain of bone joints being forced apart by his own life-giving blood. Other people I know have suffered far less. They are bitter, cynical, hateful."

Through our adversity we can either learn and grow, or we can shrivel and die. Like a rope, we can choose to climb with it or hang ourselves with it. Someone said, "The experiences in life are like a grindstone; whether they grind you down or polish you up depends on what you're made of." A hard fall can mean a high bounce if you're made of the right material.

Our trials will cause us to either lose our religion, or *use* our religion. Whether our trials deepen our spirituality or leave us bitter and cynical depends on how we choose to respond. As Louise Lake said, "There are those who choose to mope—and those who choose to hope."

It is our choice. Twelve-year-old Richard Nelson said to his grandfather some time after the accident that took the lives of his father and brother and left most of the surviving family members maimed: "Grandpa, I could be bitter and angry about what happened to our family—or I could be happy and cheerful and make the best of it. I decided my life wouldn't be very good if I was angry, so I decided to be happy."

Clarence Dickson relates: "When struck with rheumatoid arthritis at age 36, I was devastated. My third son had just been born, and I saw no 'good times' with him in the future. I became depressed.

"Then one day we visited a family in which the mother had been confined in a wheelchair for many years due to an automobile accident. I asked, 'How can you be so 'up' all the time with all your problems?'

"Her answer changed my life. She said, 'I'm stuck with this chair, and that's one problem. If I'm depressed about it, that's a second problem. I just decided I'd rather have one problem than two.'" She taught Dickson that attitude is a choice, a decision to be made, something over which we do have control.

With her positive attitude, a woman who had lost her husband could say, "My heart is heavy and sad, but my soul is of good cheer."

The first Christmas after my own father passed away, my mother recorded in her journal similar emotions: "December 24: It's Christmas Eve, Darling. In two days it will be exactly five months since your passing. I didn't believe Christmas Eve would be harder, but it is. Everyone has been so kind. There've been carolers and goodies and phone calls and letters and tapes, and I'm burning the wood you split and stacked. I'm wearing your robe over my gown. Your handkerchief is where you put it in the pocket but your chair across from mine is empty, and I'm alone." She then went on to enumerate her many great blessings and to express joy and gratitude for them, even in her aloneness and her sorrow.

How we view adversity makes all the difference as to what we become by it. So often we seek a change in our condition when what we need is a change in our attitude. "As a man thinketh, so is he."

Thinking is our way of processing and recording our human experiences. By our choice of thoughts, we create our own reality. We live the life we imagine we are living. The world outside is a mirror, reflecting the good and bad, joy and sorrow, laughter and tears within us. If we're frantic, life will be frantic. If we're peaceful, life will be peaceful. Our internal state determines our life's experiences; our experiences do not determine our internal state. Our happiness will not be determined by what goes on in the world, but in our own private world. *No Such Thing as a Bad Day* is a book written by a man who has survived three different forms of cancer.

Someone said, "What you play on the stage of your mind is a preview of a coming attraction." We can ask ourselves, "Does this thinking provide encouragement for me, or does this thinking create hopelessness about the future?"

> Life itself can't give you joy
>   Unless you really will it;
> Life just gives you time and space—
>   It's up to you to fill it.

* * * *

The power of thought is incredible. A man found himself accidentally locked inside a railroad refrigerator-freezer car. Despair filled his soul, and he knew that he would freeze to death if not rescued soon. His spirits sank lower and lower as the hours passed. He recorded his thoughts on paper: "It is getting harder and harder for me to write. . . ." Finally, he wrote a farewell note which was found on his body when the car was opened the next day.

Amazingly, the refrigerator car was out of order—it wasn't even in operation—and the temperature had never fallen below 56 degrees.

Our negative emotions are a product of our own distorted perceptions. Since we can control our thoughts and our thoughts create our emotions, we must take responsibility for the way we feel. There are no victims, only volunteers. We are not victims of circumstance—unless we choose to abnegate responsibility for our own lives.

A man who always seemed to have a happy and positive outlook was questioned, "Don't you ever get depressed?"

His reply: "No, I don't. I tried it once and I didn't like it, so I don't do it anymore."

Negative thoughts may come to us unbidden, but *we* decide

whether or not we will allow them to stay, whether or not we will entertain them. It was explained: "If you entertain a thought for ten seconds, *it* takes charge. If you can cast it out before ten seconds, then *you* are in charge."

So many of our trials involve personal loss. Divorce, unemployment, growing old, death of a loved one, forfeited goals and plans, relationships gone wrong—all personal losses. Grieving a loss is natural and necessary and healthy. Sadness, mourning, longing for what can never be—these things must be given their place. But bounds must also be set. We can ourselves decide the length of their stay, their place in our lives.

Voltaire stated: "Life is thickly sown with thorns and I know no other remedy than to pass quickly through them. The longer we dwell on our misfortunes the greater is their power to harm us."

Speaking of those with a negative mind set, C. H. Spurgeon put it in plain words: "Some people water their miseries and hoe up their comforts. Sorrows are visitors that come without invitation, and complaining minds send a wagon to bring their troubles home in."

> A crowd of troubles passed him by
>   As he with courage waited;
> He said, "Where do you troubles fly
>   When you are thus belated?
> "We go," they say, "to those who mope,
>   Who look on life, dejected,
> Who weakly say, 'good-bye' to hope;
>   We go where we're expected."
>   (Francis J. Allison)

Since adversity is an integral part of life, we may as well accept it. Kay Lindsay illustrates the importance of attitude: "When I first received word of my husband's unexpected death, I felt as if the best part of me had died, too. I penned in my journal: 'How does one write about the end of an era in life? I feel as if my whole world, my whole reason for being has just been shattered. It looks as if the sun will never shine again.' I didn't think I would ever laugh again.

"Two days after the funeral it struck me that I had a great-grandmother who lived to be 102 years old; I could have 62 years left on earth! I decided that there was no way I was going to be miserable for 62 years. I was going to do a lot more than just 'cope' with the situation. And so began our family's pursuit of happiness."

She enumerated several things their family had done that had helped them overcome their grief and then summarized the growth that had been experienced as well as the importance of attitude.

"Friends and loved ones have observed that the Lindsays are stepping a lot higher these days. We are not the same people we were before Van's death. When we are next reunited with our father and husband, we will have grown in faith, character, understanding, empathy, and love. We will have had to become more dependent upon the Lord. We will have grown in ways we would not have known through any other experience.

"Of course, the price for this growth is more than we would have chosen to pay if the decision had been up to us. But I believe that our Heavenly Father has tailored our mortal experience to help us develop our weaknesses into strengths. He doesn't permit us to choose whether we will face trials—only *how* we will face them."

> Our lives are songs; God writes the words
> And we set them to music at pleasure,
> And the song grows glad, or sweet or sad,
> As we choose to fashion the measure.
>   (Ella Wheeler Wilcox, *Choice*)

CHAPTER TWENTY-ONE

Looking on the Bright Side

"ADVERSITY MAKES LIFE interesting," observed one person. "Have you noticed that while we are in the middle of adversity we only long to get out of it, but we then spend a lifetime recounting it to anyone who will listen? This is because it spices life up a little. Imagine how boring life would be if everything always went well, if there were never a challenge, never a mountain to be climbed."

If you can look back on your life without regrets, you have one of life's most precious gifts: a very selective memory.

Being miserable will not help us avoid trials. Peace is not the absence of conflict, but the ability to cope with it. Small souls shrink with trouble; great ones rise above it. It all depends on attitude, on one's outlook.

Elaine Fairbanks related how she was not very happy when she first started kindergarten. "Then someone hit me with the idea that I was going to have to go to school for twelve *more* years after that—and that it would be for *all* day, not just half. Having that thrust on me, a five-year-old, was almost more than I could handle. But I remember thinking, 'If I have to, I have to, and there's no way I can get out of it, so I might as well enjoy it.' And I began to like school."

According to M. D. Babcock, "If God, then, puts or permits anything hard in our lives, be assured that the real peril, the real trouble, is what we shall lose if we flinch or rebel." One cannot become as God is and maintain negative emotions and actions. The scriptures speak of rejoicing in hope and of patience in tribulation.

Thomas S. Monson stated: "It is practically a law in life that when one door closes to us, another opens. The trouble is that we often look with so much regret and longing upon the closed door that we do not see the one which has opened to us. We no doubt see challenges and problems before us. Let us see, with equal clarity, the promises."

Maria in *The Sound of Music* demonstrated a positive attitude when she said, "God never closes a door but what he opens a window somewhere."

Tragedy in life does not have to mean a life of tragedy. A bend in the road does not mean the end of the road. That which appears to be the end may really be a new beginning. Every exit is an entrance to somewhere else. As Richard Bach said, "What a caterpillar calls the end of the world, the Master calls a butterfly."

Mylinda Barron thought her world had ended. "After training my body for eight years in dance—specifically ballet—I was sure that, after all the time and energy I put into it, I would one day become a professional ballerina. My dream was beginning to blossom; I had my whole life worked out and everything seemed to be going my way.

"One fateful day I was dancing and came down from a jump, dislocating my knee slightly. From that point on, I knew that I could never dance again without concerns for re-injury. Even today, my knee gives me minor pain, a reminder of my lost ballet career. But I learned one of the most valuable lessons of my life from this dramatic change that I experienced. I learned to trust the Lord to direct our paths. With that trust, we have no reason to fear any change we may be challenged with."

Hilda Baldauf also wrote about what she had thought was the end of the road: "All my life I had been productively employed and thought of retirement as something still far in the future. Suddenly, I was afflicted with a disabling illness and my working days came to an abrupt halt.

"After several weeks of agony, a new medication brought welcome relief. I devoted my new freedom to a volunteer ambulance squad. I delivered "Meals on Wheels." I was called to serve in the family history center. I now had time to get acquainted with my neighbors and to enjoy several thick books. My life is rich and full. The dreadful change turned out to be a welcome blessing." What she had thought was the end of the road was really only a bend in the road.

John Ruskin, English art critic and writer, penned an excellent analogy: "There is no music in a rest, but there is the making of music in it. In our whole life melody the music is broken off here and there by "rests," and we foolishly think we have come to the end of the tune. God sends a time of forced leisure—sickness, disappointed plans, frustrated efforts—and makes a sudden pause in the choral hymn of our lives, and we lament that our voices must be silent and our part missing in the music which ever goes up to the ear of the Creator.

"How does the musician read a rest? See him beat time with unvarying count and catch up the next note true and steady as if no breaking place had come between. Not without design does God write the music of our lives. But be it ours to learn the time and not be dismayed at the "rests." They are not to be slurred over, nor to be omitted, nor to destroy the melody, nor to change the keynote. If we will look up, God Himself will beat the time for us. With the eye on Him we shall strike the next note full and clear."

Rachel Grant, though she lived 150 years ago, is still a marvelous example of looking on the bright side in adversity. In her middle years, Rachel suffered an attack of quinsy (abscessed tonsils) that made her deaf. Although her health and longevity would carry her through her eighty-seventh year, she spent the last forty years of her life in almost total silence, except the loss of hearing was accompanied by terrible head noises, "like a steam engine going night and day."

Although her deafness prevented her from hearing the music she loved, it did not stop her from singing. Her spirit is reflected in her statement, "I'm glad I can see; I feel blindness would be a great affliction." She made up for her loss of hearing by writing letters and reading magazines and other "good thoughts and good books."

George Bernard Shaw advised, "Better keep yourself clean and bright, for you are the window through which you must see the world." What lies behind us and what lies before us are tiny matters compared to what lies within us. As one observed, "It's not the mountains ahead of us, but the sand inside our own shoes that cause the most trouble."

The really happy man is the one who can enjoy the scenery

when he has to take a detour. Popcorn kernels all appear to be alike. But when the heat is on, they react differently. Some explode with promise and can then bring joy to others. Others remain hard and are fit only to be cast out. Our attitude "when the heat is on" determines what we will become.

"Be like the tea kettle; it sings even when it's up to its neck in hot water."

The most extraordinary thing about the oyster is the fact that he turns irritations into lovely pearls. If there are irritations in our lives today, we can do the same—even if they be pearls of patience, courage, and compassion.

I recall, as a child, reading the *Little House on the Prairie* books. Father Ingalls demonstrated a bright outlook when he taught that there is no great loss without some small gain. When grasshoppers descended and destroyed the family's crops, seeing the abundance of insects, they commented that at least they didn't have to feed the chickens!

Defeat is simply education, the first step to something better. George Washington viewed defeat as only a reason for greater exertion.

This same indomitable spirit was repeatedly demonstrated by Thomas Edison, the man who patented over 1,000 inventions including the phonograph, electric light system, and moving picture camera. While working on the incandescent light bulb, an employee expressed his discouragement after repeated failures. Typically positive, Edison's cheerful response was, "Yes, but now we know that many things that won't work!"

Thomas Edison had two serious ear injuries as a boy, and later, a third. Then he began to lose his hearing. As he grew older and his deafness increased, he said he really didn't mind; it actually helped him concentrate on his work without being bothered by outside noise. This same positive spirit was further demonstrated by Edison through his life, as revealed by Jeffrey Holland:

"He had devoted ten years and all of his money to a particular project. Then one night the terrifying cry of fire echoed through the plant. Spontaneous combustion had ignited some chemicals. Within moments everything had gone up with a whoosh. Fire companies from eight towns arrived, but the heat was so intense and the water pressure so low that the fire hoses had no effect.

"Edison was 67 years old—no age to begin anew. His daughter was frantic, wondering if he could handle a crisis such as this at his age. She saw him running toward her. He spoke first. He said, 'Where's your mother? Go get her. Tell her to bring her friends. They'll never see another fire like this as long as they live.'

"At 5:30 the next morning, with the fire barely under control, he called his employees together and announced, 'We're rebuilding.' One man was told to lease all the machine shops in the area, another to obtain a wrecking crane from the Erie Railroad Company. Then, almost as an afterthought, he added, 'Oh, by the way, anybody know where we can get some money?'

"Virtually everything you now recognize as a Thomas Edison contribution to your life came after that disaster." I am reminded of Caleb in the Old Testament who, at 85 years of age, pled, "Give me this mountain." Give me these challenges.

* * * *

Even in extreme adversity, one can look on the bright side. One man related how his family's home had burned to the ground. While they were grateful that there was no loss of life, still it was a difficult and bewildering experience to suddenly find themselves without any earthly possessions, without even a change of clothing. The man spoke of his appreciation for a friend who brought to them a small plaque she had made. Depicted on it were the charred remains of a house, sunrise in the background, accompanied by these words: "Since my house burned down, I have a better view of the rising sun."

It's all in how you look at things. The U. S. Marines were in a precarious position. This is the message the commander sent: "At last we have the enemy just where we want him. We are surrounded and we can fire in every direction."

The Persians, in an effort to intimidate the Spartans into surrendering, sent messengers saying they had such a large army they could darken the sky with their arrows. The Spartans replied, "So much the better. We shall fight in the shade."

Perspective makes all the difference. A shoe company sent a salesman to Alaska to open up the market there. He reported back: "I can't do it; nobody up here wears shoes." The top salesman was then sent to the same location. His enthusiastic request was immediate: "Send a truckload of shoes! Nobody up here wears shoes!"

Learn to look on the bright side. If you think you're getting too much government, just be thankful you're not getting as much as you're paying for!

Not long after my brother opened a music store, someone broke in and stole over $6,000 worth of musical instruments, including his own violin. With a large family to support, he might have been devastated, as there was no insurance to cover his loss. Yet I was amazed at his attitude, as he looked on the bright side. His comments included these: "Oh, each one of our children is worth so many more times than what they took," and "All these things will be for my experience. And who knows what good may come of it?" He even jokingly said that this was a quick way to liquidate his inventory.

Joy can attend even adversity. A bitter-sweet joy, perhaps— but it comes. And if you keep your face to the sunshine, the shadows fall behind you.

> Be like the bird who,
> Halting in his flight
> On a limb too slight
> Feels it give way beneath him;
> Yet sings
> Knowing he hath wings.

William James said that "the path to cheerfulness is to sit up cheerfully and to act and speak as if cheerfulness were already there." If you have to be blue, be a bright blue. You can't stop the waves, but you can learn to surf.

Albert R. Lyman, himself terminally ill, in an effort to encourage another, wrote in a letter these thoughts: "Christ so often said, 'Be of good cheer.' That was not simply a meaningless salutation; it was a command—the very command that people need most often. I think of the times when I was cast down in gloom and in depression from the adversary, but I recall how I have prayed and how into my dark world, cheer and hope and purpose have come to me.

"The sorrow that comes over us is a call from the Lord to rise above it; it is our opportunity to see that the Lord is watching over us. We get encouragement from the Spirit of light; discouragement comes from the spirit of darkness.

"Right now, at this time, I am suffering with a heart ailment which may take me away at any moment, yet I am enjoying an assurance and a calmness that I have never had before. You are precious in His sight. There is nothing so comforting as the extension of cheer and hope and courage that you will get by your own prayerful, resolute efforts."

* * * *

How about a practical pointer? If you don't feel like smiling—if you just don't feel like raising the corners of your mouth—try letting the middle sag.

I heard of a woman who was always smiling. No one ever saw her without a smile on her face. One day she was questioned as to why, and she replied that she had been in a terrible accident that had left her face scarred and disfigured. "But," she said, "I discovered that when I am smiling, the scars are much less noticeable. So I smile."

Another woman used her scars to her advantage in a different way. After a fire that had nearly claimed her life, she said, "At the time, I never believed I would think of the fire as a blessing, but I see now that it was." She looks upon her few remaining scars as "beauty marks of the soul," for they remind her of what might have happened and of the value of life. "I look upon my scars as a reminder of the blessings in my life and of my need to rely on my Father in heaven. If I didn't have the scars, I might possibly forget the miracles in my life."

* * * *

Donna Turley's life is an inspiration, as reported by Bruce C. Hafen. Donna formed a dream for her life. There would be an education, prosperity, and a home with flowers and fruit trees. There would also be children, good health, and happiness. This dream contained seeds of both disappointment and fulfillment, because so much of it would never be hers—yet she would find unforeseen richness in adversity's crucible.

Donna grew up in pioneer-like conditions, reading by candlelight and bathing in a washtub. She believed her family was rich because her mother had two pairs of shoes. After graduating from college in 1953, Donna taught high school. She went without a car for her first three years of teaching to help with her family's finances. Donna taught clothing and child development at Dixie College from 1955-58, but found her real love in being appointed Dixie's first girls' dorm "mother." One Christmas she made housecoats for her forty-eight girls out of surplus GI material that had been given to the school. The girls proudly wore them down the main street of the town in an impromptu midnight parade. Her role as gifted confidant to the Dixie girls steered her toward a career as a professional counselor.

This sunny picture of life began to darken in 1959, when Donna was stricken with crippling rheumatoid arthritis while working as a service volunteer in New England. With characteristic grit, she simply tried to outwork her illness, but her condition only worsened. In the physical deterioration that followed, Donna gradually came to know the world of doctors, medication, surgery, incessant pain, and the frightening specter of total immobility.

Amid a worsening illness and an urban life far from the flowers and fruit trees of her childhood, Donna worked and groped and grew. In 1968, she became a school psychologist, working with educationally handicapped and emotionally disturbed children. After years of professional intimacy with troubled families, nothing surprised her any more. She remembers the shy little boy who lived with grandparents, after having watched his father kill his mother; the child who vowed not to live if his parents divorced; the girl with a seventy-five-year-old father and a young retarded mother who begged to stay at school because her parents said not to come home that day.

Motherhood never came to her, but, she says, "my children have been the children of the world. I have had my private moments with trusting, shining eyes. I have felt their hugs and known the sweet sharings of little hurts and joys."

Donna Turley grew up wanting life to be perfect, then discovered through bittersweet experience that she could make life perfect, however it comes. To the outside observer, she has not had an easy time of it. But Donna knows that she spends herself fully, all the days of her demanding life. Whatever she has to give, she gives. "I am determined," she once wrote, "not to leave this life with an ounce of anything left in me that could be a stepping-stone or a light to another." As many elements of her childhood dream have slipped from her grasp, she has reached deeper to find new ways to dream. For Donna, happiness is not a place, but a way of seeing life. She is happy for being alive, having work to do and gifts to give. She wrote, "Does everyone love life as dearly as I do?"

CHAPTER TWENTY-TWO

Have Some Fun Along the Way

SOMEONE QUIPPED, "LIFE is too important to take too seriously." A sense of humor goes a long way in facing trouble. Humor is to life what shock absorbers are to automobiles—it make the "bumpy ride" a little more tolerable.

From *Cradles of Eminence*, the book reporting the challenging childhoods of famous people, I learned that a surprising number of comedians had alcoholic or abusive or desertive fathers. Their childhoods were tragic. Perhaps humor became their way of coping with the pain in their lives. George Bernard Shaw expressed his attitude toward such a situation with these words: "If you can't get rid of the family skeleton, make it dance."

Susan Trainer doesn't let life's pitfalls keep her down, the article heading read. As Susan Trainer jams the receiver into the cradle, her telephone sidles over to the edge of the table and goes over the edge. "Whoops," she says, then laughs. "People would probably say that happened because I'm blind," Trainer says. "But that's not true. It happened because I'm clumsy." She's amused.

Her sense of humor—described by friends as "slightly bent"—was present long before her eyesight departed over 30 years ago. And whether she's at work, puttering around her apartment or indulging in her all-time number one passion—watching *Jeopardy!* ("I have a terrible time with the video Daily Double questions," she says)—Trainer usually has a joke, a zinger or a self-deprecatory story to share. Her ability to accept—and laugh at—life's tortuous detours has come in handy.

"You take what life gives you and do the best you can," says Trainer. "What choice do you have? And you might as well have some fun along the way."

This philosophy comes from a person who was six years old when she first injected herself with insulin to control her diabetes. A person who battled the disease during childhood and adolescence but still had enough gumption and brains to qualify for the National Honor Society, despite attending only 40 days of classes one year. A person who lost her sight "overnight" at age 24—an event that coincided with the birth of her second child and the disintegration of her marriage.

Diabetes. Divorce. Blindness. A lesser person might have spent more time wringing her hands and less time learning new Helen Keller jokes. Not Trainer.

She doesn't like to talk much about the past. No point. It happened. It's over. What's next? But when she does reminisce, Trainer does so with mirth.

She talks about how much fun her children had growing up with a blind mom: "We'd go outside and play around with balls—nothing more fun than watching me trying to catch a ball."

Not that Trainer experienced a seamless transition to the realm of sightlessness. "It was a frightening time. I felt immensely sorry for myself for a time. Then I woke up one day and decided, 'This is really boring. Let's get on with it.'"

James Thurber defines humor as "emotional chaos remembered in tranquility." Indeed. Pulling into my garage after an exhausting day at work, I was momentarily distracted, and my foot slipped off the clutch. My car then propelled itself into the upright freezer located at the back of the garage. Sick inside, I backed the car up, got out, and saw the sizeable dent in my previously beautiful freezer. I then opened the freezer door to assess the internal damage and was horrified when the heavy door literally came off in my hand and fell to the floor, frozen juice cans rolling everywhere.

I hurried into the house and looked in the Yellow Pages under *Refrigerator Repair* and the frantic telephone call was made. When I described to the repairman what had happened and the pathetic condition of my freezer, he began laughing so hard he could barely get the words out: "Lady, we don't *do body* work!"

We need to step back from the trials that we face in order to see the humor in them, for they certainly don't seem funny at the time. Large or small, humor makes the experience more palatable.

I heard about a mother who was sick in bed with the flu. Her little daughter wanted so much to be a good nurse. She fluffed the pillows and brought a magazine for her mother to read. She even showed up with a surprise cup of tea.

"Why, you're such a sweetheart," her mother said appreciatively as she drank the tea. "I didn't know you even knew how to make tea."

"Oh, yes," the little girl replied. "I learned by watching you. I put the tea leaves in the pan, and then I put in the water, and I boiled it, and then I strained it into a cup. But I couldn't find a strainer, so I used the fly swatter instead."

"You *what?*" the mother exclaimed.

The little girl said quickly, "Oh, don't worry, Mom, I didn't use the *new* fly swatter. I used the old one."

Small trials or large tragedies, a sense of humor helps. In 1999, the tornado in Oklahoma left behind scenes of utter devastation as 7,000 homes were leveled and destroyed. "You can't imagine the amount of damage. Aerial photos can't even come close to explaining what it is like," said one helper. People's humor was incredible. The wreckage of one home had a sign in front: "FOR SALE—SOME ASSEMBLY REQUIRED."

"Humor is tragedy plus time," observed Mark Twain. Tears and laughter are so closely tied together that it's sometimes hard to separate them. "Comedy is an escape, not from truth but from despair, a narrow escape into faith," wrote another. Annette Nelson, some months after the family's tragic accident, wrote in a letter to me: "In Caroline's psychology class, they took a stress test for fun. If you scored over 100, you needed HELP. She scored 538. I scored 680! We laughed!"

Many people seem to find my descriptions of some of my own adversities rather entertaining. Like the osteoporosis (brittle bone disease) that I acquired after our two miracle children were born when I was 41 and 44 years old. Being either pregnant (building little skeletons) or nursing (with my calcium-rich milk) for four-and-a-half years straight in my declining years, and avoiding exercise at all costs, I developed osteoporosis "like a 70-year-old woman," said the doctor. It resulted in several broken bones within a three-year period, including three broken legs. (I'm just telling you this so you'll feel really sorry for me.) I'm not complaining, mind you, because I heard once that the more you complain, the longer the Lord makes you live.

Anyway, once two of my—both of my—*all* of my legs were broken at the same time. I had to stay off them for a full month in order for them to heal. The only time I moved from the bed was to crawl to the bathroom which was only a few feet away. When Sunday came, Merrie Anne, who was four at the time, inquired if I were going to church. When I answered in the negative, she asked innocently, "Why? Don't they like mommies crawling around at church?"

During this trying time, my husband Micheal did everything for me. He not only went to work, but he also did all the things to keep the household running: the shopping and errands, caring for the children (ages 4 and 1), cooking for a household of nine (we had boarders at the time), and cleaning—well, no, scratch the cleaning part. (Now I know why he forbade me to go downstairs during that time.)

He said, "There are two things I have learned about raising babies. First, if you can't get a baby to take a pill, just put the pill on the floor. And the second thing I've learned," he said, "is that you have to change a baby's diaper _every day_." He paused. "And when those disposable diaper packages say 'Six to twelve pounds'—they're not kidding. That's all those things'll hold!"

It is said that angels can fly because they take themselves so lightly. Said one person, "As I learn to laugh at myself, I gain a wonderful new perspective about life and the sometimes almost overwhelming situations in which I find myself." As someone else quipped, "Would it be so bad to die laughing?"

MUSIC

According to Dick Clark, "Music is the soundtrack of your life."

In times of heartache, music can lift and inspire—or it can deepen one's depression, depending on the choice of music, perhaps. Whenever I hear a song that was popular in the 1970's, "There's got to be a morning after, if we can hold on through the night. . . ." I re-experience my feelings of deep sorrow. The song was popular at a time when my own brother was going through a severe trial. His pain was mine, as well, and my own heart was heavy. I shall never forget that song nor the feelings of sadness that overcome me each time I hear it.

Kay Lindsay wrote of her discovery regarding the importance of the right kind of music in overcoming grief after the unexpected loss of her husband: "I had always had a song in my heart. I would wake up in the morning ready to burst into song, much to the chagrin of my children. I often found myself singing during the course of the day. But after Van died, the song in my heart seemed to die, too, and all we could sing as a family were songs like *God Be with You 'Till We Meet Again*. Even three-year-old Christopher knew the words.

"After several months, however, I realized that these songs were actually contributing to our grief rather than helping us find joy in life. I forced myself to start singing *You Are My Sunshine* and *Zip-a-dee-doo-dah*. At first, my children and I were singing empty words, but after days of singing, "My, oh my, what a wonderful day!" we couldn't help but start to believe it."

CHAPTER TWENTY-THREE
In Everything Give Thanks

I HAVE GAINED a tremendous appreciation for the quality of gratitude—or confessing God's hand in all things—even in the face of adversity. Gratitude can heal and transform heartache. Not only does gratitude help us get *through* adversity, but ultimately adversity provides opportunities to *attain* gratitude.

I always thought that gratitude was simply a nice feeling to have, that it comes naturally when something wonderful happens, or when we really focus on it at times like Thanksgiving. But I thought it sort of an optional thing. Not so. Have you heard of "the *sin* of ingratitude?" I suppose most of us have not thought of that as a great sin. But scriptures tell us, "In nothing doth man offend God, save those who confess not his hand in all things." Another says, "Beware, lest thou forget the Lord."

Ingratitude is a sin, because *sin* can be defined as anything that separates us from God. We separate ourselves from God when we fail to acknowledge his hand in our lives. We sometimes have a short memory of past blessings. Interesting how those with the shortest memories have the longest list of complaints. Rather than feeling grateful for the many blessings that are ours, we focus on the one blessing that is missing.

If ingratitude is numbered among the serious sins, then gratitude takes its place among the noblest of virtues. Indeed, Cicero said that gratitude is not only the greatest of virtues, but the parent of all the others. He called it the mother of all virtues.

Why is gratitude so important? Gratitude is the very essence of worship. It is an indication of the relationship we have with God. Someone said, "Your first thank you may turn out to be your first real conversation with God."

In Thessalonians we read: "Rejoice *evermore*. In *everything* give thanks: for this is the will of God in Christ Jesus concerning you." It doesn't say to rejoice when things are going well for you; it says rejoice *evermore*. It doesn't say, "for the pleasant things, give thanks; it says in *everything* give thanks. And that is what is so exciting to me: that we are to rejoice and give thanks in *everything*, even the hard times, the hurtful times, the heart-wrenching times. And that is a good thing, because that means that we can be happy, no matter our circumstances. A thankful heart will find in every hour some heavenly blessing.

I have never met a happy person who was not grateful, and I have never met a grateful person who was not happy. Gratitude and happiness are inseparably connected. Joy flows freely into grateful hearts that rejoice in God's goodness. Sadness may *visit*, but it can never *possess* a heart where God's love lingers and where we recognize and acknowledge that love.

While there are many things in life that we cannot control, our happiness is something that we *can* control through cultivating a spirit of gratitude regardless of our circumstances. I sensed the gratitude of a tender heart when one little girl listed the things for which she was thankful, including "electricity—and if the electricity goes out, I'm thankful for flashlights." Even in adversity, we can be grateful.

One very interesting paradox is that oftentimes the less we have, the more grateful we are. Children seem to be grateful in inverse proportion to the amount they receive, as witnessed on any given Christmas. "Is that all there is?" they ask, after opening the last of their gazillion glittering gifts.

As one of fifteen children, my mother recalled from her childhood: "It was those *half* chocolates and *small* dishes of Jello that made them so special. It isn't special at all when you can have all you want."

I recently tested this premise with my own children. I'd received a box of chocolates when I'd spoken to a group and decided to cut the chocolates into fourths for sharing with the children. They would have been grateful for a fourth of a chocolate, but when they were told they could choose *four* different pieces, they were thrilled. But the thing that amazed me most was when one of the chocolates was divided imperfectly, making one of the little pieces larger than the others. Four-year-old Evan selected it, exclaiming excitedly, "Wow! This one is humongous!"

One salesclerk in a candy store always had customers lined up waiting, while other salesclerks stood around with nothing to do. The owner of the store noted her popularity and asked for her secret. "It's easy," she said. "The others scoop up more than a pound of candy and then start taking away. I always scoop up less than a pound and then add to it." There may be occasions when God does the same for us. We are more grateful when we start out with less and are then added upon.

Is it coincidence that in our deepest extremity we gain the most gratitude for the blessings that are ours? Might it be that adversity actually helps us become more grateful? Is there a correlation between the size of our trials and the depth of our gratitude?

Shortly after World War II ended, Ezra Taft Benson went to distribute food and clothing to people in war-torn Europe. The man who accompanied him, Frederick Babbel, told of having pointed out to him "a rather timid and emaciated sister. She had burlap sacks wrapped around her feet and legs in place of shoes. Even these were now in shreds. Her clothing was patched and tattered. As I looked at her purple-grey face, her swollen red eyes and protruding joints, I was told that I was looking at a person in the advanced stages of starvation.

"This woman had lived in East Prussia. During the final days of the frightful battles in that area, her husband had been killed. She was left with four small children, one of them a babe in arms. Under the agreements of the occupying military powers, she was one of 11 million Germans who were required to leave her homeland and all her basic possessions, and go to Western Germany to seek a new home. She was permitted to take only such bare necessities, bedding, etc. as she could load into her small wooden-wheeled wagon—about 65 pounds in all—which she pulled across this desolate wasteland of war. Her smallest child she carried in her arms, while the other small children did their best to walk beside her during this trek of over a thousand miles on foot.

"She started her journey in late summer. Having neither food nor money among her few possessions, she was forced to gather a daily subsistence from the fields and forests along the way. Constantly she was also faced with dangers from panicky refugees and marauding troops.

"Soon the snows came and temperatures dropped to about 40 degrees below zero. One by one her children died, either frozen to death or the victims of starvation, or both. She buried them in shallow graves by the roadside, using a tablespoon as a shovel. Finally, as she was reaching the end of her journey, her last little child died in her arms. Her spoon was gone now, so she dug a grave in the frozen earth with her bare fingers.

"As she was recalling these and other difficulties, she explained that her grief at that moment became unbearable. Here she was kneeling in the snow at the graveside of her last child. . . . In this moment of deep sorrow and bewilderment, she felt her heart would break. In despair she contemplated how she might end her own life as so many of her fellow countrymen were doing.

"As these thoughts assailed her, something within her said to pray. She then rapturously explained how she prayed more fervently than she had ever prayed before. She then stated that of all the ailing people in her saddened land, she was one of the happiest because she knew that God lived, that Jesus is the Christ, and that if she continued faithful and true to the end she would be saved in the kingdom of God. She stood before us in her emaciated condition, her clothing shredded, her feet wrapped in burlap, and bore testimony of God's love and how blessed she was."

As I pondered this amazing account of gratitude in the midst of incredible suffering, I thought of the scripture that says: "None of them that trust in Him shall be desolate," and I wondered about this woman who had lost her husband, all four of her children, all her possessions, her health, and her homeland. Surely *she* was desolate. But only in an earthly sense. With an eternal perspective, she considered herself incredibly blessed because she possessed the knowledge that her Father in heaven and Jesus Christ loved her and had provided the gift of eternal life.

* * * *

Dutch-born Corrie ten Boom and her sister Betsy were prisoners in Nazi concentration camps during World War II because of their involvement in hiding Jews in the "underground." Demonstrating a great deal of courage, they shared their unwavering faith and love with other prisoners in those

incomprehensibly inhuman conditions and amidst hideous
deprivations. Yet they were somehow able to maintain an attitude
of gratitude. They said that perhaps they might someday even find
a reason to be grateful for the fleas that infested their
overcrowded barracks.

It wasn't until later that they learned that the fleas were,
indeed, a blessing in disguise. They were the reason the guards
refused to enter the barracks, ensuring the prisoners enough
privacy to enable them to carry on their religious study groups
with their smuggled Bible, undetected.

* * * *

Another touching example of one who felt deep gratitude
even in his greatest extremity comes from my husband's home
town, as told by Kathy Jenkins in *Tragic Lehi Tale Recalled*.

Winter came early to Utah Valley in 1918, and froze much of
the sugar beet crop in the Old Field west of Lehi on the Saratoga
Road. Faced with closure of the sugar factory, Lehi farmers were
trying desperately to get one load of beets per day out of the
ground. The tedious process involved plowing the frosty soil,
digging out the beets, cutting the tops off the frozen vegetables,
and tossing them, one by one, into the huge red beet wagon.

Added to the challenge of frozen fields were two additional
problems that created a severe manpower shortage: many of the
Valley's men were enlisted in the armed forces, and many more
were too sick to farm—the "black plague" had spread its deadly
fingers across fields and townships.

According to Les Goates, a Lehi resident, "While my dad and
brother Francis were thusly engaged in harvesting the family's only
cash crop and were having their evening meal one day, a phone
call came through our eldest brother bearing the tragic news that
nine-year-old Kenneth had been stricken with the dread flu, and
after only a few hours of violent sickness, had died on his father's
lap. He wanted Dad to go to Ogden and bring the boy home so he
could be buried in the family plot in the Lehi Cemetery."

When he arrived in Ogden, he found his son Charles,
Kenneth's father, sprawled over the little boy's cold form. The
ugly brown discharge of the black plague was oozing from the
father's ears and nose, and he was virtually burning up with fever.

"Take my boy home," muttered the stricken young father, "and lay him away in the family plot and come back for me tomorrow."

Mr. Goates brought the tiny body home in his old flap-curtained touring car. He made a coffin in his carpenter shop and went to dig the grave while his wife and daughters made a cushion and a lining for the coffin.

The next day Mr. Goates received news that three more of the family had succumbed to the sickness. He made two more journeys to Ogden to bring Charles and his two little girls home to Lehi.

The next morning at breakfast, Dad said to Francis, "Well, son, we had better get down to the field and see if we can get another load of beets out of the ground before they get frozen in any tighter. Hitch up and let's be on our way."

They hitched up the four-horse outfit. As they drove along Saratoga Road they passed wagon after wagon load of beets being hauled to the factory and driven by neighborhood farmers.

As they passed by, each driver would wave a greeting: "Sure sorry, George;" "Tough break, George;" "You've got a lot of friends, George." On the last wagon was the town comedian, freckle-faced Jasper Rolfe. He waved a cheery greeting and called out, "That's all of 'em, Uncle George."

George turned to Francis and said, "I wish it was all of *ours*."

When they arrived at the field gate, George drove onto the field, stopped the team, paused a moment, and scanned the field. There wasn't a sugar beet on the whole field. Suddenly it dawned on him what Jasper Rolfe meant when he called out, "That's all of 'em, Uncle George!"

Then Dad got down off the wagon, picked up a handful of the rich, brown soil he loved so much, and then in his thumbless left hand a beet top, and he looked for a moment at these symbols of his labor, as if he couldn't believe his eyes.

Then Father sat down on a pile of beet tops—this man who brought four of his loved ones home for burial in the course of only six days, made caskets, dug graves, and even helped with the burial clothing—this amazing man who never faltered, nor flinched, nor wavered throughout this agonizing ordeal—sat down on a pile of beet tops and sobbed like a little child.

Then he arose, wiped his eyes with his big, red bandanna handkerchief, looked up at the sky and said, "Thanks, Father, for the elders of our ward."

CHAPTER TWENTY-FOUR

Think of the Blessings, Not the Losses

A MOTHER TELLS of her five-year-old daughter who slipped on the rug in the living room and hit her head. Her mother comforted the crying child as she applied cold compresses to the lump that had already appeared. Soon the tears stopped and the little girl ran off to play.

That night after dinner, the mother went to her little girl's room to tuck her in and to hear her prayers. Always she thanked God for the nicest thing that happened that day. It could be the movie she had seen or the ice cream or a car ride or the snow. This particular night when her mother asked, "What do you want to thank God for tonight?" she answered, "For my bump."

"Why do you want to thank Him for that?" her mother asked.

"Because now he can make it well." With that, she gave her mother a kiss, turned over, and closed her eyes.

The mother sat there thinking: "Yes, Father, how often we forget to thank Thee for the rough, hard times. But it's through them we often learn the greatest lessons of Thy healing love."

As another said, "I'm glad to know about hurts and healing, or else how would I know the Healer?"

"Behold, happy is the man whom God correcteth: therefore, despise not thou the chastening of the Almighty: For he maketh sore, and bindeth up: he woundeth, and his hands make whole" (Job 5:17,18).

In Samuel we read, "The Lord maketh poor, and maketh rich: he bringeth low, and lifteth up." And in Lamentations: "But though he cause grief, yet will he have compassion according to the multitude of his mercies."

There are those who give thanks for the pleasures
And comforts which come to their door;
But repine at the trials and hardships,
And complain that their burdens are sore.

There are souls who accept all the bounties
Bestowed by One gracious and just. . .
But lament if the road is o'ershadowed
Or obscured by the storm and the dust.

Shall we then, accept only the good things,
The ones which are easy to bear. . .
And revile at the fate which requires us
To remove from the path thorn and snare?

Not alone for the easy and pleasant
Should our praise and thanksgiving ascend;
For the Father in sending us trials
But proves He's more truly our friend.

So let us give thanks for the heartaches,
For the briar-strewn way and the tear;
They are stepping-stones higher and farther,
They are helping us grow year by year.

And instead of lamenting and grieving
When difficult things come our way,
Let us fasten our armor the closer
And cheerfully, calmly obey.

Thank God for the beauty of labor;
The glory which follows the strife;
For the strength which is born of our weakness—
Thank God for the hard things in life!

(Nancy Smith Lowe,
Give Thanks for the Hard Things in Life)

One man expressed his feeling that, rather than fighting adversity, we can gain an appreciation for the "sweetness" of adversity.

> And when we count the blessings
> That God has so freely sent . . .
> We will find no cause for murmuring
> And no time to lament . . .
> For our Father loves His children
> And to Him all things are plain.
> So He never sends us pleasures
> When the soul's deep need is pain.

Sir Isaac Newton said, "Trials are medicines which our gracious and wise physician prescribes, because we need them; and he proportions the frequency and weight of them to what the case requires. Let us trust his skill and thank him for his prescription." It is so natural for us to react negatively to adversity in our lives. We feel pain; we seek to ease that pain by focusing on the thing that caused it. Correct description, wrong prescription.

When an elderly gentleman learned of the tragic death of my exemplary sixteen-year-old nephew in a car accident, his response stunned me: "What a blessing!" He went on to explain, "He won't have to go through the trials and temptations of this world."

Then this man in his eighties shared the origin of his philosophy of life. He related how, as a young married man during the Depression, he had gone to a grand opening of a grocery store. Every hour a drawing was held; one had to be present to win.

The man's name was one of those drawn the first hour. He won a 100-pound sack of sugar. He was thrilled! Now they would have sugar to bottle their fruit, as well as for baking and other needs. He hurried home to tell his wife the wonderful news.

While he was gone, the second drawing was held. Once again, his name was among the winners, but because he was not present, he could not claim the second sack of sugar and only learned of it upon his return. When he heard of his win/loss, he was miserable. To think what he might have had filled him with despair.

But then he changed his thinking. Rather than dwell on what

he had lost, shouldn't he be grateful for the sugar that he had won in the first drawing? He adopted for his lifetime motto that day, "Think of the blessings, not the losses."

There is the story of the old farmer whose eyes still sparkled with an inward happiness. "I wish you would tell me how you've kept the twinkle in your eyes."

His answer was immediate: "I make the most of all that comes and the least of all that goes."

LaDawn Jacob's grandmother was one who possessed the delightful habit of feeling grateful. She said, "I spend half my time counting my blessings and the other half thanking the Lord for them, and that leaves no time to feel sorry for myself."

LaDawn wrote of her: "Near the end of her life, as her body was wasted away with cancer and she lay on her bed, weak and in a considerable amount of pain, my own mother leaned over and expressed the wish that somehow they could relieve Grandma of some of the burden and the pain she was experiencing. Grandma looked up and smiled in a most reassuring way and said, 'This is such a small thing to go through for one who has been blessed as much as I. The Lord has been so good to me.'

"I said to myself, 'Blessed!?' I thought of her life as a widow for nearly 40 years, the mother of ten children raising many of them alone after the death of her husband. She had endured the loss of two homes, one in a flood, and one when they were driven from Mexico. She had lived much of her life in what might be considered dire poverty. Yet, to her, the Lord had blessed her beyond measure, for all she could see were the blessings. Such was her grateful heart."

LaDawn continued on the subject of gratitude: "We have each been in a situation where a gift we had lovingly given was appreciated. We glowed with happiness and felt a desire to give again. I'm sure we have also known the disappointment of giving and realizing that our work was hardly noticed."

She told of how she sometimes prepared a good supper and felt dismayed when children complained. It made her feel like giving them nothing but bread and gravy. "I have often wondered if perhaps the Lord may not also get tired of providing feasts for us and having us complain because there was no salt on the peas. Perhaps the reason we are unable to receive more fully the blessings of the Lord is that we are not appreciative of what we have."

Even in the midst of affliction, our table surely is spread.

Laurie Thornton focused on the blessings rather than the losses. A diabetic, she went blind during her second pregnancy. Adding to her emotional anguish, the baby was born prematurely and lived only two and a half days. Doctors then warned her that she could not survive another pregnancy.

"I had always wanted 12 children. I was so jealous, so envious, so bitter that I couldn't have any more children," she recalled. "Friends would tell me that they were pregnant, and I just couldn't feel happy for them. I finally realized that the opposite of gratitude is not ingratitude; it's envy. One day the Spirit said in my mind, 'You've got to realize that you are blessed.'"

Among the blessings she treasured most were her husband, her son, and her adopted daughter—and the fact that she had her sight for 29 years. "I miss seeing a ballet or art work. You can touch a bird, but you can't feel what a bird looks like in flight. I miss seeing autumn leaves and crystal snow. But at least I saw those things at one time. At least I have that," she said.

Laurie mentioned an advantage to being blind: "Everyone I've met since I went blind is just gorgeous in my mind. What a person looks like isn't important to me. Sometimes people let appearance stand in the way of seeing how beautiful a person's soul is."

Finally she said, "You truly realize your dependence on the Lord when something like this happens. I'm convinced that there are certain experiences I will have in this life connected with being blind that I have to have. I really believe that some day I'll be grateful for those experiences."

P.S. Since publication of the previous edition of this book, Laurie Thornton passed away suddenly and unexpectedly. I'm sure she is "grateful for those experiences," as she receives the rewards earned through her grateful endurance.

* * * *

Gratitude is our gladness. We were born to it. Inside every

heart there is an aching need to feel grateful. And once we have felt it, we know that there is no pleasure on earth like it.

I will always remember the large picture I had many years ago. It depicted a family preparing to enjoy Thanksgiving dinner—a bounteous feast featuring a large, golden turkey. The words attached to the picture were: "O Thou who gives us all, give us one thing more: a grateful heart."

CHAPTER TWENTY-FIVE

Gratitude in Adversity: Practical Pointers

IF IT SEEMS difficult to gain feelings of gratitude, perhaps we should begin at this level: If you don't get everything you want, think of the things you don't get that you don't want. If you can't be content with what you have received, be thankful for what you have escaped.

> We thank thee, Father, for the care
> That did not come to try us;
> The burden that we did not bear,
> The trouble that passed by us;
> The task we did not fail to do,
> The hurt we did not cherish;
> The friend who did not prove untrue,
> The joy that did not perish.
>
> We thank thee for the blinding storm
> That did not lose its swelling;
> And for the sudden blight of harm
> That came not nigh our dwelling.
> We thank thee for the dart unsped,
> The bitter word unspoken,
> The grave unmade, the tear unshed,
> The heart-tie still unbroken.

One of my favorite methods of gaining a grateful heart is to simply think how happy I would be if I had lost everything I value—everything precious and dear to me—and then just got it all back again!

Something very much like this was experienced by Nedra Redd, as reported by Ardith Kapp. A deep brain tumor was discovered at the base of her skull. It appeared to be inoperable, especially risky in her weakened condition. Yet the doctors gave her only two weeks to live if they didn't remove the growth. The situation seemed desperate. Surgery was scheduled for Christmas Eve.

Anxious family and friends waited through the nightlong vigil following the surgery. Dawn broke; it was Christmas morning. The tumor had been removed.

"I had a very special thinking time as I regained consciousness," Nedra explained. It was in the twilight time between life and death that the gifts of life came back. They returned one by one with enough space between each to allow time for cherishing and savoring.

"I'm all right! I didn't die in surgery! I'm alive!" was her first realization. "But everything was black, and I couldn't hear anything. I tried to speak, and I couldn't speak. I thought, 'I'm blind. I can't hear. I can't speak. But I am alive.' I can remember such a surge of gratitude that I was alive, and then I sank into unconsciousness again.

"When I realized later that I was conscious again and that there was a sort of grayness around me, I thought, 'I am not totally blind. I can see some light.' I can remember praying and telling my Father, 'Thank you. I'm alive and I'm not totally blind.' I couldn't have lived in darkness. So I gave thanks again. Then I realized I could see Phil's face. My husband was talking to me, but I couldn't hear him. But," she said with intensity, "I could see him. I was grateful that I could see his face.

"Soon I realized I could hear him speaking to me, so I prayed again and gave thanks that I could see and hear. I thought, 'I can't speak, but it's enough. I can see and I can hear.'"

Then came the ecstasy of her final treasure. "The doctor was there. I had been trying to speak. I heard him ask my husband, 'Can she speak?' He shook his head just slightly. 'I was afraid of that,' the doctor said. 'We had to destroy quite a bit of her vocal chords to get the tumor. I was afraid she would not be able to speak.'

With a happy tone in her now clear, full voice, Nedra Redd

recalled her thoughts at that moment: "'Oh, so that's it,' I thought. 'I can't talk. But I can hear and I can see.' I had such a deep feeling of joy and gratitude. Then the doctor put his finger on the hole in my throat where the tracheotomy was and said, 'Now try.' I could make sounds! I knew I was not mute. It was such a good feeling. We knew the Lord had blessed us.

"It was Christmas morning. Phil had spent the night with me when I needed him so much. With my whole soul filled with gratitude and thanksgiving, I asked him to go home and be with the children. It was a wonderful Christmas."

> When upon life's billows you are tempest-tossed,
> When you are discouraged, thinking all is lost,
> Count your many blessings; name them one by one,
> And it will surprise you what the Lord has done.
> (Johnson Oatman, Jr., *Count Your Blessings*)

Another thing that helps me feel grateful amidst the personal trials of my life is to think about trading for different ones. One day I said to my mother, "I wish we could choose our own trials; I'm sure I would have chosen different ones than the ones I have." But then she asked me what ones I would prefer.

I thought of what I considered your basic big trials in life and came to a realization that, while I viewed my own trials as rather serious, I would rather keep the ones I had than trade for others. At least I felt comfortable with them; they were familiar to me.

An attitude of gratitude can be consciously cultivated. If it requires the use of the "sour grapes" method, so be it. When the most popular color for new cars was my then-favorite color of forest green, I thought them beautiful and wished for one. I reminded myself that a new car would be too costly—not only because of its purchase price, but for sales tax, property taxes, auto insurance, etc.—not to mention the stress of worrying about possible dings that would mar its perfection. Sour grapes. I remember, as I passed yet another shiny, forest green car, of consciously thinking how thankful I was for the dependable, economical, paid-for little car I was driving—and of how I liked its color of burnt orange, since it blended in so well with the rust spots.

Many people consider a lack of money to be a great adversity. Yet Henry David Thoreau looked at it this way: "Most of the luxuries, and many of the so-called comforts of life, are not only not indispensable, but positive hindrances to the elevation of mankind. . . . Love your life, poor as it is. The setting sun is reflected from the windows of the alms house as brightly as from the rich man's abode."

Here's something you can do: Joe Christensen suggests you take a sheet of paper and write on it a list of the blessings you consider to be important to you, in whatever order they come to your mind. Then place them in order of priority, beginning with your most precious blessings. Probably somewhere near the top of your list will be the four "Fs"—your faith, family, freedom, and friends.

Now look at your list again and see how far down the list you go before you come to any blessing that you can buy for money. The most precious blessings are without price; indeed, they are priceless.

You can feel grateful for your situation, whatever it may be, for you can always find someone much worse off than you are!

Annette Nelson told of a woman she had become aware of when she was in the hospital recovering from the accident that had left her paralyzed. The woman's wails could be heard up and down the corridors during most of the long days.

Annette made it a point to become acquainted with the woman and to befriend her. And when the time was right, Annette said to her, "You know, there is something about being in this hospital that could be a blessing. You can look around and see so many others who are worse off than you are." The woman's attitude began to change; her complaints diminished as she recognized her blessings.

We can realize that everything is relative. Once, in a country with rather primitive living conditions, a distressed family went to visit the wise man of the village. They complained that life was unbearable with nine people sharing their tiny, two-room hut.

The wise man's counsel to them was to obtain a goat and let it share their living quarters for two weeks. The family followed his instructions and returned to him after the time had ended. They reported that life was wonderful now that they didn't have to live with the goat anymore!

Everything is relative. At one time we were asked to take in a neglected baby for foster care, joining the baby and other children we already had. It was a trying ordeal. From my journal comes this: *Only in the last few days has Joey become secure enough that he can be happy for short periods of time without dragging himself after me and screaming. That strap-the-baby-to-your-front contraption that was loaned me has proven to be a life saver. He seems to smile more and be happier and calmer now, and he doesn't quiver now (caffeine withdrawal, since they fed him only coffee?).*

But I can say this: If life seems to be going by too fast, and you want to slow it down, just get an extra baby that screams all the time. This has been a very long two and a half weeks. The days drag by sometimes. . . .

Two blessings will come from this, in addition to any good we might be doing for little Joey: (1) I will appreciate more the blessing of having such a good *little angel as our own baby is, and 2) life will seem so _easy_ with only one baby!*

Yes, everything is relative. A long-term cast and permanent limp aren't so bad when compared to double amputation, as Richard Nelson could tell us. Divorce may be considered a positive thing, if the marriage was sufficiently horrible. Having a miscarriage, though cause for grief, is better than carrying a baby full-term if it would not have been able to survive its birth.

Peter Jeppson exemplified this "theory of relativity." He also demonstrated his sense of humor and his sense of gratitude in coping with his own tragedy. Peter related how, in his recovery from the terrible auto accident in which he had been burned so badly, one of the first surgeries performed was to remove the scar tissue from his eyes. Alone that night, he became anxious to know the outcome; he didn't want to wait until morning to find out whether or not he would be able to see.

Awkwardly, because his hands were wrapped in bandages, he started to remove the wrappings from his eyes. He flipped the lamp switch and the light exploded in his eyes. He could see! He raised a shiny metal pan and looked at his reflection. "There, in all my excitement was this horrid face. Because my family had been told that I didn't have a chance to live, they hadn't told me about some other things. They hadn't told me that I had lost most of one ear and all my eyelids and all my facial features. My nose was gone; all my mouth was gone. In my excitement to see, I hadn't thought about what I would see. I couldn't handle it emotionally. I let out a big yell."

Peter spent all night talking with a sympathetic nurse about all his questions and fears. Then, abruptly, he started to laugh.

He was remembering three years before when, as a junior in high school, he had excitedly dressed for the Junior-Senior Prom. Full of anticipation, he'd started getting his tuxedo on at 2:00 in the afternoon. Then he had noticed on his chin a blemish just starting to appear. "I remember how angry I got. 'Why today? Why not tomorrow? Any day but today!'" Throughout the entire evening, Peter had positioned himself so his face was turned away from his date.

"Now, here I was in the hospital, remembering how silly and immature I had been about that blemish. Here I was, having fought for my very life, for everything I had. And even though my face didn't look very good, that didn't seem so important when I thought of the miracle that had taken place. There really had been no chance that I would see again; yet now I could see! I took a little moment to say a prayer of thanks to my Father in heaven because he had answered that prayer."

* * * *

Linda Eyre, mother of nine, offered a suggestion. "Sometimes I get discouraged—even depressed—because things aren't going well. My melancholy ranges from little discouragements, like a child who keeps losing his homework, to the bigger ones of not being able to rise to the standard of people's expectations. I discovered an unbelievably helpful remedy lately, however, which I can't believe I didn't know before: Count your blessings. Be grateful for what you have!

"Tell the rebellious teenager that you're grateful he at least listened to you before he contradicted your wishes. Be glad your three-year-old is healthy enough to create such a mess. Be thankful that the broken arm was the left one, or not his neck."

Gratitude *does* help us get through adversity, because it connects us with God. One woman advised: "Spend more time offering prayers of gratitude. When I did, I felt His presence, love, and guidance more completely." Redecorate your life with God's gifts. Awe and wonder surround you.

If only we could learn to feel gratitude for the blessings of this day expressed by Mary Jean Irion: "It has been a normal sort of day, common. . . It was routine mostly—washing, ironing, a trip to the store, meals, dishes, the common denominators of women's days. It was pleasant here and there—a letter from an old friend, my husband's telephone call for no reason, a back fence chat with my neighbor, half an hour with a good book, some loud laughs with the children at dinner time.

"It was irritating now and then—a sticky ocean of spilled maple syrup, mealtime with one greedy child and one finicky one, the arrival of a bill unexpectedly high, a persistent salesman's theft of fifteen beautiful minutes.

"It was deeply joyous at times—the whole house glorified with the strains of the new *Greensleeves* record, our unliterary twelve-year-old's first book with its dedication to his parents, our eight-year-old and her friend playing dress up, painted and perfumed, scarved and veiled, clattering through the kitchen in spiked heels.

"It was sobering and frightening in some ways—Mom's waning health and increasing discouragement, the big blow-up after dinner about homework and learning to accept responsibility, and the guilt that followed my hasty words. . . .

"It was blessed with love throughout—in a pig-shaped breadboard made and presented to me by my son; in the wave of feeling as I watched our little daughter sleeping in soft moonlight, her long lashes shadowing her cheek; in an hour alone with my husband at the end of day.

"Just a normal day. A normal day! It is a jewel! In time of war, in peril of death, people have dug their hands and faces into the earth and remembered this. In time of sickness and pain people have buried their faces in pillows and wept for this. In time of loneliness and separation, people have stretched themselves taut and waited for this. In time of hunger, homelessness, want, people have raised bony hands to the skies and stayed alive for this.

"Normal day, let me be aware of the treasure you are. Let me not pass you by in quest of some rare and perfect tomorrow. Let me hold you while I may, for it will not always be so. One day, I may dig my nails in the earth, or bury my face in the pillow, or stretch myself taut, or raise my hands to the sky and want more than all the world—your return."

CHAPTER TWENTY-SIX

To Bring Thee Closer Still to Me

IT IS INTERESTING. In the previous edition of the book, this chapter consisted of eleven poems or hymn texts, with nary a word from my own personal experience. *Experience* is defined by the dictionary as "personal proof or practical knowledge gained by trial." I speak now more from experience.

Seven months after my husband Micheal and I were married, I was scheduled to have a craniotomy for a brain tumor. The specialists who were to perform the surgery explained that this procedure was "about as sophisticated as they get," comparable to open heart surgery. I was understandably apprehensive.

One evening, we were at a gathering where a woman was discussing the benefits and power of visualization. She asked for a volunteer for a demonstration—someone who was in a situation about which they would like to feel differently. I raised my hand, explaining that I was scheduled to have a tumor removed two weeks from that very day, and I would like to feel more positive about that.

From my journal comes this: *She asked me to close my eyes and envision the scene—the negative scene. I saw myself in the corridor of the hospital being wheeled down the hall on the bed. It was cold, the lights were harsh and glaring, and I felt so alone. She had me experience that scene three times and to signal when I was done with a deep breath.*

Then she asked me to envision a positive scene to replace the negative one. I decided I would visualize Micheal being there, which I did—but I was surprised when that new scene lasted but a second. Instead of Micheal, I immediately felt the presence of Christ. He put his hand on my shoulder. I felt his warmth and strength and comfort. I felt his light and his love.

No longer did I fear the surgery. I knew that Christ would be with me.

No longer did I need to feel alone. I remembered that Christ is my strength and that I can give my cares and concerns and my life to him. It was such a wonderful experience, tears fill my eyes even now as I record it this morning.

"He hath said, I will never leave thee, nor forsake thee. . . . The Lord is my helper, and I will not fear what man shall do unto me" (Heb. 13:5-6).

Two weeks later, even as I was being prepared for the brain surgery, I was filled with peace and I felt no fear. The seven-hour procedure went well—but then, I had no doubts that it would.

At about the same time as my craniotomy, my family of origin decided to ostracize me because of a tragic and ugly issue that split our family asunder. My physical suffering and recovery from the craniotomy for the brain tumor were nothing compared to the emotional anguish of being cut off from the family I had thought of as extremely close and loving and had leaned on for my own strength and security and sense of self. Each offense brought renewed pain, repeated disappointment, fresh heartache. It was the most difficult experience of my life.

I was obsessed by the pain. My feelings toward my family were feelings of bitterness. I instructed Micheal that if I should die, he was not to inform my siblings of my demise. If they didn't want to see me alive, I certainly didn't want to give them the satisfaction of seeing me dead!

I knew that I needed to forgive, even if only for my own benefit. I searched, studied, pled, wept, and prayed. I read everything I could about forgiveness, counseled with others, and struggled. For over three years I struggled.

But it wasn't until the night that I was viewing a video depicting the last days and events of Christ's life, that the breakthrough finally came. Perhaps it was the music that reached the depths of my troubled soul, or perhaps my heart was finally prepared.

As I witnessed my Savior and what he was willing to suffer for me—as I watched the cruelty forced upon him, so undeserving of such treatment in his utter innocence and total purity—as I felt his love for me—my own heart overflowed with sorrow and love and gratitude for him. I began to weep openly. As the tears flowed, I felt as though my own heart was broken. My spirit was also contrite, and I felt ashamed.

I wrote in my journal of the experience: *I had been praying all along to be given the gift of the pure love of Christ and a forgiving heart. Now I realized that Christ had offered me that gift a long time ago. He had invited me to partake of his love and the healing power of his Atonement, but until now I had simply not accepted his offering, his great gift. Until now, I had rejected his invitation to carry my burdens for me, to take upon himself my pain, and to allow me to partake of his peace. I decided at that moment to accept his invitation, to let go of my pain and to turn the entire situation over to him.*

From that point on, I was no longer tortured by the pain that I had felt for so long. Although the exclusion by my family continues to this day, nine years later, my life is full and rich. Although there may always be a kind of sadness, in some strange way my heart is also filled with gratitude as I recognize that I truly am surrounded by everything I need for joy. The Lord can fill our aching hearts with love and peace which passeth understanding.

> Where can I turn for peace? Where is my solace
> When other sources cease to make me whole?
> When with a wounded heart, anger, or malice,
> I draw myself apart, searching my soul?
>
> Where, when my aching grows,
> Where, when I languish,
> Where, in my need to know, where can I run?
> Where is the quiet hand to calm my anguish?
> Who, who can understand? He, only One.
>
> He answers privately, reaches my reaching
> In my Gethsemane, Savior and Friend.
> Gentle the peace he finds for my beseeching.
> Constant he is and kind, love without end.
>   (Emma Lou Thayne, *Where Can I Turn for Peace?*)

One woman who had experienced adversity said, "When I prayed the bitterness out and the lingering peace of the Savior in, I had nothing but gratitude." We *will* experience love and joy and peace if we go to the Source. Even in the midst of adversity.

Christ said, "These things I have spoken unto you, that in me ye might have peace. In the world ye shall have tribulation: but be of good cheer; I have overcome the world" (John 16:33).

In Isaiah we read, "Thou wilt keep him in perfect peace, whose mind is stayed on thee: because he trusteth in thee. Trust ye in the Lord for ever: for in the Lord Jehovah is everlasting strength."

Trust in the Lord. Base your peace and happiness on a relationship with the Savior. He is the only constant in life. Everything else is subject to change. He said, "I will not fail thee, nor forsake thee." He will not desert us. He cannot. It would be a contradiction of his eternal nature.

Jeffrey R. Holland said: "On that very night, the night of the greatest suffering that has ever taken place in the world, the Savior said, 'Peace I leave with you, my peace I give unto you. . . Let not your heart be troubled, neither let it be afraid' (John 14:27).

"I submit to you," he said, "that may be one of the Savior's commandments that is, even in the hearts of the faithful, almost universally disobeyed; and yet I wonder whether our resistance to this invitation could be any more grievous to the Lord's merciful heart.

"As a parent I can tell you that I would be devastated if I felt that my child could not trust me to help or thought his interest was unimportant to me or unsafe in my care. In that same spirit, I am convinced that none of us can appreciate how deeply it wounds the loving heart of the Savior of the world when he finds that his people do not feel confident in his care or secure in his hands or trust in his commandments.

"Considering the incomprehensible cost of the Crucifixion, Christ is not going to turn his back on us now."

One woman wrote: "In coping with personal tragedies, I found strength in many things, but my greatest strength came from my Lord and Savior Jesus Christ who lifted me up from the depths of despair."

Christ said that his purpose was "to preach the gospel to the poor, to heal the brokenhearted, to preach deliverance to the captives, and recovering of sight to the blind, to set at liberty them that are bruised." And another time he said, "I have heard thy prayer, I have seen thy tears: behold, I will heal thee."

The word *healing* comes from the same root as "to make whole," or "to become holy." Christ wants to lift us to where he is. Christ faced adversities and suffered afflictions that neither the human mind can comprehend nor the human body could endure. In the hollow of his hand is the mark of the cross. Yet often, so concerned are we with the blisters on our own hands that we forget the nail prints in *his*.

Christ has invited us to "Come unto me, all ye that labour and are heavy laden, and I will give you rest. Take my yoke upon you, and learn of me; for I am meek and lowly in heart: and ye shall find rest unto your souls. For my yoke is easy, and my burden is light."

Someone said, "Why don't you quit trying to be your own savior and let your Lord carry your burdens? Take his yoke upon you—it is so much lighter than what you impose upon yourself."

A man was carrying a heavy basket. His son asked to help him. The father cut a stick and placed it through the handle of the basket so that the end toward himself was very short, while the end toward the boy was much longer. Each took hold of his end of the stick, and the basket was lifted and easily carried. The son was bearing the burden with the father—they shared the yoke together—but the son found his work easy and light because his father assumed the heavy end of the stick. Just so it is when we bear the yoke with Christ; He sees to it that the burden laid on us is light; He carries the heavy end.

Isaiah said of the coming Christ: "He hath borne our griefs and carried our sorrows."

Do you believe that Christ *can* take your burden? Do you believe Christ *will* take your burden? Can you give it to Him? One woman recovering from the effects of childhood sexual abuse said, "Once I decided to love the Lord more than I feared the pain, He healed me."

We are invited to "Cast thy burden upon the Lord, and he shall sustain thee." And again the invitation: "Come unto me, all ye that labour and are heavy laden, and I will give you rest."

Wendy Ulrich stated, "I believe that Christ respects the suffering and pain of each individual so thoroughly that his

Atonement was not complete until he had felt the full effect of every discomfort and agony of every soul.

"The Atonement's purpose is not to minimize but rather to validate our anguish. The Savior joins us fully in every agonizing moment of our life. Christ voluntarily endured the Atonement that he might fully experience, in his body and soul, every sickness, infirmity, struggle, distress, torment, and grief we undergo."

Deep within every child of God the light of Christ resides—guiding, comforting, purifying the heart that turns to Him. There is nothing of emptiness or isolation or fear in this great plan.

Yet, to every one of us, from time to time, there comes a sense of utter loneliness. And would you know the reason why this is? It is because the Lord desires our love. In every heart He wishes to be first. So when we feel this loneliness, it is the voice of Jesus saying, "Come unto me."

"And when beneath some heavy cross you faint, and say, 'I cannot bear this load alone,' you say the truth. Christ made it purposely so heavy that you must turn to Him. And those who walk with Him from day to day can never walk a solitary way."

We can better appreciate Christ's unsurpassed sacrifice as we experience our own private Gethsemanes.

> There's a lonesome place against the sky
>   Where sometimes all alone
> We stand and watch the world go by—
>   A strange world not our own.
> For deep, heartbreaking sorrow
>   We never fully share.
> Alone we stand on that bleak hill,
>   Lost in our deep despair.
> But the cry that comes from a burdened heart
>   Is heard—there is peace if we will.
> For God's own Son knew the dreadful pain
>   Of a cross on a lonesome hill.
>
> He understands and He stands by
>   With comfort in our grief,

> To ease the pain and bring new hope
> And give the heart relief.
> There is a lonesome place and all
> Must stand there now and then,
> But if we place our hand in His,
> He'll help us smile again.
>
> (Unknown, *A Lonesome Place*)

It is comforting to know that if our lives and our faith and our hearts are centered upon Jesus Christ, nothing can ever go permanently wrong. "Lord, keep us safe in the hollow of thy hand."

How comforting to know that we are not alone, that another has been there before, has experienced sorrow in depths and degrees we cannot even comprehend. As stated so eloquently by Neal A. Maxwell: "Can we, even in the depths of disease, tell Him anything at all about suffering? We have never been, nor will we be, in depths such as He has known. Can those who yearn for hearth or home instruct Him as to what it is like to be homeless or on the move? Can we really counsel Him about being misrepresented, misunderstood, or betrayed? Or what it is like when even friends falter? Or can we inform Christ about feeling the sting of ingratitude when one's service goes unappreciated or unnoticed? Only one leper in ten thanked Him. Cannot the childless who crave children count on His empathy? For He loved children. . . . And when we feel so alone, can we presume to teach Him anything at all about feeling forsaken?"

Christ responds fully to our slightest invitation. With our prayers we invite Him in, He who is already there. In speaking of one couple who had totally changed their lives, it was said, "Their lives are proof that no matter how far people may run from the Lord, the moment they turn around, they'll realize He's been with them all along."

Ultimately, it is Jesus Christ who will make us whole. Our cry for healing is an opportunity to turn to Him. He knows the depth of our suffering; we can know the depth of His love.

> I know thy sorrow, child; I know it well,
> Thou needst not try with broken voice to tell.

Just let Me lay thy head here on My breast,
And find here sweetest comfort, perfect rest;
Thou needst not bear the burden, child, thyself,
I yearn to take it all upon Myself;
Then trust it all to Me today—tomorrow,
Yes, e'en forever; for I know thy sorrow.

Long years ago I planned it all for thee;
Prepared it that thou mightest find need of Me.
Without it, child, thou wouldst not come to
Find this place of comfort in this love of Mine.
Hadst thou no cross like this for Me to bear,
Thou wouldst not feel the need of My strong care;
But in thy weakness thou didst come to Me,
And through this plan I have won thee.

I know thy sorrow and I love thee more,
Because for such as thee I came and bore
The wrong, the shame, the pain of Calvary,
That I might comfort give to such as thee.
So, resting here, My child, thy hand in Mine,
Thy sorrow to My care today resign;
Dread not that some new care will come tomorrow—
What does it matter? I know all thy sorrow.

And I will gladly take it all for thee,
If only thou wilt trust it all to Me,
Thou needst not stir, but in My love lie still,
And learn the sweetness of thy Father's will—
That will has only planned for the best;
So, knowing this, lie still and sweetly rest.
Trust Me. The future shall not bring to thee
But that will bring thee closer still to Me.
(Unknown, *I Know*)

With a spirit of divine trust, a serenity, and a surrender to God's will, we strive to make His mind and His heart and His love our own. We will have love and peace if we go to the Source. May we find our way home, from pain to peace, from fear to love.

CHAPTER TWENTY-SEVEN

Letting Go of the Pain

IN THE TWELVE years since writing the previous edition of this book, I have—I'm searching for the right words here—passed through, endured, borne, suffered, undergone, abided, stood, met with, found, encountered, tolerated, gone through, sustained, submitted to, experienced, tasted, been effected by, been presented with, and fallen in the way of more adversity than I ever hoped to become acquainted with. In other words, a lot more "stuff" has happened.

My thoughts regarding adversity have changed, my lessons having given me a new perspective. I now believe that we have more control over the adversity that comes into our lives than I had previously thought. There are situations in which we may feel victimized by the actions of others, helpless and powerless to control the resulting hurt. Yet, in a very real sense, our suffering is optional; it is a choice we make, a burden we *choose* to carry. There are no victims, only volunteers.

A number of years ago, I wrote some articles about growing older. I interviewed several elderly people and found most of them to have happy, positive attitudes. One woman, however, seemed to revel in recounting to me every offense that had come to her in life. She recalled all the pain that had been the result of others' mistreatment of her. Her feelings toward her grown children were bitter and she was filled with resentment, her judgment of them blaming and accusative. She expressed a hope that one day her life could be made into a movie, it had been so exceptionally fraught with undeserved heartache. It appeared that the accumulation of the hurts was a great and heavy burden for her. Considering herself to be an innocent victim, she seemed miserable indeed.

How much happier would we find ourselves, free of the burden of old wounds, old grudges, old judgments and negative feelings. Why drag dead wood, scars, and thorns with us into our future—the future that we create for ourselves? To be wronged is irrelevant unless we continue to remember it.

The past is no longer here to hurt you. What happened then is simply not happening now. You are what you are today. Remembering the past is not a spiritual necessity.

I have met people who could recite long lists of grievances and hurts collected throughout their lives. None of them has seemed to be very happy people, however, considering themselves to be the helpless victims of the cruelty of others. Bitterness always destroys. When we nurture our grievances, we become slaves of the very persons we hate. We are bound to them with chains that leave us no peace. Yet, the harm others have done to us in the past only matters to the extent that we allow it to affect us today.

To forgive does not just mean to pardon; it means to let go. Jesus used the Aramaic word *shaw* when he spoke of forgiveness. *Shaw* means "to untie." If you are tied to a rock that is pulling you down in the water, all you have to do is *forgive* it—untie it—and swim toward the light. When you forgive the past, you untie yourself from the past, and you are free.

You might also think of forgiving as being *for* (in favor of) *giving*. When you forgive, you affirm that you are in favor of giving. To whom do you give? Another? Sometimes. Yourself? Always. When you release another to go his or her own way, you free yourself to do the same. The process of giving yourself this gift of freedom is forgiveness.

Forgiveness is not conditional on someone else's behavior. If we insist that it is, we cannot move out of the victim position. Holding onto the victim role is the surest way of staying stuck and blocking our own healing. Thus, we create and then nourish our own adversity.

Even if the one forgiven does not change, even if he never asks for forgiveness, the one who forgives will have attained peace within his own heart. There is no true forgiveness without forgetting, without letting go of the past. Forgiveness is giving up the hope that the past can be different. Forgetting may be difficult, but the remembering is worse. What you believe you have lost is nothing compared to what you will lose if you refuse to let go of it.

I learned that forgiving others is really an act of self love, that it is a healing gift we give ourselves. It was a long and painful lesson, but it changed my life. The book, *Forgiveness: The Healing Gift We Give Ourselves* was the result of my own intense struggle to learn how to forgive.

Trouble has no life of its own, except that which we give it by nourishing it with our thoughts and emotional energy. Mentally going over old grievances, recalling the details, savoring the injustices, and cherishing the pain, revitalizes that which would have otherwise quietly withered and died of neglect.

But when we take responsibility for our own lives and allow others to take responsibility for theirs, we will not feel threatened by their mistreatment of us. We're affected by other people's lovelessness only to the extent to which we judge them for it. Otherwise, we are invulnerable.

Forgiveness provides the missing "peace" that has eluded us, the peace that we long for. Marianne Williamson wrote, "Peace isn't determined by circumstances outside us. Peace accompanies forgiveness. Pain doesn't stem from the love we're denied by others, but rather from the love that we deny *them*. It feels as though we're hurt by what someone else did. But what really has occurred is that someone else's closed heart has tempted us to close our own, and it is our own denial of love that hurts us.

"At a certain point, we forgive because we decide to forgive. Healing occurs in the present, not the past. We are not held back by the love we didn't receive in the past, but by the love we are not extending in the present."

Blame keeps wounds open; forgiveness heals. Blame only brings bitterness. It is a self-deceptive excuse for not moving forward. Blaming ourselves or others for our circumstances serves no useful purpose. While we may always feel some twinge of regret, we can learn from the past and then let go of it. Are we mature and strong enough to love and forgive the person who was the instrument of the adversity?

Unfortunately, by refusing to forgive, we give another person power and permission to not only hurt us once, at the time he did his dreadful deed, but to *continue* controlling our lives, blocking our passage to peace and happiness. We may believe we are helpless—powerless to control the hurt we feel as a result of the actions of others. Not so! If you don't do your own negative thinking, nobody is going to do it for you. Our own resentment is a burden we have elected to carry. It is a painful affliction that we choose to bear. We perpetuate our own pain.

When we become aware that we can remove ourselves from the victim role, that we can choose to let go and forgive, we are actually freeing ourselves. We're not the product of our past; we are the product of our choices. Few people have wronged us like we're wronged ourselves. We create our own lives, our futures, our happiness or misery by what we invite to occupy our minds and with what we choose to fill our hearts.

Jill Heasley wrote of finding peace, even through incredible adversity. "My husband of 22 years was murdered at work during an armed robbery while he and I were talking on the phone. I can't say it wasn't difficult, but I did feel peace through the many prayers and acts of service on our behalf. I gained a testimony of why my mother had told me many times before and throughout my life, 'The only real tragedy in this life is sin.'

"As I sat in the courtroom during the murder trial, I realized that no matter what anyone does to us in this life, they cannot take away our inner peace; they cannot take away the truth that we know; and they cannot take away our families forever. As I watched the families of the defendants, including their very small children, I had to admit to myself that I felt more sorry for them than for the loss that I and my family had experienced. We have the gospel and are blessed daily by it. My four sons have a father that they can honor and respect and look forward to seeing again."

* * * *

So many of our problems as adults are reactions to our childhoods. If we can choose to be damaged by our past, we can also choose to be healed by it. Our childhood is not causing the problems—because our childhood is over and no longer exists—but our reactions to it may continue in the present. And because our reactions are within our control, healing is always possible.

Daniel Judd declared: "Many people have come to believe and teach that we would be in a state of peace and prosperity if our parents hadn't been alcoholic, abusive, emotionally distant, or enmeshed. Influenced by these ideas, many of us have grown up with the idea that our problems are the result of our environment. In other words, our problems are always someone else's or someone else's fault. We deny individual responsibility and accountability for our problems and solutions. "Sadly, by blaming our circumstances for our problems, we also give up any real hope for peace. For in thinking this way, our happiness is dependent upon circumstances which may be largely, or even completely, out of our control. This isn't to say that the sins of our parents, or other difficult circumstances of life don't influence us and bring us pain. They have, they do, and they will. But these circumstances need not make us evil nor ruin our lives. . . . They provide opportunities for growth that we couldn't experience any other way."

Patsy Heaps experienced an incredibly painful childhood. She speaks of her determination to take responsibility for her own life, despite her tragic beginnings.

Patsy is an attractive woman—pretty face, beautiful long, red hair, a former model. She moves and speaks with confidence, her mannerisms and expressions full of life and good humor. Perhaps that is why her story was so powerful to me.

Patsy never knew her real father; he went to prison when she was three years old. She lived in an orphanage for three years of her life, and nurseries before that. She lived in a total of twelve homes as she was growing up, being made a ward of the court when she was twelve years old. She attended 12 schools: six elementary schools, four junior high schools, one high school, and one university.

Her mother was killed when Patsy was 16 years old; her stepfather burned to death one year later when he was smoking in bed and caught fire.

She came from a home where there was alcoholism, prostitution, physical and sexual abuse. Her sister was sent to reform school for four years. Her mother later had two children out of wedlock. Both of these children were taken from her a number of times for abuse; she eventually gave them both up for adoption.

In her first foster home, age twelve, the father felt she was too vain with her long, beautiful, waist-length hair, so he had her hair cut close to her head. As her hair dropped on the floor and was swept into the garbage bag, Patsy's self-confidence went with it. "I felt I was nothing," she said.

That night she nearly succeeded in killing herself. After the trip to the hospital, she was placed in the county jail, waiting to be sent to reform school. Patsy found the farthest corner of the cell, fell to her knees, and prayed that God would either release her from this earth or give her an opportunity to make something special of her life.

"That was a great turning point for me," she said. "I was still on my knees when the door opened and the matron announced that there were two members of the Mormon Church who had come to take me home with them."

As time passed, when Patsy went to bed at night and was all alone she would begin to sob and pray that somehow her life would turn around and she would be someone very special. "I prayed that people would respect me, admire me, and want to be around me," she said. "That desire became a force in my life.

"People had always assumed that I was exactly as my environment was," she said. "I was judged as though I was truly a part of that lifestyle, so I always acted guilty, because I knew they thought I was."

She determined that she would take responsibility for her own life, that she would not live her life according to the expectations of others. "I believe with all my heart that every person born into this world has the capacity to succeed, that we have everything within us to be successful.

"Even though experiences can make us feel bad, make us hurt, make us cry, make us ache inside—still, we are the ones who determine how we're going to handle the situation. We really can handle hardships by maturing our thought processes. Our thoughts are shaping exactly how we're going to be in five years. Think good thoughts, not negative, depressing thoughts. In order for circumstances to change, *you* have to change.

"I decided to go after the things I really desired and pay the price." Patsy improved from failing grades to a "B" average her last two years of high school. She also became a model in St. Petersburg, Florida.

When Patsy was still a teenager she was converted to the Church of Jesus Christ of Latter-day Saints. During one visit, the missionaries challenged her to set a high goal for herself. She told them she wanted to make it to church every Sunday, to never miss a meeting. The missionaries told Patsy her goal wasn't high enough.

"They didn't realize what that commitment meant for me. Because I lived so far from the chapel, I had to ride two different city buses and then walk a mile down a road with nothing on it. It was a frightening experience to me in the dark, a great sacrifice to set such a goal. And those Utah missionaries said it wasn't good enough.

"I was mad! So I thought of something that would fix them good! My new goal was going to be to attend Brigham Young University. Sure enough, those missionaries said, 'That's great!'"

But for a girl who had earlier been assumed to be retarded because her grades were so poor, the goal loomed large. "What have I done? What if BYU won't accept me?

"But the more I thought about it, the more powerful and important that goal became to me. It meant more to me than just getting an education. The more I thought about it, dreamed about it, wanted it desperately—it became something to me that said, 'Patsy, if you can get into BYU, never again will you question yourself mentally, never again will you feel as though you are inferior to other people.' It became a symbol of self-fulfillment that I was a good enough person, that I could stop fighting so hard.

"I was working five jobs as well as going to high school at this time. I was so proud to be self-supporting and also saving the money for college. I was thrilled with the prospects of what my life was going to be. Then my mother was killed in a car accident."

Patsy had to go to the bank and withdraw the money that she had put aside so she and her sister could fly from Florida to California to attend the funeral.

"When I came back, there were many people who thought that that would be the thing that would make me give up and quit trying. I did have a few days of self-doubt and self-pity, but prayed and received the assurance that I would go."

At a church meeting soon after, an elderly couple asked to see Patsy after the meeting. "The dear little couple came out arm-in-arm. The man held out his hand as though he was going to shake mine. But in his hand he held a check for the entire year's tuition at BYU."

Patsy spoke of her philosophy of life: "If you want something bad enough and long enough and you are willing to pay the price for it—then it's yours!

"There is no getting through life without working through your problems. At some point, you are going to have to face them. So why not just take them head on, handle them and get them behind you? If you don't learn to cope, to deal with the frustrations and the natural burdens of life, you're going to just give up—not because you *can't* handle it, but because you are a coward and didn't want to take responsibility for your own life. You can't blame anyone else.

"All of us have our own set of screwy circumstances in our lives. Everybody has problems. It's what you do to solve these problems—how you react to them—that determines your success or failure.

"There has been intervention in my life. And the intervention came because I was prepared, because I wanted it so desperately. Our capacity is virtually unlimited if the desire is strong enough."

Patsy is a living visual aid. She speaks from experience.

CHAPTER TWENTY-EIGHT

The Journey Will Be Joy

AT ONE POINT in his life, Abraham Lincoln wrote in despair: "I am the most miserable man on earth. If what I feel were distributed to others, there would not be a cheerful face anywhere. I don't know if I'll ever get better, but it is impossible to stay as I am." Twenty years later he could say, "I've come to believe that most people are about as happy as they make up their minds to be."

I would be very interested to know the circumstances that led to Lincoln's despair, and I would love to learn what caused the transformation in his way of thinking.

Every person has the choice of becoming a fountain of joy or a fountain of sorrow. Our attitudes determine our altitudes. Just as beauty is in the eye of the beholder, so also is ugliness in the eye—and mind and heart—of the beholder. It is our own thinking, our own perspective that determines whether we will sink or swim as we are tossed to and fro on the seas of life.

Although adversity is inescapable, we *can* control our happiness. Regardless of what happens to us, we can cultivate a cheerful heart. It has been said that the clearest sign of wisdom is continued cheerfulness. Not that it's an absence of adversity; it's just that one has the wisdom and the faith to handle it.

Even calamity can be faced with a cheerful attitude. In June, 1976, the Teton Dam broke, flooding the small community of Rexburg, Idaho. A letter addressed to a university admissions office contains this illustrative account:

"Dear Sirs: Please forgive this handwritten letter on this somewhat austere paper, but when you haven't got much, you've got to make the best of it. I never received a class schedule nor a catalog so that I could register. I believe you did send me this material but it either floated majestically away in my hapless mailbox or it went down with the post office. Please send these materials as soon as possible.

"I imagine you are wondering what is happening up here, so I'll tell you. June 5. You should know approximately 80% of us here either totally lost our homes, businesses, or both. Like many, many others, my family and I returned to our residence that night of the flood. Rexburg was still under two to four feet of water, but we had to see what happened to our homes.

"As we drove through our once beautiful city, we were brought to the ugly realization of the catastrophe which had visited us. Cars smashed through homes, houses piled into other houses, buildings aflame, trailers flung like match boxes hanging in trees or just torn into minute pieces. The smell of ruptured gas lines and the repugnant stench of contamination hung heavy on the still night air. It was as though a watery 'A' bomb had hit our community.

"Our house, like many others, was completely destroyed with almost everything therein. I jumped out of our pick-up into the numbing cold water. There, before me, stood a broken witness to the fact that most everything I had since my birth to the present was now gone. The only thing I could do was try to comfort my mother and put her back in the pick-up. She only said, "My beautiful home," then she quietly wept. For the first time in my life I realized the poignant feeling of being homeless.

"Well, Sunday and 'the ox was in the mire.' All of Rexburg was a mire! We worked 16 hours that day and the only thing I really remember is standing in a puddle of water (which was once our dining room), muddy from head to toe, chuckling. I was pitying poor old Noah. All my mind could dwell on was what must have met his astonished eyes when he opened the doors to that ark! It makes me wonder how anxious Noah really was about getting out. At any rate, I figure the reason Noah lived another 400 glorious years after the flood was to clean up the mess! Any man that put up with all that *had* to be 'perfect in his day.'

"The week dragged on endlessly. Hours and hours, days and days and still the muck and debris was endless. At this point a miracle started to happen. People from Southern Idaho came to our aid like manna from heaven, but in school buses, not loaves. They worked! Oh, did they work! Many of us tired, muddy refugees shed tears and rejoiced. The good people had to go that day, but in leaving, they said more were coming. And they did come! Thousands! From Idaho, Utah, Montana, and Wyoming, they came to our stricken valley bringing strong hands and big hearts. Over 20,000 have come and they are still coming, God bless them.

"I've truly learned one of the greatest lessons I'll ever learn. I've only lost a house and worldly items, not my home. You see, 'home is where the heart is,' and when your heart is with the Lord, you're always at home. No disaster or enemy can take home away from me—or you. God bless you all."

* * * *

Many people think happiness just happens to us, like the weather. The truth is, we create our own inner climate. If we don't have joy in this life, it's our own fault. Man is not the creature of circumstance; circumstance is the creature of man. We aren't victims of the world outside us. Each of us chooses the background hues of his or her own portrait. As hard as it is to believe sometimes, we are always responsible for how we see things. We *can* know peace and joy, even amidst adversity.

We get hooked into believing that if we aren't feeling happy now, then happiness will surely be just around the next corner, at the top of the next mountain, when we have solved our current problems. We know that big moment will come one day. On that day, you'll wake up and say, "Wait a minute; something feels different. Could it be? Could this be it? Oh my goodness; I think it is. I made it! I'm finally happy!" It just doesn't happen that way. The day we decide to *create* joy will be a turning point in our lives.

Patch Adams wrote: "The most revolutionary act anyone can commit is to be happy. It takes no greater effort to be happy every day than to be miserable. Rejecting joy and beauty takes great effort; it is not a passive act. With all the potential for happiness in this world, it is astounding that people are so bored and lonely. I do not intend to trivialize sadness and anxiety but simply to say that we choose these ways of life. People who feel sad tend to blame external events over which they have no control. This is irresponsible. They *choose* to live in a paradigm of pain. Yes, the terrible things that happen are painful. Choosing to give up, however, is what makes these experiences continue to wound us. . . ."

Although it seems like the outside world is making you unhappy, it is an illusion. Look *within* to find love, joy, confidence, and peace, and gain the power to attract and create what you want in your life. Very little is needed to make a happy life. It is all within yourself, in your way of thinking.

LouAnn Hoffman is thankful for the joy she finds in simple things: "When I express gratitude each day, it always includes 'a bit of land' to work with, a cozy home, and beauty in all its forms. . . . I have been barefoot with water trickling across my feet and down a row of green beans and have had my heart melt and have totally forgiven the world. . . . Would that I were always outdoors—if only in my heart."

Since our minds can construct any reality we want, why do we so often choose to make up a painful reality rather than one that is peaceful and joyful? Why do we do negative affirmations? Even when difficult things are forced upon us, we still have the ability to interpret them as we choose. We alter our destiny by altering our thoughts. The best thing we can do is to become accountable for our thoughts.

When we feel anxiety, fear, resentment, frustration, anger, worry, irritation, uneasiness—it's only our thinking patterns that set us up for creating unhappiness time after time. It's only our negative mental habits, our selected memories of how we think things are that keep us from viewing things in our lives in a more positive, more harmonious way.

Misery is more than sorrow; it is the ultimate state of disharmony with God. How many times in the scriptures did the Lord tell us to be of good cheer? It is a commandment, not merely a suggestion, and our level of spirituality is directly related to how well we obey the injunctions to "be of good cheer" and "lift up your heart and rejoice." We, too, should say with the psalmist: "This is the day which the Lord hath made; we will rejoice and be glad in it."

> Oh, help me learn the gracious art
> Of living with a happy heart,
> And open up my eyes to see
> Thy blessings here on earth for me.
> (Joy Saunders Lundberg)

Things are never quite as bad—or as good—as they seem. Every silver lining has a cloud. Trouble will come, sure enough—but the more amiably you greet him, the sooner he will go away. On the other hand, "when I dwell upon my problems and repeat them o'er and o'er, God may think I like them and give me more and more!"

My neighbor is a member of a "Tragedy Group," old friends who get together every two or three months. "What do you do—talk about your tragedies?" I asked. "No; we talk about how life is getting better," she smiled.

We, too, can focus more on positive things than on those that are giving us trouble. As someone said, "Start living now. We often form a habit of procrastination. Not only do we put off unpleasant activities, but we also tend to put off the enjoyable ones, too. We dole out pleasure, contentment, and happiness as though they were somehow rationed. The supply of these is limitless (as, by the way, is the supply of misery, pain, and suffering). We do the rationing ourselves. The only thing that has to be different for you to enjoy your life is where you focus your attention. Look for all the positive things taking place in and around you *right now*. As you find them, naturally you'll feel more joyful."

Enjoy life! This is not a dress rehearsal. C. S. Lewis mused, "Joy is the serious business of Heaven." According to the Talmud, a person will be called to account on Judgment Day for every permissible thing he might have enjoyed but did not. Be happy, cheerful, delighted, pleased—as often as you can, as much as you can, for as long as you can. Be a vessel of joy! My friend has a saying at her house that goes like this: "Be pretty if you are, be witty if you can, but be cheerful if it kills you."

When the challenges of life tempt you to think negatively, ask yourself, "Is what I am putting myself through worth the effect it is having on me?" Louise Hay observed: "Many of us terrorize ourselves with frightful thoughts and make situations worse than they are. It's a terrible way to live, always expecting the worst out of life."

It is easy to get into the habit of "catastrophizing." But a bad business meeting does not become a ruined day. It is simply a bad meeting. A conflict does not become a failed relationship. It is simply a misunderstanding with a loved one. A negative performance appraisal does not become a failed career. It is simply information, a learning experience, not a sign your life is falling apart. People who don't do well in negative situations tend to "catastrophize" problems—magnifying them and letting them gain control over their lives.

Another trap we may get caught in: Many of us have a knack for personalizing events that are beyond our control. The solution: QTIP—Quit Taking It Personally! For instance, realize that the IRS isn't out to get you—it's out to get *all* of us.

Happiness is not necessarily the result of good fortune. It is the grace to accept life gratefully and to make the most of the best of it. Gordon B. Hinckley, now ninety years old, shared his outlook: "Things will work out. They always do. If you want to die at an early age, dwell on the negative. Accentuate the positive, and you'll be around for awhile."

Perhaps another older man's choice to be happy is a factor in his longevity. He said: "Each morning when I open my eyes, I say to myself, 'I, not events, have the power to make me happy or unhappy today. I can choose which it will be. Yesterday is dead, tomorrow hasn't arrived yet. I have just one day, today, and I'm going to be happy about it.'"

Charles Swindell wrote: "The longer I live, the more I realize the impact of attitude on life. It is more important than appearance, giftedness, or skill. The remarkable thing is that we have a choice every day of our lives regarding the attitude we embrace for that day. We cannot change our past. We cannot change the fact that people will act in a certain way. We cannot change the inevitable. The only things we can do is play on the one string we have, and that is attitude. I'm convinced that life is 10% what happens to me and 90% how I respond to it." When you can't change the direction of the wind, adjust your sails.

When I get up and look into the mirror, I may not like what I see. But the solution is not to break the mirror. The solution is to change myself so the mirror will reflect something different. Thoreau observed, "Things do not change: *we* change." Rather than pushing so hard against life, we can see how graceful life can be. Birds sing after a storm—why can't we?

Things are only as important as we want them to be. The

defeats in our lives don't have to define us—unless we allow them to. We don't have to remain in mourning for what happens to us unless we *choose* to. Cultivating a joyful outlook will help us get through adversity. A Chinese Proverb states, "One joy scatters a hundred griefs."

Elizabeth Fetzer Bates, writer of children's songs, went blind as a young mother. Later in her life, she recounted her experiences and wrote of the evolution of her mental posture: "In the beginning, everything can seem impossible to us. In 1951, when I went blind, I would not have believed that all the living and working and problem solving that has given me so much pleasure could have been accomplished." Then she added, "I feel that it is a great sin to be unhappy. We can always be happy if we develop our appreciation and gratitude, and remember that problems are only opportunities and that joy will come to those who work through every day and endure to the end."

It is not the adversity itself that is to be the reason for our joy. Rather, it is the potential result—the development of our character—that allows us to rejoice in adversity.

Henry Van Dyke expressed his happy hopes for life, even through adversity:

> Let me but live my life from year to year,
> With forward face and unreluctant soul
> Not hastening to, nor turning from the goal;
> Not mourning for the things that disappear
> In the dim past, nor holding back in fear
> From what the future veils; but with a whole
> And happy heart, that pays its toll
> To youth and age, and travels on with cheer.
> So let the way wind up the hill or down
> Though rough or smooth, the journey will be joy.
> Still seeking what I sought but when a boy,
> New friendship, high adventure, and a crown,
> I shall grow old, but never lose life's zest,
> Because the road's last turn will be the best.

* * * *

Reading this chapter could make you feel a lot happier. Not that the book itself will make you happy—external things never do. But it will, hopefully, help you to realize that happiness is a choice, regardless of outer circumstances. That you must take responsibility for your own thoughts, your own outlook, your own life. Find out what you need to let go of in order to be free, to feel joy in the journey.

Pain is inevitable; suffering is optional. Tribulation is mandatory, but misery is a choice.

Marianne Williamson wrote in *A Return to Love*: "God's will is that we be happy now. In asking that God's will be done, we are instructing our minds to focus on the beauty in life, to see all the reasons to celebrate instead of mourn. . . . Happiness isn't circumstance-dependent. The key to happiness is the decision to be happy."

Chapter Twenty-Nine
This Too Shall Pass

ANN LANDERS REVEALED: "If I were asked to give what I consider the single most useful bit of advice for all humanity it would be this: Expect trouble as an inevitable part of life and, when it comes, hold your head high, look it squarely in the eye and say, 'I will be bigger than you. You cannot defeat me.' Then repeat to yourself the most comforting of all words, 'This too shall pass.'"

This, too, will pass.
O heart, say it over and over,
Out of your deepest sorrow,
Out of your deepest grief,
No hurt can last forever—
Perhaps tomorrow will bring relief.

This, too, will pass.
It will spend itself—its fury
Will die as the wind dies down
With the setting sun;
Assuaged and calm,
You will rest again,
Forgetting a thing that is done.

Repeat it again and again,
O heart, for your comfort,
This, too, will pass
As surely as passed before
The old forgotten pain,
And the other sorrows
That once you bore.

As certain as stars at night,
Or dawn after darkness,
Inherent as the lift of the blowing grass,
Whatever your despair or your frustration—
This, too, will pass.
                    (Grace Noll Crowell)

It is comforting to know that the darkest hour is only sixty minutes long. Surely we can last for an hour—an hour at a time.

God broke the years to hours and days,
That hour by hour and day by day,
Just going on a little way,
We might be able all along
To keep quite strong.
                    (George Klingle)

H. E. Manning offers these comforting words: "We never have more than we can bear. The present hour we are always able to endure. As our day, so is our strength. If the trials of many years were gathered into one, they would overwhelm us; therefore, in pity to our little strength, He sends first one, and then another. But all is so wisely measured to our strength that the bruised reed is never broken. Each trial is sent to teach us something, and altogether they have a lesson which is beyond the power of any to teach alone."

William Cowper said, "Beware of desperate steps; the darkest day, lived till tomorrow, will have passed away."

Evils have their life, their limits. Say to yourself, "My patience will outlast my pain. No pain that I experience will last me forever. This feeling will pass; I can count on that." I love the innocent wisdom of the little child's simple words: "When it stops hurting, it will feel better."

When things are bad, we can take comfort in the thought that they could always get worse. And when they do, we can find hope in the thought that things are so bad they have to get better.

Today's troubles are just that: today's troubles. Crises pass. Circumstances change. Situations evolve. It may not seem so now, but given the perspective of time, the pain will have eased and we will see things more clearly.

Did you know that the sky is always blue? It is! It only looks dark and dull and dismal when it is overcast by gray clouds. The clouds move in front of the blue sky and hide its beauty from us until we think that the sky itself is gray. We must remember that gray skies are just clouds passing over.

> If I can endure for this minute
> Whatever is happening to me,
> No matter how heavy my heart is
> Or how "dark" the moment may be—
> If I can but keep on believing
> What I know in my heart to be true,
> That "darkness will fade with the morning"
> And that *this will pass away, too*—
> Then nothing can ever disturb me
> Or fill me with uncertain fear,
> For as sure as night brings the dawning
> "My morning" is bound to appear.

One person reflected, "I do not experience much fear in the face of trial, because I have felt myself in the jaws of hell and, through our Lord's mercy, did not get swallowed up, after all. When we are in pain, all we can think about is the hurt. We need to remember that pain ends. The morning *will* come."

I find it interesting that in the account of the earth's creation, the scriptures tell us, "And the evening and the morning were the first day. . . . And the evening and the morning were the second day," and so forth—connected together, the morning *after* the evening. So one would not make the mistake of thinking that anything ended without being also a new beginning.

> Let there be love; let there be light,
> Let there be hope in the dark of the night.

We can trust, even when our hearts would groan, even when the shadows darken—that this too shall pass, that it is better farther on. I am encouraged by the promise in Psalms 30: "Weeping may endure for a night, but joy cometh in the morning."

Janet Lee wrote of her despair in contemplating the impending death of her husband. "Feeling more alone than I had ever felt before, I wandered away. . . . Then, as I continued down the little road and saw the sun hanging heavy in the western sky, I began to feel the dirt and rocks through my sandals. My mind turned to another who had walked the earth in sandaled feet, and I began to feel ashamed about feeling so alone. Then, as I recalled the Savior's promise to always be with us, I sat down on an old stump and contemplated that while the sun would set, it would also rise again—that there is an unerring dependability in these sequences of nature.

"And then it occurred to me. My life was not out of control. The same God who set in motion the rising and the setting sun controls the universe, of which I am a part. And he had granted me my agency, my right to choose. So while I was faced with circumstances I did not understand and could not will away, I still had the ability to make choices in my life. The agency was mine, even if my ability to exercise it was limited to simply controlling my reaction to the events I was facing. No one, I knew, could take that away from me, and I prayed silently for strength."

But sometimes the journey seems long. I recall a time some years ago when I had received a crushing blow—one that had destroyed a deep trust I had held and that had held me for a long time. I wanted to die; I just wanted to go Home. My mother wept with me from 1200 miles away. By telephone she encouraged and pled with me to be strong and assured me—*promised* me—that this life is short, that it would pass quickly. That it would seem only a short time before it would be over. In my very depths, I clung to that.

> For life seems so little when life is past,
> And the memories of sorrow flee so fast.
> And the woes which were bitter to you and to me,
> Shall vanish as raindrops which fall in the sea;
> And all that has hurt us shall be made good,
> And the puzzles which hindered be understood,
> And the long, hard march through the wilderness bare
> Seems but a day's journey when once we are there.
>   (Susan Coolidge, *Hurrying Years*)

We live forward; we understand backwards.

You're very young, my dear, to sorrow so.
This grief of yours is very real, I know,
And if I told you how that you'd forget;
That you and Trouble, here have scarcely met,
I'm very sure that you would not believe;
Nor if I said you're not the first to grieve
Because your tinsel was not gold.

But you are young, and Trouble's very old,
And wiser, kinder even, than you know.
Believe me, dear, although it hurts you so,
Some day you may look back, before life's end
And know this Trouble truly was your friend.

There is nothing we can do with suffering but suffer it. Disliking difficult times does not necessarily mean you have little faith. It just means you haven't completely unwrapped the gift yet. What's miraculous is that, regardless of how willingly or unwillingly you move through it, move through it you will—and on the other side, when the trial has passed, new strength and wisdom will be waiting. You have experienced a loss, faced it, and have survived. You have learned that the pain does lessen and that healing does occur. Now's the time to see what lessons you learned from your loss, and what possible good is contained within the loss. The final stage in healing is gratitude. Gratitude is felt when the gift is finally and fully unwrapped.

Even as tears bedim our eyes, we know that this, too, shall pass. The pain will leave, but the beauty will last.

After the tempest—calm.
After the darkness—light.
And the golden dawn breaks clearly
After the long, long night.
After the rain, the sunshine,
After the tears, the laughter.
And when this life is over,
Life eternal follows after.

CHAPTER THIRTY
A God of Loving Purpose

MRS. VANCE'S LILAC bushes were precious to her, but they had grown too tall, robbing the Vance's tiny home of sunlight. Her husband, a large, strong, grandfatherly man, told Mrs. Vance that the bushes needed to be moved. He would have to cut them back to ground level and move the roots to a new location. She vigorously protested his decision, fearing for their survival, but he felt it was necessary.

He performed the painful but loving task of pruning the bushes, preparing the soil in the new location, and finally digging up the roots and planting them in the new bed. Then came his almost daily ritual of weeding, watering, and anxiously looking for signs of new life.

Finally, early one morning, he was relieved to find green evidence that the roots were alive and growing. He brought his wife to see her lilacs and offered a prayer of thankfulness for the budding results of his work.

There are times in life when it seems as though the Lord cuts us back and even moves us to unfamiliar soil. When times of fear and pain come into our lives, his plans for us unfold. As we fervently pray and study, we find new power and purpose in our challenges. Struggling to redevelop, we become stronger than if we had never been challenged.

No affliction would trouble a child of God if he knew God's reasons for sending it. Suffering ceases to be suffering when we form a clear and precise picture of it. Yet, our own view is limited. We see only the present and some of the past. Our outlook is as from inside a cave at the foot of a mountain. God's view is as from the mountaintop in all directions; it is unlimited. He sees all the past, present, and future. We are inclined to peer through the prism of the present only, thus distorting our perspective about things.

An ancient prophet taught: "Believe in God; believe that he is, and that he has all wisdom, and all power, both in heaven and in earth; believe that man doth not comprehend all the things which the Lord can comprehend."

And from Isaiah: "For my thoughts are not your thoughts, neither are your ways my ways, saith the Lord. For as the heavens are higher than the earth, so are my ways higher than your ways, and my thoughts than your thoughts."

On the wall of a doctor's office was displayed a plaque containing these words: "It has taken all my life for me to understand that I don't need to understand everything."

God reckons time differently than we do. This life is so short, though to us, the journey sometimes seems long. In truth, mortality is like a clothespin on a clothesline that has no beginning and no end, a parenthesis in eternity. "Peace be unto thy soul; thine adversity and thine afflictions shall be but *a small moment*; and then, if thou endure it well, God shall exalt thee on high."

> Your moment may seem to linger,
> But my moment is only brief.

With our finite wisdom, we assume that trials are bad because they cause us pain, while all things that cause us to feel happy must be good. A little boy questioned his Sunday School teacher: "How come my sister got so sick? God doesn't like her, I guess."

The teacher's reply: "God loves all of us, especially children. Sometimes He lets painful things happen to us now that help us later on. Maybe if your sister hadn't stayed home in bed she would have been hit by a car that day and been hurt even worse. Or maybe by being sick she learned what it feels like to be sick, so when she grows up she'll become a doctor to help other people. Or maybe when she was sick she had more time to stay home and be with you so that the two of you could become better friends.

"You see, things aren't always what they seem when you're talking about God's plan. Even though something hurts now, it may end up helping you later. God always knows best."

Today,
Dear Lord,
I knelt to pray for one afflicted—
But paused with words unsaid
For I (in my limited wisdom)
Had been about to ask,
As always,
That the sick be healed;
That all suffering cease.
In short, That all should have
A happy ending
All the time.

Oh, dear Father, instead I give thanks
That Thou, (in thine infinite wisdom) Art able to
Edit my prayers,
Lest, in my well-intentioned concern
I should shield those I love
From the very trials
They may need
To bring them
Close
To thee.
(Teresa Anselm Spring, *Interrupted Prayer*)

If we give way to discouragement, we are questioning God's love for us. Albert Schweitzer said, "Don't vex your mind trying to explain the suffering you have to endure in this life. Don't think that God is punishing you or disciplining you or rejecting you. . . . You are always his child and he has his protecting arms around you. Does a child understand everything his father does? No, but he can confidently nestle in his father's arms and feel perfect happiness, even while tears glisten in his eyes, because he is his father's child."

We must cling to the fact—and it *is* a fact—that all that God gives us is for our good. Even shadows can be manifestations of God's light and love.

To us, adversity may appear completely senseless and irrational, but to God, it is neither senseless or irrational. He has a purpose in every pain or sorrow he brings or allows in our lives. We can be sure that in some way he intends it for our good. God's training is no random work. Every trial that comes to us, large or small, is intended to help us grow in some way. Even adversity has some sweet uses.

> I learn, as the years roll onward
>   And leave the past behind,
> That much I had counted sorrow
>   But proves that God is kind;
> That many a flower I had longed for
>   Had hidden a thorn of pain,
> And many a rugged bypath
>   Led to fields of ripened grain.

We can be thankful that we don't always get what we want. Ben Franklin observed, "If a man could have half his wishes, he would double his troubles."

With our limited perspective, we may not even be able to tell which events of our lives are blessings in disguise. (What I am looking for is a blessing *not* in disguise.)

I wish I could better recall the story of the man in Civil War times who was given a mule. His neighbors told him how fortunate he was. He replied: "Maybe so, maybe not." The next day, his son was thrown from the mule when he tried to ride it, breaking his leg. The neighbors bemoaned his bad luck. The man replied, "Maybe so, maybe not." The next day, an officer rode up, commissioned to enlist men to fight in the war, but because the son's leg was broken, he was not required to go. What a good thing, said the neighbors. "Maybe so, maybe not." The story continues. . . . Wish I knew the rest of it!

James E. Faust offered perspective on trials and tragedies: "Into every life there comes the painful, despairing days of adversity and buffeting. There seems to be a full measure of anguish, sorrow, and often, heartbreak for everyone, including those who earnestly seek to do right and be faithful. For some, the refiner's fire causes a loss of belief and faith in God, but those with an eternal perspective understand that such refining is part of the perfection process."

During a tour of a factory in England where fine china was produced, it was noticed that at the end of the inspection line stood a large container where the pieces of china that did not meet the standard of excellence were tossed. The blemished china would be reground and used again; nothing would be wasted.

Similarly, God told Jeremiah to go down to the potter's house to be taught. There, Jeremiah observed the potter at work. The vessel that the potter produced was imperfect, flawed, so he reworked the same clay, making it into another vessel that pleased him. Then God said, "Cannot I do with you as this potter? Behold, as the clay is in the potter's hand, so are ye in mine hand." (see Jeremiah 18:1-6)

What a wonderful lesson for us. When we are flawed or misshapen, God can still mold us into something useful, something wonderful, if we will allow it. If we place our trust in him and put ourselves in his hands, we will feel assured that the end product will be beautiful, though the reshaping may be painful.

Every burden is a blessing. "Troubles are often the tools by which God fashions us for better things," reflected Henry Ward Beecher. Someone else observed, "When trials are not consequences of your own disobedience, then they are evidence that the Lord feels you are prepared to grow more. He allows you to have experiences that polish and refine you. To get you from where you are to where he wants you to be requires a lot of stretching, and stretching usually involves some discomfort, even pain."

According to John Pontius, "Until we can see with God's perspective, we 'see through a glass darkly,' and our trials seem immense. We must remember that Father has a single purpose in our lives, which is to bring us to Him. Anything which moves us nearer to that goal is valuable, even pain and suffering. From His divine perspective, worldly possessions, jobs, careers, health, happiness, even life itself, is expendable if the outcome is exaltation. After we share His divine viewpoint, we will shout praises to His holy name for his wisdom and love."

The Apostle Paul demonstrated his understanding of the larger, eternal perspective. Near the end of his ministry, times were very difficult for him. To the saints in Corinth, he described his personal trials: five times he was scourged with the 39 lashes that sometimes killed the victim; three times beaten with rods, once stoned, three times shipwrecked, constantly imperiled by robbers, by his own countrymen as well as by heathen, by the wilderness, by the sea, by false brethren. Soon, he would die a martyr.

Yet, with an eternal perspective, he could say: "We are troubled on every side, yet not distressed; we are perplexed, but not in despair; Persecuted, but not forsaken; cast down, but not destroyed. For our light affliction, which is but for a moment, worketh for us a far more exceeding and eternal weight of glory" (2 Corin. 8-9).

Victor Frankl elucidated: "To live is to suffer; to survive is to find meaning in the suffering. Suffering ceases to be suffering in some way at the moment it finds a meaning. . . . Man's main concern is not to gain pleasure or to avoid pain, but rather to see a meaning in his life."

It is natural for us to avoid pain and seek pleasure. But God knows that the pathway through adversity is the safest way to heaven.

The adventure of adversity includes being able to look at the events of our lives with a larger perspective. Ralph Sockman declared: "There are parts of a ship which taken by themselves would sink. The engine would sink. The propeller would sink. But when the parts of a ship are built together, they float. So with the events of my life. Some have been tragic. Some have been happy. But when they are built together, they form a craft that floats and is going someplace. And I am comforted."

According to Neal A. Maxwell, "What may seem now to be mere unconnected pieces of tile will someday, when we look back, take form and pattern, and we will realize that God was making a mosaic. For there is in each of our lives this kind of divine design, this pattern, this purpose that is in the process of becoming, which is continually before the Lord but which for us, looking forward, is sometimes perplexing."

Who knows but what we knew, before we came here, of the challenges we would face. Hazel M. Thomson wrote:

You agreed to accept earth's sadness and pain,
So when troubles come, why do you complain?
Know that all things shall be for thy good,
Have courage to face them; you promised you would.

Someone worded it this way: "Never mind the little things, my dear. And the big things we agreed to before we came here." That same sentiment was expressed by Carol Lynn Pearson:

When some new pain pierces my life
Rebellion begins to cry,
"God knew this would come and He approved!"
But wait, long ago, so did I.
    (*A New Dimension to Faith*)

Carol Lynn Pearson's poem was written before it was learned that her husband was gay. Later, although they were divorced, she cared for him in her home where he died of AIDS.

Sometimes the lessons seem pretty tough in this earth-school. Life is boot camp. Satan would have us perceive suffering and injustice as indications that God does not love us. Yet we do not need to understand why God allows things to happen in order to know that he loves us. The very fact that he *does* allow suffering and sickness to occur should indicate that opposition is needed for our growth. Because He loves us so much, he is willing to do whatever it takes to help us obtain a greater faith, humility, courage and strength—both now, in this earthly adventure, and in eternity, as well. This is important for those who struggle with adversity while trying to believe in a God of loving purpose.

As Janice Perry said to me once, "The Lord will not cut short a trial that is for your good, regardless of your prayers of faith."

How much easier our lives would be if, rather than questioning God's love or his purposes when trials come to us, we could simply trust him. "Trust in the Lord with all thine heart, and lean not unto thine own understanding. In all thy ways acknowledge him and he shall direct thy path."

If we can trust God and know that He is there and that he loves us, then we can cope well and endure well. "If I could just be sure, I know I could endure."

When I was single, I gained great comfort from this scripture: "Trust in the Lord and do good; Delight thyself also in the Lord; and he shall give thee the desires of thine heart. Commit thy way unto the Lord; trust also in him; and he shall bring it to pass. Rest in the Lord, and wait patiently for him: fret not thyself."

How we wish sometimes that we could arrive at the destination without having to make the journey! We don't always pick our route. But we *can* choose our guide.

I know not what tomorrow holds
And I may not understand
But I know who holds tomorrow
And I know who holds my hand!

CHAPTER THIRTY-ONE
He Maketh Me to Lie Down

ONCE, A SPIRITUALLY insightful man from Russia evaluated me and said, "You should appreciate more what you have. You have a wonderful smile, but your heart is not smiling. You take things too seriously. You shouldn't push so hard against life—because then life will also push back hard against you."

How did my Father in heaven teach me to appreciate what I have? How did He teach me about the things that really matter? Many of us do receive blessings in disguise—sometimes in such terrible, terrible disguise.

Just last autumn I had two major abdominal surgeries simultaneously; some body parts were moved, and some body parts were removed. It was a horrible ordeal and a dreadful recovery with many complications and incredible pain. It was, physically, the worst experience of my life, and for a time, I seriously thought that death would have been preferable.

My way of coping was to read about others who had it worse than I. After reading one very, very sad account recorded by a pioneer woman, I identified with her parting comment: "I only lived because I could not die."

Twelve days after the surgery, in pain and with an angry red infection raging along the entire 23-inch incision, my spiritual leader visited me at our home. He gave me a blessing in which I was promised that good would come of this suffering. I remember thinking, "Yah, right. I can't think of a single good thing that could come from this."

Some time later, in a telephone conversation, a friend quoted to me, "He maketh me to lie down in green pastures. . . . He restoreth my soul." Then she repeated, "He *maketh* me to lie down." I immediately grasped the scripture's personal application to myself. I thought how in my own life I've always been so busy. So busy and so task oriented. Now, with my inability to be up and doing, time to re-examine my priorities was forced upon me.

Someone suggested, "Imagine that you are hanging pictures in your living room. You become so absorbed in your task that you don't take time to stop, stand back, and notice if the pictures are hung correctly. You just keep banging those nails into the wall. Taking time for introspection means standing back far enough so you can determine if the pictures in your life are crooked or straight. It will help you see clearly, sometimes for the first time, exactly what is out of balance in your life."

Over time, my spirit had become numbed to the point that I was unable to *feel* much. So God had to *make* me lie down before He could restore my soul.

I remember sitting in my chair reading, in the middle of the night because I could not sleep, a pioneer mother's heartbreaking account of losing her precious little three-year-old boy after a wagon accident. I was literally sobbing, tears streaming down my face, my own heart aching for that poor mother. The only thing that brought me comfort was to realize that that event had occurred 150 years ago, and that those parents and their little boy have long since been reunited in a better place.

Perhaps I was so touched by that story because of my own dear little boy. After the surgery, our young children were not allowed to touch or even come close to me where I sat in my easy chair, for fear of hurting me, so we blew each other kisses. But one day four-year-old Evan looked at me with longing and said, "Mommy, can I just hug your arm?" The memory of that expression of childlike love and the adoration in his eyes will warm my heart forever.

One time after falling asleep in my chair, I awakened to find a rolled up paper in my lap. Seven-year-old Merrie Anne had written: "Der mommy get well soon. I fill soo sory For you. I want to give you soumthing. But I dont know wat. So I will giv you this note. I love you."

With no insurance coverage, I had been very concerned about the medical expenses for this surgery. But I wrote in my journal: *"Suddenly I realized that despite my physical problems and the fact that correcting them will cost many thousands of dollars and leave us bereft—that I have things worth more than money. I have all that matters, the things that money cannot buy. I have the love and adoration of precious, beautiful children, as well as the devotion of one good husband. I felt so blessed."*

Pioneer stories weren't all I cried about. I wept during *Oprah!* I cried during parts of *The Today Show*. After five weeks, Mike took me out of the house for the first time other than doctor's appointments, and we went to see the movie *Life Is Beautiful*. I wept for an hour after that.

Now, Micheal and the doctor thought that all this crying was a lack of hormones—but I prefer to believe it to be "a heart grown tender in my breast," a line taken from this poem, a favorite of mine:

> Pain stayed so long I said to him today
> "I will not have you with me anymore."
> I stamped my foot and said,
> "Be on your way!" and paused there
> Startled at the look he wore.
>
> "I, who have been your friend," he said to me.
> "I, who have been your teacher?
> All you know of understanding, love, or
> Sympathy and patience, I have taught you.
> Shall I go?"
>
> He spoke the truth, this strange, unwelcome guest.
> I watched him leave, and knew that he was wise.
> He left a heart grown tender in my breast.
> He left a far, clear vision in my eyes.
> I dried my tears and lifted up a song—
> Even for one who'd tortured me so long.
> (Samuel Butler)

I recall, six days after the surgery, awakening in the middle of the night so thirsty, so miserable, so filled with pain. I didn't want to disturb Micheal, but finally I felt I could endure it no longer, and I awakened him, crying, "I can't do this anymore! What do people do when they reach the end?"

Micheal, in addition to doing everything he could to make me more comfortable, reminded me of the people who were praying for me, of all those who loved and cared about me. The thought had not occurred to me. Feeling so engrossed in my own pain, I had felt I was carrying this burden alone.

And so, among the disguised blessings that came was a heightened gratitude for friends. There were the meals brought in, the cards, the visits, the encouragement, the treats delivered, the telephone conversations—each one invisibly stamped with the message, "We care about you," and "you can do this." I felt such gratitude for the love I felt during this most difficult experience.

I also gained a much greater appreciation for good health. It sounds trite, but it is true, that we never fully appreciate our health until we have lost it. It, too, is something money cannot buy. Even John D. Rockefeller, with all his millions, could eat only pureed baby food because of severe stomach ulcers.

I recall the night, weeks after the surgery, that I lay in bed conscious of the fact that for the first time I was able to breathe deeply without pain. Imagine! Being able to breathe without hurting! Do you thank the Lord every day for this blessing that you may take for granted? Now, take a deep breath—and as you exhale, say "Thank you."

Finally, I learned to more fully celebrate the incredible beauty of this earth. Never an "outdoor person," I marvelled at the newfound appreciation felt for bright sunshine, azure skies, soft clouds, for the glorious colors of autumn leaves and the crisp, cool air.

I could identify with this story: A happy, cheerful waitress greeted the man who came into the restaurant: "It's a great day, isn't it?"

The man snarled, "What's so great about it?"

The waitress' smile never wavered as she responded, "Well, sir, you just try missing a few, and you'll find out."

I had missed a few—several weeks, in fact. Six weeks after the surgery I wrote, *Each day I go for a walk, I rejoice that the warm weather this year was prolonged and I can still enjoy the beauty of the autumn after being inside for so many weeks. . . .* And another time: *How I love the fresh, crisp air and the gorgeous autumn sunshine! It felt so good as I began again to take my little walks each day.*" Over and over I wrote of the gratitude I felt for this priceless blessing of being able to finally enjoy the beautiful autumn after so long indoors.

And finally—this is my favorite part—I will share what I call "the miracle of the pennies." Once a man said to me, "I think that God is more involved in our day-to-day lives than we ever realize. Every day he sends us love notes—and if we are grateful, we begin to see them."

In the past when I used to take walks fairly regularly, almost every day I would find one "lucky penny." Just one. Almost every day. Now, on November 27, I went for a walk, the bright sunshine of the prolonged autumn warming my heart and soul. As I carefully moved along the sidewalk, I looked down and saw not *one* lucky penny, but many of them! I bent over and picked them all up, every one that I could find on the sidewalk and in the grass next to it, counting them as I did. My hands were full; there were 42 of them. And then I realized that that number was exactly six weeks' worth of lucky pennies—the amount of time that I had been recuperating and had missed taking my regular walks outdoors.

I thanked God for this "love note," this symbolic message for me. It was as though He were saying to me, "I love you, and I am mindful of the time you have lost—and I will make it up to you."

* * * *

God loves and cares about us, each one, individually. He is aware of and cares about our feelings. He will encourage and comfort us and calm our troubled hearts. Recently I had a painful experience in which I felt misunderstood and rejected. It had to do with the book I'd written called *His Law Is Love*. The hurt was deep, and I felt discouraged. I wondered why I had opened my heart and traded a year of my life to write that book. I was pretty discouraged about my reaching out at all.

The next night, just after midnight, I sat down at my desk, preparing to pour all my feelings into my journal. At 12:08, the telephone rang. It was a woman calling long distance who had dialed the number in the back of the book expecting to get a recording. When I answered, she expressed surprise and then began weeping as she shared with me her story. Of how she had been filled with despair, of praying aloud in her car for help to know what to do, promising that she would listen and obey.

She had then driven to a favorite bookstore where she had always felt peace; she sat down with a favorite book. "I looked up and your book *His Law Is Love* almost literally jumped out at me from the shelf. I started reading and could hardly put it down. I took it home and read and read and read and marked and marked and marked. In fact, my book is all yellow. You are an answer to my prayers. . . ." (In my joy and astonishment, I wrote all this down in shorthand.)

And then she said, "*You need to know* that you are doing what is right—sharing what needs to be heard." She went on to say, "Oh, Cheryl, I've had wonderful experiences in my life. But of all the times I've needed my Savior, this surpasses them all. I know and you know this didn't come about by chance. . . ."

This story was not only hers, it was mine, as well. God reached out to her, in her despair, at exactly the right moment in leading her to the book. He also reached out to me, in my own discouragement, at exactly the right moment, through her incredibly encouraging telephone call. God does send us "love notes." He does intervene and He does heal us with His love. We simply need to learn to recognize it more often. Open your spiritual eyes to a myriad of miracles taking place around you. Feel the divine love of the Lord.

God cares about *each* of us, individually. Recently I learned of a young man from Northern Utah serving time in the Utah State Penitentiary south of Salt Lake City. He enrolled in a religion class being offered in the prison. Used scriptures that had been donated by individuals or groups were distributed to members of the class for their use. Imagine the astonishment of the young man when the scriptures passed to him were the very ones that he had used in seminary—a religion class for high school students—years before and many miles away. He received a "love note" that day about God's caring for him personally.

It has been said that a coincidence is a small miracle in which God chooses to be anonymous. Celebrate the coincidences in your life; they may be miracles.

CHAPTER THIRTY-TWO

The Race

LIFE IS TRULY known only to those who suffer, lose, endure adversity, and stumble from defeat to defeat. It's a common mistake to think of failure as the enemy of success. Instead, look on it as a teacher—a pretty rugged one, but the best. You can become discouraged by failure, or you can learn from it. Failure is really success if we learn from it. Indeed, Soichiro Honda, founder of the Honda Motor Corporation, said that success is 99% failure.

Kurt Bestor, acclaimed composer, was asked, "What lessons have you learned from failure and success?"

His reply: "I've learned that there really is no such thing as success unless you've failed. The reason I've been successful is that I've kept getting up after I would fail. And I don't think I've ever really failed, because failing just means that you didn't try again."

Abraham Lincoln said it well: "My great concern is not whether you have failed, but whether you are content with failure."

The Rabbi Harold S. Kushner enjoined, "Life is not a trap set for us by God so that He can condemn us for failing. Life is not a spelling bee, where no matter how many words you've gotten right, if you make one mistake, you are disqualified. Life is more like a baseball season, where even the best team loses one-third of its games and even the worst team has its days of brilliance. Our goal is not to go all year without ever losing a game. Our goal is to win more games than we lose, and if we can do that consistently enough, then when the end comes for each of us, we will have won it all."

No one has really failed as long as he doesn't lose faith in himself. In Romans we read, "Happy is he that condemneth not himself."

Curt Brinkman was a tall, strong, 16-year-old Idaho farm boy when he was nearly electrocuted in a farming accident that resulted in the loss of both his legs.

When Curt and pretty, talented Bonnie met at Ricks College, his physical handicap was not a detriment in her feelings toward him. "Everyone has handicaps of one kind or another, including me, of course," she said. "Curt's is just more obvious than many people's. Anyway," she added, "I didn't marry the wheelchair; I married the man."

What she saw in Curt was strength of character. She saw courage and determination—qualities that would later enable him to win the Boston Marathon in his wheelchair. The Brinkmans spoke at a conference where Bonnie presented the poem, *The Race*, by Dee Groberg. It so influenced my life that I have shared it with many audiences on numerous occasions.

"Quit!" "Give up, you're beaten!"
They shout at me and plead.
"There's just too much against you now;
This time you *can't* succeed."
And as I started to hang my head
In front of failure's face,
My downward fall is broken by the memory of a race.
And hope refills my weakened will
As I recall that scene,
For just the thought of that short race
Rejuvenates my being.

A children's race, young boys, young men;
Now I remember well.
Excitement, sure, but also fear;
It wasn't hard to tell.
They all lined up so full of hope.
Each thought to win that race
Or tie for first, or if not that,
At least take second place.
And fathers watched from off the side,
Each cheering for his son,
And each boy hoped to show his dad
That he would be the one.

The whistle blew and off they sped,
As if they were on fire.
To win, to be the hero there
Was each young boy's desire.
And one boy in particular,
His dad was in the crowd,
Was running near the lead and thought,
"My dad will be so proud."
But as he speeded down the field
Across a shallow dip,
The little boy who thought to win,
Lost his step and slipped.
Trying hard to catch himself,
His hands flew out to brace
And mid the laughter of the crowd
He fell flat on his face.

So, down he fell, and with him hope.
He couldn't win it now.
Embarrassed, sad, he only wished
To disappear somehow.
But, as he fell his dad stood up
And showed his anxious face
Which to the boy so clearly said,
"Get up and win the race!"
He quickly rose, no damage done,
Behind a bit, that's all,
And ran with all his mind and might
To make up for his fall.
So anxious to restore himself,
To catch up and to win,
His mind went faster than his legs.
He slipped and fell again.

He wished that he had quit before
With only one disgrace.
"I'm hopeless as a runner now,
I shouldn't try to race."
But, in the laughing crowd he searched
And found his father's face,

That steady look that said again,
"Get up and win the race."
So, he jumped up to try again.
Ten yards behind the last.
"If I'm to gain those yards," he thought,
"I've got to run real fast."
Exceeding everything he had,
He regained eight or ten,
But trying so hard to catch the lead,
He slipped and fell again.

Defeat! He lay there silently,
A tear dropped from his eye.
"There's no sense running anymore.
Three strikes, I'm out. . . . Why try?"
The will to rise had disappeared.
All hope had fled away.
So far behind, so error prone,
A loser all the way.
"I've lost, so what's the use?" he thought.
"I'll live with my disgrace."
But then he thought about his dad,
Who soon he'd have to face.
"Get up," an echo sounded low.
"Get up and take your place.
You weren't meant for failure here.
Get up and win the race."
With borrowed will, "Get up," it said,
"You haven't lost at all.
For winning is no more than this. . . .
To rise each time you fall."

So up he rose to win once more.
And with a new commit,
He resolved that win or lose,
At least he wouldn't quit.
So far behind the others now,
The most he'd ever been,
Still he gave it all he had
And ran as though to win.

Three times he'd fallen stumbling,
Three times he rose again,
Too far behind to hope to win,
He still ran to the end.

They cheered the winning runner
As he crossed the line, first place.
Head high and proud and happy;
No falling, no disgrace.
But, when the fallen crossed
The finish line, last place,
The crowd gave him the greater cheer
For finishing the race.
And even though he came in last,
With head bowed low, unproud,
You would have thought he won the race,
To listen to the crowd.
And to his dad he sadly said,
"I didn't do so well."
"To me you won," his father said,
"You rose each time you fell."

And now when things seem dark and hard
And difficult to face,
The memory of that little boy
Helps me in my race.
For all of life is like that race,
With ups and downs and all,
And all you have to do to win
Is rise each time you fall.
"Quit!" "Give up, you're beaten!"
They still shout in my face.
But another voice within me says,
"Get up and win that race."

* * * *

The Apostle Paul wrote, "Let us run with patience the race
that is set before us." Regardless of our defeats and despite our
failures, may we be able to say as did Paul to Timothy: "I have
fought a good fight, I have finished my course, I have kept the
faith."

CHAPTER THIRTY-THREE
Making It Through

EVERYBODY HAS A story at least as deep and as strong as my own. I feel a great admiration for those who carry a heavy load and still carry on. There is a wholeness about the man or woman who has learned that he or she is strong enough to go through tragedy and survive—and still feel like a complete person. At that point, nothing can scare you. You have been through the worst and come through it whole.

> Somehow strength lasted through the day,
> Hope joined with courage in the way;
> The feet still kept the uphill road,
> The shoulders did not drop their load,
> The unseen power sustained the hearts
> When flesh and will failed in their part,
>   While God gave light
>   By day and night,
> And also grace to bear the smart.
>   For this give thanks.

GRIEVING

I hope you can find the healing power in grieving. First there is the shock and denial, then the pain and anger, followed by acceptance, and finally, gratitude. People may try to escape the stages of grief, feeling that it is weak to cry or it is not good to feel angry, or it is self-indulgent to mourn. Wrote Afton Day, "While it is true that any of the stages of grief, if carried out for a long period or totally surrendered to, can prove destructive, it is also true that to refuse to acknowledge the feelings in any of the stages can cause harm." She illustrates:

"When I do my laundry, if I set the dial at the beginning of the cycle and let it run its course, the clothes will be clean and free from detergent at the end of the cycle. If, however, I move the dial and skip one of the steps, I can't blame my washer if the clothes are still dirty, or are stiff from inadequate rinsing.

"By accepting each stage as it comes, by understanding that our feelings are not abnormal and by knowing that they will pass, we are allowing ourselves to participate in a cleansing process that can roughly be compared with the process we put our clothes through when we wash them. By refusing to accept one of the steps, we refuse to let the cleansing take place, and we make it difficult for ourselves ever to come to the point of acceptance of the loss or resolution of the problem.

"Strength and bravery are great qualities, but true strength is developed through an acceptance of natural laws. . . . Children must be taught that a period of mourning is acceptable. Don't encourage your child to 'be brave, now, don't cry' when his puppy is run over or when his friend moves to another city. We accept an increase in body temperature when we are ill; we should as readily accept the methods our body provides for us to adjust to traumatic events."

It is helpful to know that there are aids to help us move through the grieving process. What are some of the sources for peace and healing?

NATURE
Some find healing in nature:

> I heard a woodthrush in the dusk
>   Twirl three notes and make a star:
> My heart that walked with bitterness
>   Came back from very far.
> Three shining notes were all he had,
>   And yet they made a starry call:
> I caught life back against my breast
>   And kissed it, scars and all.
>   (Sara Teasdale, *Wood Song*)

PRAYER

Prayer is another source of peace and healing. Prayer enlarges the heart and keeps it pliable. And it is comforting to realize that people pray for you whom you don't even know.

SCRIPTURE READING

In addition to prayer, we can find strength in the scriptures. One wrote: "I read the Psalms every morning. The Psalms are a treasure of praise, promises, pleas, and comfort. They became my daily worship journal. . . ."

FAITH

We make it through by relying on our faith. Wrote one: "I don't believe that faith means God will remove all tragedies from our path or solve all of our problems for us. I believe it means that he will be with us, suffering with us and grieving with us and waking with us as we deal with our own tragedies and work our way through those problems."

"If I could just see around the bend," said another. To trust means to obey willingly without knowing the end from the beginning. We can be comforted with the knowledge that our Heavenly Father knows the rest of the story.

> When you come to the end of everything you know
> And the next step is into the darkness of the great
>   unknown
> You must believe that one of two things will happen:
> Either you will step out onto firm ground
> Or you will be taught how to fly.

FROM OTHERS

We gain strength by observing others who have overcome the same kinds of trials that we face, receiving insights that we are not alone and that it is possible to triumph over tragedy. We can see the immense progress they have made and feel hopeful that we, too, can make it through. "I learned of the importance of reaching out to others for comfort and moral support in times of need," said one.

A mother prepared to go to a meeting one evening. Her

husband said the children were in the back yard. She moved the bikes and toys from behind the car and backed out, killing her little two-year-old Jamie, who loved to hide from Mommy and had been hiding under the car. The mother spoke of her own self-loathing: "'How could I have done such a horrible thing?' I was haunted by 'should haves' and 'what ifs.' I was beside myself. I didn't know where to turn." Others tried to help.

"Then Earlene came. She knocked on my door unannounced. Someone had offhandedly mentioned our accident to her. She had found out where we lived and started to call one day the week before, but put the phone down before it started to ring. She didn't want to intrude. But she didn't feel right. Restless. Dissatisfied. Finally she put on her make-up, curled her hair, put on her favorite dress, and came to my house. She sat in the car for nearly forty-five minutes. She almost hadn't come in.

"She told me she had been doing the wash while her children were playing in the back. Somehow her three-year-old got through the gate and wandered into the front yard. He fell into an irrigation ditch, and two agonizing days later his body was recovered six miles from home. It was four years ago. It still hurt to talk about it.

"I broke down and sobbed. We cried together. And we prayed together. She left two hours later. She was just what I needed, a confirmation that the Lord loved me and heard my prayers.

"I don't know why I needed her to tell me, 'It's okay to cry, to feel bad.' And knowing that Earlene had survived, had gone on, gave me tremendous hope. . . .'"

A SPIRITUAL RELATIONSHIP WITH DEITY

There is no safety in the world. Wealth cannot provide it, enforcement agencies cannot assure it. We must find quiet, inner havens where the storm cannot penetrate.

Wendi Bergin shared her story: "I was 16 years old when my grandpa was murdered and the murderer was later acquitted due to 'lack of evidence.' He had confessed to the murder without his lawyer present; thus, his testimony was inadmissible.

"Later, my brother and I were serving missions [for the LDS Church] at the same time. I was in Finland, and he was in Arizona. About a year into our missions, my brother was struck and killed by a drunk driver.

"Both incidents have compelled me to understand my own relationship with the Father. I am on the path to live eternally with my Father in heaven, but I wouldn't be able to do that if I stayed grieved because of these experiences. My faith had to be strengthened. Reading the scriptures helped me to do that.

"I did my best to concentrate on the good that came out of the tragedy. I'm amazed at how much good can stem from a moment of such horror. The Lord loves us, and I have learned to turn to Him for my peace; I think that is the greatest good."

* * * *

Janet Christensen wrote of yearning for a baby as a young bride. She recounted the pain, despair, disappointment, the doubting of her own worth—and, finally, her path to peace: "I will be forever grateful for the healing of my heart that came as I humbled myself and sought the Lord through prayer and scripture study. As life goes on and my joy is mingled with new sorrows, rather than hide from the pain and focus on myself, I have learned to rely on our Savior to find healing balm. My life, with all its challenges and unmet expectations, is much richer and deeper now than I ever dreamed possible as a young bride so full of hope."

* * * *

Tessa Santiago wrote of grief after a miscarriage and of the healing power of Christ: ". . . The pregnancy ended in death. It was a long November Monday morning when I labored for ten hours, knowing that the end would produce only a misshapen fetus, that my body in its wisdom knew to dispel. I don't have a name for that desolate feeling that covered my spirit as my body labored. I only knew my baby would not be born, and I grieved for what was not to be."

She described various kindnesses shown her, and then: "Most of all, I was given a husband who held my hand and stood by, waiting and watching, feeling helpless to stop my pain, wishing he could endure for me. Who waited for me in surgery, and who I found sobbing in his office three days later: he too had lost a child. In all my pain, no one had noticed his. Yet, I believe we felt the healing arms of the Savior around our hearts that week: our neighbors' tears and hearts broken for our pain, faint whisperings of another child in time, lessons of peaceful patience from Him who would gather us in his arms as a mother hen would gather her chicks.

"Could I have had my heart broken to the will of the Lord another way? Would I have come so heavy laden and willingly to the Savior's yoke? I don't know. I do know that the loss of this baby brought light to my soul that perhaps I could not have seen any other way. . . . When the pain subsides or is grown accustomed to, one realizes that some time during the darkest of nights knowledge has descended like the dews from heaven and enlarged the soul."

* * * *

Yesterday I sat in the hairdresser's chair and listened as she shared with me some of the painful challenges of her life. I asked her, "Did those things make you stronger? Did you learn from them?" And, finally, "Would you do it all again?"

Her reply caught me off guard: "Heck, no! Do you think I'm *stupid*? Yes, I'm stronger now, and yes, I learned. And I did have spiritual experiences along with the trials. But *no*, I'd never be willing to go through any of it again."

Then she added, "You know, I love Job. Everyone thinks that Job was perfect in his adversities. But I love Job because he was so human. He hated his afflictions—he cursed and he swore—but he never cursed God."

Her remarks piqued my curiosity to know more about Job, to learn the rest of the story. I was familiar with the first part of the story—and the last. But I don't recall having ever read the entire account, all 42 chapters of the book that bears his name. Beyond my curiosity in wanting to know if he really did get angry and swear, I wished to know more of the emotions he felt. How was he able to come through his adversities? Is there something we can learn from him?

"There was a man in the land of Uz, whose name was Job; and that man was perfect and upright, and one that feared God, and eschewed evil." Job had seven sons and three daughters. He was extremely wealthy, owning "7,000 sheep, 3,000 camels, 500 yoke of oxen, 500 she asses, and a very great household; so that this man was the greatest of all the men of the east."

But Satan contended that Job feared God only because he

had things so good, that if Job were tried, "he would curse thee to thy face." And so, as the story goes, Job lost everything. His servants came to him, one after another, reporting that robbers or fire had taken or destroyed all of his animals. And that a great wind had caused the collapse of the house where all his children were gathered; none had survived. Job's reaction? Though heartbroken, he fell down and worshipped, saying "Naked came I out of my mother's womb, and naked shall I return thither: the Lord gave, and the Lord hath taken away; blessed be the name of the Lord."

Satan then said that it is one thing to lose your possessions, even loved ones, but it is another to lose your health and suffer intense physical pain. Surely then Job would buckle and lose his faith. So Job became covered with sore boils from head to foot. The pain must have been incredible. Even his wife suggested that he curse God and die. Still, Job's first reaction was to say, "What? Shall we receive good at the hand of God, and shall we not receive evil?"

But the pain must have gotten to him, for Job "cursed his day," cursed the day he was born, even the day he was conceived, wished he'd died at birth. So miserable that he "longed for death, but it cometh not. . . . For my sighing cometh before I eat, and my roarings are poured out like the waters."

The nights were long; he reports tossing and turning. Because of his physical affliction, his "days are spent without hope and mine eye shall no more see good." Indeed, Job did complain: "I will not refrain my mouth; I will speak in the anguish of my spirit; My soul is weary of my life. I will complain in the bitterness of my soul." Still, Job acknowledges the greatness of God—"who should question Him?" Yet, he also felt that God had condemned him; he was full of confusion, since he had always tried to live a good life. He had to acknowledge that "He destroyeth the perfect *and* the wicked."

But, while the loss of all his possessions and all his children is reported in only seven verses, and the physical afflictions and his suffering and longing for death is included in greater detail, the trials that would yet come would take many chapters to report.

His three friends who had come "to mourn with him and comfort him" were far from comforting. Instead, in effect, they said, "You've taught and strengthened many, but now *you're* the one who's suffering, and it's getting to you." His "friends" contended that he was suffering because he was wicked, evil: "God exacteth of thee less than thine iniquity deserveth." They said, in effect, "If you weren't wicked, you should be able to lift up your face and be steadfast and not fear. You would be able to forget your misery and be bright and feel secure and have hope and could rest in safety and not be afraid—but you fail because you are wicked."

Repeatedly, Job found it necessary to defend himself: "You think you're so wise—but I have understanding as well as you. I am not inferior to you. Who knows but what this is the hand of the Lord? With him is strength and wisdom. He is all powerful. Though he slay me, yet will I trust in him. He also shall be my salvation. What are my sins? Tell me! You say bitter things against me when you judge me."

His friendly "comforter" responded: "You think you're so righteous! Let me tell you again: the wicked man travaileth with pain all his days. Trouble and anguish shall make him afraid—He shall not be rich. He's a vain hypocrite."

Job responded, "You're all miserable comforters. If I were the one trying to comfort *you* I would strengthen you with my words and try to assuage your grief. Instead, you have reproached me, judged me, even as I weep and approach death, not for any injustice in mine hands: also, my prayer is pure. My witness is in heaven, and my record is on high. My friends scorn me: but mine eye poureth out tears unto God."

It seems that Job's most difficult trial was the betrayal of his friends, the alienation of those who had once respected him so much: "My brethren are far from me, and mine acquaintance are verily estranged from me. My kinsfolk have failed, and my familiar friends have forgotten me." His maids count him a stranger and an alien. His servant ignores him when he entreats him. He feels isolated from his wife, even as he speaks to her of the children they had had together. Even young children despise and speak against him. His closest friends abhor him "and them whom I loved are turned against me." This must have been his darkest hour.

He recalled the days of his prosperity when he was respected and admired, when he had been able to fill his life with many good deeds—the days when he was happy, when people eagerly came to him for counsel—when *he* was the one to comfort the mourners. But now even the lowliest hold him in derision. Now even the most vile mock and scorn and abhor him, even spitting in his face. Now "the days of affliction have taken hold upon me."

He wrote of how his disease had changed his life. Of his discouragement when his prayers for deliverance seem to go unanswered: "I cry unto thee, and thou dost not hear me." He reports feeling confusion and despair: "When I looked for good, then evil came unto me: and when I waited for light, there came darkness."

But despite the verbal assaults on his character, and notwithstanding the terrible physical affliction that still remained, he reasserted his faith: "I know that my redeemer liveth, and that he shall stand at the latter-day upon the earth: And though after my skin worms destroy this body, yet in my flesh shall I see God: whom I shall see for myself, and mine eyes shall behold."

Job speaks of his efforts to seek and find the Lord. He reveals his determination to endure to the end: "But he knoweth the way that I take: when he hath tried me, I shall come forth as gold. My foot hath held his steps, his way have I kept, and not declined. . . . Till I die I will not remove mine integrity from me. My righteousness I hold fast, and will not let it go: my heart shall not reproach me as long as I live."

Apparently, Job passed The Test, for God finally spoke to him, assuring him of the eternal plan from before this life and beyond it. God reminded Job that, before coming to earth, and with an eternal perspective, "the morning stars sang together, and all the sons of God [including Job] shouted for joy."

After the trial of his faith, Job felt God's love and acceptance. God then suggested that Job pray for his friends who had caused him such grief. He knew that Job's forgiving his friends would set him free from the prison of bitterness he must have felt toward them. "And the Lord turned the captivity of Job, when he prayed for his friends: also, the Lord gave Job twice as much as he had before." Now he had twice as many sheep, camels, oxen, and asses as he had had before the calamities that took them. Eventually, there would be seven more sons and three more daughters.

Then, interestingly, there came to Job all his brothers and sisters and acquaintances who were willing to associate with him once more. They even bemoaned and comforted him, each one bringing money and a gold earring.

"So the Lord blessed the latter end of Job more than his beginning." Job lived 140 years more, saw four generations of his posterity. "So Job died, being old and full of days."

"There was a man in the land of Uz, whose name was Job; and that man was perfect and upright, and one that feared God, and eschewed evil." Even through the loss of all his possessions, the deaths of all ten of his children, even through his incredible physical suffering, even through the false accusations and judgments, through the extreme mistreatment that brought him such emotional pain, and even with the humanness that caused Job to question, to complain, to weep, to long for death because of his adversities—Job remained firm in his faith in God and allowed his adversities to refine him: "God has softened my heart," he said. His relationship with Deity became a personal one: "I have heard of thee by the hearing of the ear; but now mine eye seeth thee."

May we learn from the life of Job as we make it through our own adversities.

CHAPTER THIRTY-FOUR
Evidence of a Father's Love

BEECHER SAID, "DIFFICULTIES are God's errands, and when we are sent upon them, we should esteem it a proof of God's confidence." We needn't look upon adversity as a punishment. Trials are an evidence of a Father's love.

It would help, wouldn't it, to think of our trials as a compliment rather than a curse. Elva Cowley recounted an incident that illustrates:

"A young mother came into the hospital with the most pitifully deformed baby I had ever seen. I was amazed that she was in such good spirits. I asked her how she managed such a trial.

"She replied, 'I know that my Heavenly Father loves me because he knew that he could send this little spirit to me and that I would really love it and care for it.'"

Elva adds: "That was the day I saw with new eyes. I began counting my store of blessings that proved Heavenly Father loved me, too. I knew that I must not give in to the negativism that Satan tempts us with."

> God,
> Before He sent His children to earth
> Gave each of them
> A very carefully selected package
> Of problems.
>
> These,
> He promised, smiling,
> Are yours alone. No one
> Else may have the blessings
> These problems will bring you.

And only you
Have the special talents and abilities
That will be needed
To make these problems
Your servants.

Now go down to your birth
And to your forgetfulness. Know that
I love you beyond measure.
These problems that I give you
Are a symbol of that love.

The monument you make of your life
With the help of your problems
Will be a symbol of your
Love for me,
Your Father.

(Blaine M. Yorgason, The Monument)

* * * *

The womb is a comfortable place, warm and cozy and secure. We're pleased and content to be where we are. The muffled sounds we hear from outside are our only indication that there is something beyond. But there comes a time that we begin to feel restricted and constricted—an undeniable need to move on—a time for birth. It is difficult, and we struggle. But who would ever want to go back?

Perhaps some serious introspection might be in order, including these questions: Who am I? Am I living as the person I want to be? What have I really been doing with my life? Am I happy? What brings me joy? What do I need to let go of to be free? Facing these questions may bring about the contractions in your rebirth process that will push you through to a new, free-er, happier existence.

There are times in our lives that we sense something beyond, as we go through a painful refining process in order to realize a new freedom. What we had earlier thought was wonderful, we now see as only a prelude to something more. Would we want to go back? No, because to miss the misery is to miss the joy, and to miss the joy is to miss it all.

Epictetus said, "Ask not that events should happen as you will, but let your will be that events should happen as they do . . . and you shall have peace." Inner peace is accomplished by understanding and accepting the inevitable contradictions of life—pain and pleasure, success and failure, joy and sorrow, birth and death. Embrace the irony. It takes both rain and sunshine to make a rainbow. Enjoy when you can and endure when you must.

In our society we think having problems is a problem. Realize that life isn't fair. Maybe it's not supposed to be. One cannot get through life without pain; you can't hire someone to go through your sorrow for you.

Our very lives are beset with disruptions. Despite the setbacks, the temporary failures, despite the detours, we must not lose hope. If we retreat or give up, if we become embittered when things seem so unfair—if we lose faith in the Lord or in ourselves—then Satan has won the victory just as if we are sinning. And that is the battle we are facing.

We all have adversity in our lives. Although the personal burdens of life vary from person to person, every one of us has them. There is no way to go but through; there is no way around.

Some of our trials may be violent and damaging and destructive. Yet, we cannot have an experience that will destroy us unless we choose to let it. One man said, "I am bigger than anything that can happen to me. All these things, sorrow, misfortune, and suffering, are outside my door. I am in the house and I have a key."

While adversity is inevitable, we *can* choose how to use the pain life presents to us. It is our choice whether or not we will respond well to the tremendous opportunities for growth that are offered here. God kindly allots us what is our will. One woman wrote: I have a different understanding of adversity now, viewed not with despair or anguish or regret but with confidence that my loving Heavenly Father is earnestly trying to allow me to learn something very important—so important that he is actually willing to let me suffer in order to learn the lesson."

When we follow the divine road map, we need never fear or become lost. We can know that every detour is for our ultimate good and safety. With such trust, we can surrender to God our will—which is the only thing that is really ours to give. Everything else already belongs to Him. Surrendering to God is the ultimate victory.

If we are fortunate, we have approximately 80 years—29,200 days to experience life and all it offers. How many of us, as we breathe our last breath, will truly be able to say, "I feel fulfilled with who I was, and with what I did. I learned to trust God, to appreciate all the moments He gave me."

No mortal can escape death; life is bound by the cradle and the grave. One can face death with wisdom only after one has learned to face life with courage. One woman whose mother died of cancer said of her: "I did not think such courage possible. She looked out on eternity with trust and perfect faith. He who had taught her how to live surely taught her how to die."

"Whether I shall turn out to be the hero of my own life, I do not know," mused one young man.

A woman reflected, "I've sustained some significant life wounds by this point. Haven't we all? But I want to have done more than suffered with these pains. I want to know I've turned them into learning, character-building experiences. I want to develop 'beauty for ashes' as my life unfolds."

We don't develop courage or increase our strength by having easy, carefree days. We develop courage and strength by facing adversity and surviving difficult times. A schooling in hardship can burn from our souls the dross, leaving only the gold of character and faith—tried, tested, and refined. God has never worked out his purposes through the pampered victims of ease and luxury. Always He has used those in whom hardship and difficulties have built strength of character and determined wills. God shapes His servants in the forge of adversity.

> In the furnace God may prove thee,
> Thence to bring thee forth more bright,
> But can never cease to love thee;
> Thou art precious in his sight.
> (Thomas Kelly)

A mother related how her little three-year-old daughter had been abducted from the park adjacent to their backyard when she was playing there with her two brothers. Three weeks later, her little body was found, bound and gagged, up a canyon. "My husband and I had always tried to live good lives and always expected Heavenly Father's protection in return. I felt angry, betrayed. It was so unfair, so wrong."

She spoke of blaming herself, of 'what ifs' and 'if onlys.' "But, just weeks before Becky was taken from me, I had felt a confirmation from the Lord, in a very personal way, that I was a respected and loved daughter of His—a confirmation of my own self-worth. The Spirit bore witness to me that He lived.

"I later recalled and clung to that experience as I explored my hurt and anger. I wanted again to feel those feelings. That gave me something to strive for, a place in my memory to return to and be refreshed. For if God lived, so did my Rebeccah."

If we place our trust in Him, the Lord will direct us through every obstacle of life, give us strength we never could have imagined before. We go to Him because we have nowhere else to go. And then we learn that the storms of life have driven us, not upon the rocks, but into the safe haven where we find hope, relief, safety, love, and great mercy.

Jesus was not spared grief and pain and anguish and buffeting. We cannot even comprehend the unutterable burden he carried. We cannot expect our prayers of faith to eliminate the very difficulties that will prepare us to become more like him. What allows us, as human beings, to psychologically survive life on earth, with all of its pain, drama, trauma, and challenges, is this sense of purpose and meaning.

We must trust; we must have faith; we must endure for the whole journey, the entire experience, the fullness of our life. We must not stop before we've sung the whole song. If we stay the course, the promise is great: "And all they who endure in faith, fear not, for in this world your joy is not full, but in me your joy is full. And seek the face of the Lord always, that in patience ye may possess your souls, and ye shall have eternal life."

A young mother was in the hospital, having given birth to her third child. Her husband came to visit her and the new baby, leaving the other two children with a kind neighbor who offered to care for them. While the father was gone, the two-year-old drowned in the neighbor's swimming pool.

Attempts were made to revive him. In the hospital, he was put on life support to help him breathe. Great faith was exercised in behalf of the little boy. His mother fully expected that he would be made whole. She stroked his little body and sang to him. He was kept on life support for two months before the tubes were pulled; he lived another two weeks before he died. In her anguish, the mother lashed out at God. She cried, "I asked for a fish, and I got a serpent. I asked for bread and got a stone. Is that what the scriptures promise?"

Yet, at her little son's graveside, she could finally say: "I know God lives and loves us, that He is mindful of us. We do not suffer out of his view. He does not inflict pain upon us, but He sustains us in our pain. We are safe with Him. I used to think we were safe from grief and pain here because of our faith. I know now that is not true, but we are safe in His love. We are protected in the most ultimate sense of all—we have a safe home forever. That is my witness."

One man, well acquainted with sorrow, counseled another from his own experience: "Go to Heavenly Father often and cry unto the Lord in secret prayer. Those are the times of release from pain, the times that Heavenly Father is so close that his love and presence can be felt. He loves us so very much. He weeps, too, as he watches us in our growth experiences. He understands our distress; he too has felt the pain of loneliness. We are not truly alone. Jesus literally sent the Comforter to assuage our grief, to whisper our worth, to sustain and strengthen our souls.

"You will draw closer to dependence upon the Lord, stronger in the exercise of your faith, more resourceful in the development of your gifts and potential, more charitable and understanding through adversity, opposition, struggles, and the refiner's fire than through any other means. If it were not so, Heavenly Father would not allow it to be. He must love us greatly to present such challenging opportunities."

"For lo, I am with you always, even unto the end of the world." God is with us always, even through—*especially* through—our pain, even though we may not realize it at the time. The stars are constantly shining, but often we do not see them until the dark hours. What a comfort to read in Psalms 139: "Whither shall I go from thy spirit? Or whither shall I flee from thy presence? If I ascend up into heaven, thou art there: if I make my bed in hell, behold, thou art there. Such knowledge is too wonderful to me." It is a great blessing to know our suffering and travail has purpose. It is the peace of knowing we are being lovingly led through the furnace of our afflictions. Pure gold fears no fire. Because our trusting, submissive attitude in spite of adversity allows us to draw closer to Christ, we will come to treasure that adversity as one of our most valued experiences.

CHAPTER THIRTY-FIVE

With Strength in My Soul

IN PSALMS 8 we read: "In the day when I cried thou answeredst me, and strengthenedst me with strength in my soul. Though I walk in the midst of trouble, thou wilt revive me. Thy mercy, O Lord, endureth for ever: forsake not the works of thine own hands."

Our Father in heaven will not forsake us. When our Evan was two-and-a-half years old, my husband related this experience: "Evan wanted me to help him move his little basketball hoop. He was saying, 'Dad, help.' But I was too busy and didn't come. Finally, he said to me in a desperate tone of voice, 'Father, help me!' How could I resist that?" My husband continued: "It made me think of how our Heavenly Father cannot resist our pleadings, 'Father, help me!'—even though at times we may not recognize that He is helping us, or *how* He is responding to our pleas for help."

God, who is aware of the sparrow's fall, is also aware of our losses. He will be with us to comfort and sustain us—and as the years pass, the sharpness of today's pain will soften, and a divine balm will heal our broken hearts. He will guide our feet into the way of peace.

> We cannot judge what happens,
>   though tears and questions start—
> We only see what's visible—
>   God sees into the heart. . .
> And though there may be many things
>   that we cannot explain,
> We can be sure it breaks His heart
>   to see His children's pain.
> In loving arms,
>   He bears us to a quiet place apart

Where He mends the wounded spirit
And heals the broken heart.

Eileen Whitaker related the story of taking her six-month-old baby in for an immunization. The baby was happy, but suddenly, out of nowhere, she was jabbed with a needle, and a pain shot through her tiny thigh. "She whirled around to face me, with an expression of pure anguish. Everything in her small demeanor asked, 'Why? What on earth did I do to deserve that? Why did you let them hurt me?' Then she burst into tears.

"I could tell that most of her tears were not from the pain. She felt betrayed. I held her little body in my arms and rocked her. I soothed and comforted, but I could not tell her why what had just happened had happened. I could not explain to a six-month-old what an immunization is or why she had to have it or even that it was for her own good. And I could not explain that I had allowed it to happen because I loved her. All I could do was comfort and reassure her.

"Often, in our own lives, when something completely unexpected and seemingly unfair is hurled at us, we are tempted to scream in anguish, 'Why? What did I do to deserve this?' Just as I was unable to tell my infant why, the Lord cannot make us understand in our infancy. But he can offer comfort, peace, and love. If we can be still, we can feel the complete peace that can come *without* complete understanding, and it is sufficient."

"Verily, verily, I say unto you, ye are little children, and ye have not as yet understood how great blessings the Father hath in his own hands and prepared for you; And ye cannot bear all things now; nevertheless, be of good cheer, for I will lead you along.

"The kingdom is yours and the blessings thereof are yours, and the riches of eternity are yours. And he who receiveth all things with thankfulness shall be made glorious; and the things of this earth shall be added unto him, even an hundred fold, yea, more.

"And if you keep my commandments and endure to the end you shall have eternal life, which gift is the greatest of all the gifts of God."

Some years ago, I was at a hospital in Joplin, Missouri, where my seven-year-old nephew lay in a coma after a car accident. Jeffrey was asleep in the back of the station wagon when it was hit from the rear by a flat-bed truck. Jeffrey sustained brain injuries, and it was not known at first if he would even live. I thought, "Why Jeffrey? Why this shy little gifted boy? What did Jeffrey have to do with this event that would so alter his life?"

Jeffrey's recovery was miraculous. I have learned that it doesn't matter what happens to us in this life—It simply doesn't matter. All we need be concerned about are two things: (1) that we prove our obedience under all conditions, and (2) that we endure to the end with faith intact.

> Though visions sometimes dim,
> If we place our trust in God
> Then we may dwell with Him.
> When all the pain has passed
> And tears no longer fall,
> We will understand the reason for it all.

Neal A. Maxwell declared, "One day we will understand how we accepted the very conditions of challenge in life about which you and I sometimes complain in this school of stress. One day we will see that God indeed is perfect in his justice and perfect in his mercy. In retrospect we will even see that our most trying years will often have been our best years, producing large tree rings on the soul, Gethsemanes of growth."

> Not now but in the coming years;
> It may be in a better land.
> We'll read the meaning of our tears
> And then we'll understand.

I was promised once in a blessing that, while my "trials may well be a little extraordinary," that my strength would always be adequate to meet the trials of life and that I would see the necessity for their having been.

Malcolm Muggeridge wrote: "I feel strongly at the end of my life that nothing can happen to us in any circumstances that is not part of God's purpose for us. Therefore, we have nothing to fear, nothing to worry about, except that we should rebel against His purpose, that we should fail to detect it and fail to establish some sort of relationship with Him and His divine will. On that basis, there can be no black despair, no throwing in of our hand. . . .

"All the happenings in this world, including the most terrible disasters and suffering, will be seen in eternity as in some mysterious way a blessing, as part of God's love. . . ."

C. S. Lewis offered his perspective: "All this earthly past will have been Heaven to those who are saved. That is what mortals misunderstand. They say of some temporal suffering, 'No future bliss can make up for it,' not knowing that Heaven, once attained, will work backwards and turn even that agony into a glory. It is the opposite of a mirage. What seemed, when they entered it, to be the vale of misery turns out, when they look back, to have been a well; and where present experience saw only salt deserts, memory truthfully records that the pools were full of water."

There is a purity which only suffering can impart; the stream of life becomes snow-white when it dashes against the rocks. Even when a seeming undertow grabs us, somehow in the tumbling we are being carried forward, though battered and bruised. Maybe one day we shall be glad to remember even these hardships.

> He asked for strength that he might achieve;
> He was made weak that he might obey.
> He asked for health that he might do greater things;
> He was given infirmity that he might do better things.
>
> He asked for riches that he might be happy;
> He was given poverty that he might be wise.
> He asked for power that he might have the praise of men;
> He was given weakness that he might feel the need of God.
>
> He asked for all things that he might enjoy life;
> He was given life that he might enjoy all things.

From an Irish blessing comes this: "May your joys be as bright as the morning and your sorrows merely be shadows that fade in the sunlight of love. May you have enough happiness to keep you sweet. Enough trials to keep you strong. Enough sorrow to keep you human. Enough hope to keep you happy. Enough failure to keep you humble. Enough success to keep you eager. Enough friends to give you comfort. Enough faith and courage to banish sadness. And one thing more: enough determination to make each day a more wonderful day than the one before."

This lyrical reminder carries within it my own wish for you:

> Weeks turn to months, and the months into years.
> There'll be sadness and joy,
> There'll be laughter and tears.
> But one thing I pray to heaven above:
> May each of your days be a day full of love.
> May each day of your life be a good day. . . .
>
> And good night. . . .

The End
But remember that every ending is also a new beginning.

Please send the following item(s) to:

Name_____

Address_____

City_____ State_____ Zip_____

Phone (_____)_____

ORDER FORM

THE ANGUISH—AND ADVENTURE—OF ADVERSITY

_____ (book, 244 pages) . . . .$13.95 _____

_____ (six audio cassettes,
        entire book read by author) . . . .$27.90 _____

HIS LAW IS LOVE

_____ (book, 312 pages) . . . .$13.95 _____

_____ (nine audio cassettes,
        entire book read by author) . . . .$34.90 _____

FORGIVENESS—THE HEALING GIFT WE GIVE OURSELVES

_____ (book, 163 pages) . . . .$8.95 _____

_____ (three audio cassettes,
        entire book read by author) . . . .$17.90 _____

Subtotal _____

Shipping and handling (per order): $3.00

TOTAL _____

Please send a copy of this order form with check or money order to:

Cheryl Carson
854 East 1170 North
Pleasant Grove, Utah 84062
(801) 796-6293

TrueHeart Publishing
226 North 2370 West
Provo, Utah 84601
Tel.(801)314-5060